Praise for previous editions of *Fun with the Family™ in Texas*

"Next time you're trying to decide where you can go in Texas with your kids—and have fun . . . consult Allan C. Kimball's *Family Adventure Guide: Texas.*"
—*American-Statesman* (Austin, Tex.)

"A Texas-size helping of fun and adventure for the whole family."
—*Books of the Southwest*

"[This book] contains hundreds of ideas for trips with kids . . . [and] has something for every family to enjoy."
—*San Marcos Daily Record* (Tex.)

Help Us Keep This Guide Up to Date

Every effort has been made by the author and editors to make this guide as accurate and useful as possible. However, many changes can occur after a guide is published—establishments close, phone numbers change, hiking trails are rerouted, facilities come under new management, etc.

We would love to hear from you concerning your experiences with this guide and how you feel it could be made better and be kept up to date. While we may not be able to respond to all comments and suggestions, we'll take them to heart, and we'll make certain to share them with the author. Please send your comments and suggestions to the following address:

The Globe Pequot Press
Reader Response/Editorial Department
P.O. Box 480
Guilford, CT 06437

Or you may e-mail us at: editorial@globe-pequot.com

Thanks for your input, and happy travels!

FUN WITH THE FAMILY™

in TEXAS

**HUNDREDS OF IDEAS
FOR DAY TRIPS WITH THE KIDS**

THIRD EDITION

By ALLAN C. KIMBALL

The
Globe
Pequot
Press

Guilford, Connecticut

Fun with the Family is a trademark of The Globe Pequot Press
Cover and text design by Nancy Freeborn
Cover photograph by Julie Bidwell
Maps by M. A. Dubé

Library of Congress Cataloging-in-Publication Data
Kimball, Allan C.
    Fun with the family in Texas : hundreds of ideas for day trips with the kids / by Allan C. Kimball. — 3rd ed.
        p. cm.
    Includes index.
    ISBN 0-7627-0851-4
    1. Texas—Guidebooks. 2. Family recreation—Texas—Guidebooks. I. Title.

F384.3.K55   2001   00-051065
917.6404'64—dc21

Manufactured in the United States of America
Third Edition/First Printing

A million thanks to my wife, Madonna,
without whom I could never have written this book.

Contents

Preface

A common bumper sticker on cars in Texas proclaims, I WASN'T BORN IN TEXAS, BUT I GOT HERE AS SOON AS I COULD. That's what I did. The day after I graduated from high school, I headed south to the Lone Star State, a land of bigger proportions, bigger personalities, and bigger possibilities than where I was coming from.

Since then, I've driven, walked, flown, or paddled through just about every one of Texas's 266,807 square miles, often dragging my family with me. As a journalist I've had the advantage of getting to know Texans from all walks of life and racial backgrounds, the rich and the poor, the politicians and the farmers, the singers and the shopkeepers, and quickly discovered the state is full of fascinating people and their stories. I've never tired of traveling Texas.

I've traveled in other places, too. I've stepped foot on every continent and visited most countries, spent time in every state in the United States, but Texas stands out. Texans, you quickly discover, behave like those in no other state. Because of the state's size and diversity on nearly every scale, Texans are a separate breed, a distinct culture within America. Think about it: Almost everyone can recite a Texan joke or two—many books have compiled those jokes—but how many do you know for the other forty-nine states? It's the one state you can be sure is known in every country around the world thanks to books, films, television, and a reputation for friendliness and braggadocio that is only slightly exaggerated.

Texas is a unique place, one that takes a lifetime to know, and one that is always entertaining to visitors.

Introduction

Texas is a state so large it is the only one that can legally divide itself into five new states—or that would need to. It isn't just size that makes Texas special, it is its incredible diversity. Here, America collides with Mexico in an undeclared war of cultures that seems to be creating a whole new culture. But many more cultures than those two have influenced—and continue to influence—Texas. Africans, Scandinavians, Vietnamese, Czechs, Filipinos, Lithuanians, Japanese, Lebanese, Peruvians, Germans, Canary Islanders, Native peoples, and many others have made their presence felt so strongly in the state that an immense Institute of Texan Cultures had to be established in San Antonio just to pay tribute to them all.

Texas's diversity extends to climate and geology as well. Here the borders reach from balmy, sandy beaches to raw desert, majestic mountains, rolling hills, deep forests, grassy plains, and tropical areas filled with swaying palm trees. Four distinct geographic regions converge here: the Rocky Mountains, the Great Western High Plains, the Great Western Lower Plains, and the Gulf Coastal Plains.

These regions are home to some huge, modern metropolitan areas, and three of them (Houston, San Antonio, and Dallas) are among the ten largest cities in the United States. Yet Texas has more land dedicated to agriculture, has more farms and ranches, produces more cotton, and grazes more cattle than any other state.

In fact, Texas is so big you really can't see it all in one trip, unless your vacation lasts for months. Here's just one example of its size: Driving from Lake Rita Blanca, the northernmost state park, to Bentsen–Rio Grande State Park, the southernmost, you would travel 815 miles. You'll discover similar mileage traveling across the state from El Paso to Orange. That's like traveling from Presque Isle, Maine, to Washington, D.C., or Chicago, Illinois, to Montgomery, Alabama.

Texas Trivia The name Texas comes from *tayshas*, a Hasinai Indian word meaning "friend."

Texas spends a lot of money on its roads and highways, some of the best you will find in the United States. It also has more public roads than any state in the nation, with 294,491 miles. The state highway system encompasses 76,764 miles of state-maintained routes, of which 40,748 miles are paved farm-to-market (marked as FM or Farm Road) and ranch-to-market (marked as RM or Ranch Road) thoroughfares.

Information Center

During your trip, don't miss stopping at one of the Texas Travel Information Centers run by the state Department of Transportation. These are at entry points scattered around the state on major thoroughfares, and each one is packed with travel literature to make your trip easier and more enjoyable. They are open daily from 8:00 A.M. to 5:00 P.M., except New Year's, Thanksgiving, Christmas Eve, and Christmas.

- If you're traveling east from New Mexico or south from Oklahoma, stop at the Amarillo center on I-40 at U.S. Highway 287.

- Traveling east from New Mexico, stop at the El Paso center on I-10 in the city of Anthony.

- In Austin, stop at the Capitol Complex Visitors Center in the restored Old General Land Office Building at Eleventh Street and Congress Avenue. The building features several exhibits on the history of Texas and the Land Office, which manages state properties. One display celebrates the Land Office's most famous employee, William Sydney Porter, who wrote short stories under the name O. Henry.

- Traveling south from Oklahoma, stop in Denison on U.S. Highway 75, in Gainesville on U.S. Highway 77 at I-35, or the Wichita Falls center on I-44 at U.S. Highways 277 and 281.

- Traveling south from Arkansas, stop at the Texarkana center on I-30.

- Traveling west from Louisiana, stop at the Orange center on I-10, or the Waskom center on I-20.

- Traveling north from Mexico, visit the Laredo Visitors Center on I-35 just north of the city, the Harlingen center at the intersection of U.S. Highways 77 and 83, or the Langtry center on Loop 25 at U.S. Highway 90. The Langtry location is especially interesting because it's on the grounds of the historic Jersey Lilly Saloon built by Judge Roy Bean, the "Law West of the Pecos" back in the late 1800s.

If one of the things your family likes to do on trips is just drive around scenic areas, the state has helped you out by creating several "highway trails." These are well-marked routes that travel through the most interesting areas of each region of the state. They include the Hill Country Trail in central Texas, the Tropical Trail in south Texas, the Independence Trail along the Coastal Plain, the Forest Trail in east Texas, the Mountain Trail and the Pecos Trail in west Texas, the Plains Trail in the Panhandle, the Lakes Trail in northeast Texas, and the Forts Trail in north-central Texas.

You can get maps of these trails free from the Texas Department of Transportation at (800) 452-9292. You can also get a free road map of the state by calling that number.

If you're driving in Texas, you are required to have liability insurance. Evidence of insurance must be furnished when requested by a police officer. Texas law also requires all front-seat passengers to wear seat belts, children under four must be belted up whether in front or backseat, and children under two must be in a federally approved child safety seat.

SOUTH OF THE BORDER

Since Texas shares 1,254 miles of border with Mexico, a few words about traveling south of the Rio Grande are in order.

If you are a U.S. or Canadian citizen, you are not required to have a passport when crossing into Mexico, provided you neither stay longer than seventy-two hours nor travel farther than about 20 miles into the interior. You must have some proof of citizenship with you, however, such as a birth certificate or voter's registration card. If you are a citizen of any other country, you will need a passport and appropriate visas for both the United States and Mexico. If you are traveling to the interior of Mexico or staying longer than seventy-two hours, you must get a Tourist Card, available at Mexican consulates, travel agencies, and air, train, and bus depots in the United States around the border, or at Mexican Customs when you cross the international bridge. If you are driving a car, obtaining Mexican insurance is a must to avoid legal problems if an accident occurs while you are in Mexico. Auto accidents are considered criminal offenses in Mexico and, regardless of fault, your vehicle could be impounded. *Riders on American policies are no longer accepted.* You can purchase short-term Mexican insurance at a number of offices along the border. You will also need a Mexican automobile permit, good for 180 days. It may be obtained at the border for $10 and must be paid for with a major credit card. If traveling beyond the border area, you must stop at a Federal Inspection Point, usually 12 to 20 miles from the border, where your vehicle and baggage may be inspected.

When crossing back into the United States, you must verbally declare your citizenship. Don't be tempted to joke. Many customs officers will detain you and make you prove your citizenship, a process that could take several hours even if you are carrying proof.

U.S. dollars are readily accepted at all Mexican border cities. U.S. citizens may bring back $400 worth of goods duty free. Each person may bring back one liter of alcohol every thirty days. Alcoholic beverages in excess of the limit are subject to duty and internal revenue tax. In addition, Texas requires a state tax on all alcoholic beverages brought in from Mexico.

Foreign-made items such as cameras, watches, and jewelry acquired prior to entry into Mexico should be registered with U.S. Customs before going to Mexico. Without proof of prior purchase, such articles may be subject to duty when brought back into the United States. If you have a pet, it's probably best to leave it home or at a boarding facility while you are in Mexico since both countries have stringent regulations about animals crossing the border.

Vast expanses of the Rio Grande have no official crossings, and in these areas the boundary may seem more imaginary than real with people casually traveling back and forth despite the requirement that all travelers check in at an official U.S. Customs office. However, it is about 150 miles between the Fort Hancock and Presidio official crossings and about 250 miles between the Presidio and Comstock crossings. The U.S. Border Patrol maintains several checkpoints on all roads just north of the river, but they do not count as a customs stop.

Maps provided at the beginning of each chapter are for reference only and should be used in conjunction with a road map. Distances suggested are approximate.

LODGING AND RESTAURANT FEES

In the "Where to Eat" and "Where to Stay" sections, dollar signs indicate general price ranges. For meals, the prices are for individual entrees. For lodging, the rates are for a double room, with no meals, unless otherwise indicated; rates for lodging may be higher during peak vacation seasons and holidays. Always inquire about family and group rates and package deals that may include amusement park tickets, discounts for area attractions, and tickets for concerts and other performing arts events.

Rates for Lodging		Rates for Restaurants	
$	up to $60	$	entrees under $10
$$	$61 to $100	$$	entrees $11 to $20
$$$	$101 and up	$$$	entrees $21 and up

> The prices and rates listed in this guidebook were confirmed at press time. We recommend, however, that you call establishments to obtain current information before traveling.

Attractions Key

The following is a key to the icons found throughout the text.

 Swimming

 Animal Viewing

 Boating / Boat Tour

 Food

 Historic Site

 Lodging

 Hiking / Walking

 Camping

 Fishing

 Museums

 Biking

 Performing Arts

 Amusement Park

 Sports/Athletic

 Horseback Riding

 Picnicking

 Skiing/Winter Sports

 Playground

 Park

 Shopping

Prairies and Lakes

This is a region drenched in history with a number of fine museums to preserve its past. The Texas Declaration of Independence was signed here, the fledgling republic's first capital was here, the oldest university in the state is here, Dr Pepper was invented here, the West begins here, and the Texas Rangers—both the law enforcement agency and the baseball team—have excellent showcases here.

Except for the bucolic rolling hills along the back roads, this area doesn't have much in the way of dramatic landscapes. But when the wildflowers are blooming in the spring, the area is a festival of color and a great backdrop for photographs of children. The Brazos River Valley offers plenty of outdoor recreation, from canoeing down the river to water sports on the lakes.

The land here is given over mostly to farming, with a giant metropolitan area hulking in its midst. The Metroplex, from Fort Worth to Dallas, is one of the largest urban areas in the nation and offers families an abundance of things to do, from amusement parks to world-class zoos, from art galleries to wax museums, from planetariums to sporting events.

The easiest way to get around the Prairies and Lakes is on I-35 and I-45, Highways 281 and 290, and Route 6. Don't worry if you take a back road—virtually all Texas roads are very well maintained. This area is crowded with cities and towns, perhaps more than any other region, so a travel stop is always just over the next hill. Be aware that Highway 75 through Dallas (the Central Expressway) is under construction and will be for some time, so plan accordingly if you must take that route. Also, in the Metroplex, the majority of family attractions are adjacent to or very near I-30.

Lake Texoma

Wichita Falls

Denison

Sherman

Gainesville

Jacksboro

Denton

McKinney

Lewisville

Plano

Grapevine

Garland

Mineral Wells

Weatherford

Irving

Dallas

Mesquite

Fort Worth

Grand Prairie

Arlington

Duncanville

Mansfield

Granbury

Cleburne

Waxahachie

Ennis

Glen Rose

Corsicana

Meridian

Whitney

Clifton

West

Mexia

Waco

Killeen

Temple

Belton

Salado

Bryan

College Station

Navasota

Elgin

Washington

Brenham

Bastrop

Ledbetter

Rosanky

Round Top

Chappell Hill

Smithville

PRAIRIES AND LAKES

Allan's Top
Annual Family
Fun Events

- Southwestern Exposition and Livestock Show and Rodeo, Fort Worth, January (817-877-2400)
- Eeyore's Birthday, Round Top, April (409-278-3530)
- Scarborough Faire, Waxahachie, April through June (972-938-1888)
- Red River Rodeo, Wichita Falls, June (940-592-2156)
- Festival of Trains, Ennis, September (972-875-7070)
- Comanche County Pow-Wow, Comanche, September (915-356-3233)
- State Fair of Texas, Dallas, October (214-421-8713)
- Red Steagall Cowboy Gathering, Fort Worth, October (817-884-1945)
- Winedale Oktoberfest, Round Top, October (409-278-3530)
- Christmas in Chappell Hill, Chappell Hill, December (409-836-6033)

Bastrop, Rosanky, and Smithville

Bastrop is one of the more historically important towns in Texas. The area originally was a meeting ground for Tonkawa and other southwestern Indians, provided a vital river crossing on El Camino Real—the King's Road from Mexico City to Nacogdoches—and was the prime settlement for Stephen F. Austin, the father of Texas.

The city is named for Philip Hendrick Nering-Bogel, a land developer with no royal blood who called himself the Baron of Bastrop. He was, however, instrumental in persuading the Mexican governor of Coahuila y Tejas to allow Austin to bring American colonists into the area in 1827. That was the beginning of events that would lead Anglo settlers and many Mexican citizens to revolt against Mexico and establish Texas as an independent republic just a few years later.

Nestled among towering loblolly pines along the Colorado River, the city of Bastrop is a quaint city surrounded by parks, ranch land, and meadows alive with wildflowers in the spring. More than 125 structures in town are listed on the National Register of Historic Places. Its courthouse was built in 1889, the same year as its Opera House.

3

The nearby city of Smithville has a similar history and was once a riverboat stop on the Colorado River and an important railroad hub. It's known today as a popular place to shop for antiques.

BASTROP OPERA HOUSE (ages 6 and up)

711 Spring Street, Bastrop 78602 (512–321–6283).

The Opera House, a Victorian building with a tin roof over the balcony and main floor, has shows on Friday and Saturday evenings. Prices vary with the performances.

BASTROP MUSEUM (ages 6 and up)

702 Main Street, Bastrop 78602 (512–321–6177). Open Monday through Friday noon to 4:00 P.M., Saturday and Sunday 1:00 to 5:00 P.M. Adults $2.00, 50 cents for children under 12, children under 6 **Free**.

The museum is located in an 1850 house displaying historic documents and photographs, along with frontier tools, artifacts, and Native American relics sure to interest children.

BASTROP STATE PARK (ages 2 and up)

1 mile east of Bastrop on Route 21, via Loop 150 from Route 71, Bastrop 78602 (512–321–2101).

The 3,503-acre park is in the midst of the Lost Pines area of Texas, a loblolly pine woodland isolated from the main body of east Texas piney woods. It's the most westerly stand of loblollys in the state. The rugged hills and quiet woodlands are a perfect retreat.

Overlooking a small lake are thirteen rustic cabins with cooking facilities—the perfect place for a family to relax for a day or two. The park also has a swimming pool, two children's wading pools, a nine-hole

Annual Bastrop Events

- Yesterfest in April
- Salinas Art Show in May
- Loblolly Days Festival in July
- Bastrop Opera House Arts and Crafts Show in November
- Old Fashioned Christmas in December

For more information contact the Bastrop Chamber of Commerce and Visitor Center at 927 Main Street, Bastrop 78602 (512-321-2419).

golf course, picnic tables, and modern rest rooms with hot showers. Even if you don't golf, you might want to walk the course as it winds through tall pines and crosses steep ravines.

If you have older children, you might be interested in biking along the hilly park road system that connects Bastrop and Buescher State Parks.

CENTRAL TEXAS MUSEUM OF AUTOMOTIVE HISTORY (ages 6 and up)

South of Bastrop on Farm Road 535 off Route 304, Rosanky 78953 (512–237–2635). Open April 1 through September 30, Wednesday through Saturday 9:00 A.M. to 5:00 P.M., Sunday 12:00 to 5:00 P.M.; October 1 through March 31, Friday through Saturday 9:00 A.M. to 5:00 P.M., Sunday 2:00 to 5:00 P.M. Adults $5.00, children 6 through 12 $2.50, children under 6 **Free**.

If anyone in your family likes old cars, they are going to love this museum full of beautiful and interesting vehicles, all restored and polished to mirror finishes. Usually you'll see 100 to 115 cars on display at any time. The rotating collection traces the development of the automobile and its effect on the social and economic climate of the world. You'll see early European estate cars, town cars, limousines, and sports cars, as well as cutaway engine displays, tools, and diagnostic equipment.

Other displays include

Texas Trivia Along Texas roads you will find more than a million signs and markers, including more than 2,500 historical roadside markers and more than 1,000 rest areas, picnic areas, and scenic overlooks.

gasoline and oil pumps, automotive signs, license plates from around the world, accessories, and a large collection of models and toys.

SMITHVILLE RAILROAD HISTORICAL PARK AND MUSEUM (ages 4 and up)

102 West First Street, Smithville 78957 (512–237–2313). Open during business hours Monday through Friday. **Free**.

Who doesn't like trains, especially kids? This museum in the Katy Depot features Union Pacific and Missouri–Kansas–Texas cabooses, photos, railroad memorabilia, and a vintage motor car. Unusual for a museum are the picnic tables and children's playground outside. The park's gazebo is topped by a cupola salvaged from the 1896 city hall building.

BUESCHER STATE PARK (ages 2 and up)

On Park Road 1, Smithville 78957, 2 miles north of Smithville off Route 71 (512–237–2241).

Unlike nearby Bastrop State Park, this park on the edge of the Lost Pines has more oaks than pines. It also has picnic areas with tables and grills, a 7.8-mile hiking trail, and overnight camping facilities. Four screened shelters with water and electricity are available at $12 a night, but make reservations well in advance, especially in spring and summer.

While roaming around Buescher (pronounced "Bisher"), you might see armadillos, bobcats, white-tailed deer, opossums, rabbits, raccoons, and squirrels. The thirty-acre lake is stocked with fish, but you need a state fishing license to drop a hook. You can swim in the lake, but the park has no lifeguards, so keep a close eye on the kids.

*S*cenic Drive One of the prettiest drives in the entire Prairies and Lakes region is the 13-mile route through the Lost Pines. Directions are simple: Take Park Road 1 from either Bastrop State Park or Buescher State Park and drive to the other park. Park Road 1A loops around Bastrop State Park. The route splits into Park Roads 1C and 1E, but they both end up in the same places, so travel in one direction on one and return on the other. In some areas, the trees are so thick and the road so narrow, it appears as if you are in a wooded tunnel. Make sure your windows are down as you mosey over the hills, letting in that fresh smell of the pines, a fragrance intensified just after a rain shower. Best times are spring and fall.

Where to Eat

Bastrop Bar-B-Q & Meat Market. *919 Main Street, Bastrop 78602 (512–321–7719).* One of the better barbecue restaurants in an area filled with good ones. $

The Plantation. *912 Main Street, Bastrop 78602 (512–321–9229).* Good old American food. $–$$

Texas Grill. *101 Route 71, Bastrop 78602 (512–321–5491).* Homey place for good hamburgers. $

Where to Stay

Bastrop Inn. *102 Childress Street, Bastrop 78602 (512–321–3949).* $$

The Colony Bed and Breakfast. *703 Main Street, Bastrop 78602 (512–303–1234).* Welcomes children. $$–$$$

Pine Point Inn. *Route 71 East, Bastrop 78602 (512–321–1157).* $$

For More Information

Bastrop Chamber of Commerce and Visitor Center. *927 Main Street, Bastrop, TX 78602; (512) 321–2419.*

Elgin, Ledbetter, and Round Top

Take Route 95 north to Highway 290, then east.

If you're in the little town of Elgin in late July, take the family to the city's **Western Days and Rodeo** festival in Memorial Park and the Lost Pines Arena. You'll be treated to arts-and-crafts and food booths, dancing on tennis courts, a fun run, a kids' parade, and a championship arm-wrestling contest. Top-notch rodeoing entertains in the evening. (Elgin is pronounced with a hard g, as in *begin*.) Call (512) 285–4515 for information.

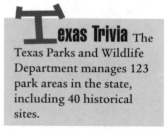

Texas Trivia The Texas Parks and Wildlife Department manages 123 park areas in the state, including 40 historical sites.

By the way, Highway 290 and Route 21—roads that connect Austin (home of the Lyndon B. Johnson Presidential Library at the University of Texas) and College Station (home of the George Bush Presidential Library at Texas A&M University)—are now designated **The Presidential Corridor,** a picturesque drive.

 STUERMER STORE (ages 6 and up)
On U.S. Highway 290, Ledbetter 78946 (409–249–3330).

Old-fashioned fun and food can be found at the Stuermer Store, which has been in operation for more than one hundred years. Its old bar has been converted to a soda fountain and ice cream parlor.

HENKEL SQUARE (ages 6 and up)

Downtown Round Top 78954 (409–249–3308; www.roundtop.org). Open daily noon to 5:00 P.M. Adults $2.00, students $1.00.

This is a nationally recognized museum village where your family can experience pioneer life. Artifacts are on display in each building, and often reenactors demonstrate pioneer crafts. Among the forty historic structures you can visit are a double-log house, a schoolhouse church, a log store, and several family homes. The apothecary shop serves as the visitors center.

Texas Trivia Texas is second only to Alaska in volume of inland water, with 4,959 square miles of lakes and streams.

WINEDALE HISTORICAL CENTER (ages 6 and up)

4 miles east of Round Top via Farm Road 1457, then Farm Road 2714, Round Top 78954 (409–278–3530; www.rtis.com/reg/roundtop/winedale.htm). Open for tours May through October on Saturday 10:00 A.M. to 6:00 P.M. and Sunday noon to 6:00 P.M.; November through April on Saturday 9:00 A.M. to 5:00 P.M. and Sunday noon to 5:00 P.M. Event admission varies. Tours: $3.00 adults, $1.00 students.

The Winedale Historical Center in Round Top is operated by the University of Texas for the study of ethnic cultures. The center itself is a restored nineteenth-century farm and homestead with log cabins, a fireplace kitchen, a smokehouse, and barns. The center holds a couple of first-rate, family-oriented festivals during the year. **Eeyore's Birthday** is celebrated in late April with food, children's games, children's costume contests, and a Shakespearean comedy. **Shakespeare at Winedale** offers a revolving repertoire of the Bard's classics Thursday through Sunday in July and August. **Winedale Oktoberfest** is held every October with demonstrations of German pioneer crafts and heaping helpings of authentic German food and music.

Where to Eat

Meyer's Elgin Smokehouse. *On U.S. Highway 290, Elgin 78621 (512–281–3331).* Elgin sausage is legendary. Sample it here along with heaping helpings of ribs, brisket, beans, potato salad, creamed corn, pickles and onions, and bread. Stars here are garlic pork sausage and their fat-free (yes, that's fat-free) barbecue sauce. $

Royer's Round Top Café. *On the square in Round Top 78954 (409–249–3611).* Pasta and salmon and great pies. $–$$

Southside Market. *On U.S. Highway 290, Elgin 78621 (512–285–3407).* One of the most authentic, and legendary,

Texas barbecue cafes. The 117-year-old eatery is known far and wide for its German-style sausage. This is way old-fashioned fare, with big slabs of meat served up on red butcher paper, side orders in cups, and drinks from a tub of ice. $

Where to Stay

Heart of My Heart Ranch. *403 Florida Chapel Road, Round Top 78954 (800–327–1242).* True family bed-and-breakfast in an elegant Victorian house. There's a log cabin, a lake, woods, hot tub, bicycles, fishing and paddle boats, and a full breakfast. $$–$$$

Ragtime Ranch Inn. *On County Road 98, Elgin 78621 (800–800–9743).* Pool, fishing pond, picnic and barbecue grounds. $$

Round Top Inn. *102 Bauer Rummel Road off Route 237, Round Top 78954 (409–249–5294).* Restored pioneer buildings; sleep amid history. $$

Brenham

Brenham is more than 150 years old and teeming with historic buildings. The downtown area has plenty of antiques shops, and the town has more than thirty bed-and-breakfast inns. The area is filled with bluebonnets and other wildflowers in the spring. Call the local chamber of commerce at (888) 273-6426 and ask for a list of historic sites, info on the bed-and-breakfasts, and a ℱ𝓇ℯℯ **Bluebonnet Trails** map so you can find the best spots to take those precious photos of your children. Visit the city's Web site at www.brenhamtx.org.

BLUE BELL CREAMERY (ages 4 and up)
On South Horton Street (Farm Road 577) Brenham 77834, 2 miles southeast of downtown Brenham (800–327–8135; www.bluebell.com). Open Monday through Friday 8:00 A.M. to 5:00 P.M., Saturday 9:00 A.M. to 3:00 P.M. March through December, closed major holidays. Tours: $2.50 adults, $2.00 children and seniors. Children under 6 admitted ℱ𝓇ℯℯ. *No tours on weekends.*

The Blue Bell Creamery is the second most sacred place in Texas, just behind the Alamo, and a great family fun place. This is where Blue Bell Ice Cream is made. Somehow, over the years, this state favorite became legendary, and to disparage it in front of an old-time Texan is to risk your health.

The "little creamery in Brenham" was founded in 1907, named for the bluebonnet flowers that cover the nearby hills in the spring. *Time* magazine pronounced Blue Bell "the best ice cream in the world." Judge for yourself with a tour and a taste. Tours are given Monday through Friday throughout the year and on Saturday March to December.

BRENHAM HERITAGE MUSEUM (ages 6 and up)

105 South Market Street, Brenham 77833 (979–830–8445). Open Wednesday 1:00 to 4:00 P.M., Thursday through Saturday 10:00 A.M. to 4:00 P.M. Admission, $1.00.

The Brenham Heritage Museum is housed in a renovated 1915 Federal building. The exhibits preserve area history and feature traveling exhibits throughout the year. Among the attractions is an 1879 steam-powered fire engine.

MONASTERY OF ST. CLAIRE (ages 2 and up)

9300 Route 105, Brenham 77833, 9 miles northeast of Brenham (979–836–9652). Open daily 2:00 to 4:00 P.M. except Holy Week (the week prior to Easter) and Christmas. Donations accepted.

The kids will love the Monastery of St. Claire, and they don't even have to be religious—they just have to love little horses. The monastery is home to a group of nuns who support themselves by raising miniature horses—some as small as medium-size dogs—and selling handmade ceramics and other crafts in their Art Barn Gift Shop.

LAKE SOMERVILLE

On Route 36, 14 miles north of Brenham (979–535–7763). Call (409) 596–1622 for information on the four Army Corps of Engineers parks; (409) 596–1122 for information on the city park; (409) 535–7763 for area information; or (512) 389–8900 for camping reservations.

Cool off at this 11,460-acre lake with seven parks surrounding it and about 500 acres of shoreline developed for boating, camping, fishing, picnicking, and swimming. Lake Somerville State Park is divided into two units, Birch Creek on the north shore and Nails Creek on the south shore. The two units are connected by the 21.6-mile Somerville Trailway System, where you can hike, bike, or ride horses.

Where to Eat

Purcell's Country Style Buffet. *2800 Route 36 at Highway 290, Brenham 77833 (979–836–9508).* Wide variety of choices. $

Tejas Cafe & Bar. *2104 South Market Street, Brenham 77833 (979–836–9554).*

Steaks and fajitas, shrimp and chicken. $-$$

Tex's Barbecue. *4807 Route 105, Brenham 77833 (979–836–3991).* Open pit barbecue, dine inside or in picnic area. $-$$

Where to Stay

Best Western of Brenham. *1503 Highway 290, Brenham 77833 (800–528–1234 or 409–251–7791).* Pool, hot tub. $$

Dewberry Hill Farm Bed and Breakfast. *(979–836–6879).* Room for the entire family in the adjacent

guest house; eighty-five-acre grounds have a large lake and wooded hiking trails. $$

Holiday Inn Express. *210 U.S. Highway 290, Brenham 77833 (979–836–4590).* Pool, gazebo, spa, Free continental breakfast. $$

For More Information

Brenham Chamber of Commerce. *314 South Austin Street, Brenham, TX 77833; (979) 836–3695 or (888) BRENHAM.*

Chappell Hill, Washington, Navasota

This area rivals the Hill Country when it comes to beautifully blooming wildflowers in the spring. Take the scenic drive along Farm Road 1155 north to **Washington-on-the-Brazos State Historical Park.** The road winds through beautiful pastoral landscapes filled with bluebonnets, red Indian paintbrush, and pink primroses along a historic route used by early pioneers and settlers.

Chappell Hill has several early Texas and antebellum structures, homes, antiques stores, and crafts shops. One standout is the **Chappell Hill Bank.** In the same building since 1907, it is the oldest continuously operating bank in the state and features rare historical photographs and documents on its walls, including an original 1899 map of the United States.

Don't miss the **Teddy Bear Parade** during the **Christmas in Chappell Hill** celebration in early December. The bears are escorted by their young owners, and several prizes are given. City merchants kick off the Yuletide with a number of events, including the arrival of Santa Claus on a fire truck and other entertainment and caroling. For more information call (409) 836-6033.

Washington is considered the birthplace of Texas. The city was the site of the signing of the Texas Declaration of Independence and the drafting of the new republic's constitution. From 1842 to 1846 this small town served as the capital of the Republic of Texas.

The famed explorer Robert Cavalier, Sieur de la Salle, is memorialized with a statue on Route 90 in downtown Navasota. He was murdered by one of his own men in what is now Navasota while on a statewide quest for the mouth of the Mississippi River.

The first week of February sees Navasota turn back the clock and celebrate **Go Texan Days** at the Grimes County Fairgrounds. Arts-and-crafts and food booths, games, and chili and barbecue cook-offs will keep your family entertained. Call (409) 825-7100.

Allan's Top Family Fun Ideas

1. Six Flags Over Texas, Arlington
2. Hurricane Harbor, Arlington
3. Texas Rangers baseball at The Ballpark, Arlington
4. Museum of Science and Natural History, Fort Worth
5. Texas Ranger Hall of Fame and Museum, Waco
6. Fort Worth Zoo, Fort Worth
7. Cowtown Rodeo and Stockyards Historic Area, Fort Worth
8. Blue Bell Creamery, Brenham
9. Dallas Zoo, Dallas
10. Dinosaur Valley State Park, Glen Rose

CHAPPELL HILL HISTORICAL MUSEUM (ages 6 and up)

Church Street, Chappell Hill 77426 (979–836–6033). Open Wednesday through Saturday 10:00 A.M. to 4:00 P.M., Sunday 1:00 to 4:00 P.M. Tours, $2.00 per site.

Housed in a 1927 school building, the museum exhibits depict plantation life, the Civil War era, life under Reconstruction, local educational institutions, and Polish immigration.

WASHINGTON-ON-THE-BRAZOS STATE HISTORICAL PARK (ages 2 and up)

Off Farm Road 1155, Washington 77880, just south of Washington (979–878–2214). Open daily 8:00 A.M. to sundown.

    This 229-acre park on the banks of the Brazos River contains a portion of the original town site; a reconstruction of Independence Hall; the home of Anson Jones, the last president of the republic; an auditorium; a pecan-grove picnic area; and an outdoor amphitheater. The park was recently renovated and has several new buildings, roads, trails, and exhibits. The new visitors center has computerized interactive exhibits. History comes alive during the annual **Texas Independence Day** celebration, when volunteers re-create the original Texas Army and display pioneer garb and crafts (usually held on the Sunday nearest March 2).

STAR OF THE REPUBLIC MUSEUM (ages 6 and up)

At Washington-on-the-Brazos State Park, Washington 77880 (979–878–2461). Open daily 10:00 A.M. to 5:00 P.M.

    The history of early Texas is preserved at the Star of the Republic Museum, built in the shape of a star. This is one of the best historical museums in the state, perhaps second only to the Institute of Texan Cultures in San Antonio. The museum presents Texas history through exhibits and multimedia presentations depicting pioneer life, agriculture, politics, transportation, and military affairs.

For More Information

Washington County Convention and Visitors Bureau. *314 South Austin Street, Brenham, TX 77833; (800)* *225–3695 or (979) 836–3695. Visit the Web site at www.brenhamtexas.com.*

Texas Trivia The state song is "Texas, Our Texas"—not, as many outsiders believe, "The Eyes of Texas" or "The Yellow Rose of Texas."

Bryan and College Station

THE BRAZOS VALLEY MUSEUM OF NATURAL HISTORY (ages 6 and up)

3232 Briarcrest Drive, Bryan 77801 (979–776–2195). Open from September through May, Tuesday through Saturday 10:00 A.M. to 5:00 P.M.; June through August, Monday through Saturday 8:00 A.M. to 5:00 P.M. Adults $5.00, children $4.00.

The museum has displays on archaeology, prehistory, and other subjects and hosts many children's activities and traveling exhibits.

TEXAS A&M UNIVERSITY (ages 10 and up)

At Texas Avenue and University Drive, College Station 77845 (979–845–5851; www.csdl.tamu.edu/). Appelt Aggieland Information Center open Monday through Friday 8:00 A.M. to 5:00 P.M. **Free**.

College Station is home to Texas A&M University, which dominates the city as few other colleges dominate towns in Texas. Among the attractions on campus are the Albritton Bell Tower, with forty-nine bells cast in France; the J. Wayne Starke Center Gallery in Memorial Student Center, which features rotating art exhibits; and the Sam Houston Sanders Corps of Cadets Center, which honors the past, present, and future of the university, celebrating its Corps of Cadets with miniature cannons, swords, guns, flags, and a Hall of Honor. The center also includes the Metzger-Sanders Gun Collection, featuring antique firearms and other weapons and a collection of Colt pistols.

The university conducts customized family tours of the campus led by students who tailor their presentation based on the ages of your children.

GEORGE BUSH PRESIDENTIAL LIBRARY AND MUSEUM (ages 6 and up)

1000 George Bush Drive West, College Station 77845 (979–260–9552; www.csdl.tamu.edu/bushl:b). Open Monday through Saturday 9:30 A.M. to 5:00 P.M., Sunday noon to 5:00 P.M. Adults $5.00, seniors $3.50 with advanced reservations, children under 16 **Free**.

The newly opened research library and museum is on the Texas A&M campus, housing thirty-eight million pages of

Texas Trivia The state flower is the bluebonnet.

official and personal papers, one million photographs, 2,500 hours of videotape, and 50,000 museum exhibit items. Included in the exhibits are a 1925 home movie of baby George taking his first steps to memorabilia from his days as a congressman, ambassador to China, head of the Central Intelligence Agency, vice president, and president. Some of the larger displays include a World War II torpedo bomber airplane, a 1947 Studebaker, a slab of the Berlin Wall, and replicas of Bush's offices.

The museum also has a classroom designed specifically for students from kindergarten through high school where kids can learn about the presidency and recent American history.

 PUTT PUTT GOLF AND GAMES (ages 4 and up)
1705 Valley View, College Station 77845 (979–693–2445). Open Sunday through Thursday 11:00 A.M. to 11:00 P.M., Friday 11:00 A.M. to midnight, Saturday 9:00 A.M. to midnight. Prices vary by activity.

In the mood for some miniature golf? Take the family to Putt Putt. The park has golf, batting cages, bumper boats, and a video-game room.

Where to Eat

Royer's Cafe. *2500 Texas Avenue South, College Station 77840 (979–694–8826 or 888–881–PIES).* Everything from burgers to quail, topped off with divine pies. $$

Tom's. *3601 College, Bryan 77801 (979–846–4275) and 2001 Texas Avenue, College Station 77840 (979–696–2076).* Steaks, catfish, hamburgers, and barbecue served on butcher paper. $$

Where to Stay

La Quinta Inn. *607 Texas Avenue, College Station 77840 (800–NU–ROOMS).* Pool, kids under eighteen stay **Free**, and **Free** continental breakfast. $$

For More Information

Bryan/College Station Chamber of Commerce. *715 University Drive East, College Station, TX 77840; (800)* *777–8292 or (979) 260–9898. Visit the Web site at www.bcs.com.*

Temple and Belton

Take Highway 190 west from Bryan.

Temple grew up around the railroads and still maintains an important railroad shop. The town is now an agriculture center with a growing emphasis on industrial products. Visit the Web site at www.temple-tx.org.

Nearby Belton is a smaller town that has retained a rustic charm. Founded in 1850, it was a central stage stop and favorite of cowboys herding cattle up the Chisholm Trail. Many of the city's buildings date to the 1860s and are well preserved, especially in the graceful old downtown area. Some homes are open to the public during the annual tour in April. The city is also home to one of the oldest colleges in the state, Mary Hardin Baylor University, founded in 1845 when Texas was still an independent republic.

If you want to find out what the weather is going to be in advance, visit the Web page at www.olgc.com/tx/belton.html.

Texas State Parks The Texas parks system has about 8,000 campsites available statewide. Most parks are generally accessible to the disabled.

Entrance fees vary from $1.00 to $5.00 at each park. Camping fees vary considerably. A yearly $50 Gold Conservation Passport allows unlimited entry for everyone in your vehicle, Free tours at historical parks, advance notice of activities and tours in the quarterly passport *Journal*, Free access to wildlife management areas, discounted subscription price of $10.50 to the monthly *Texas Parks & Wildlife* magazine for a year, and other benefits. A Free, lifetime Texas State Parklands Passport allows entry to park lands at no charge for seniors sixty-five and older and to veterans with a 60 percent or greater disability.

Get comprehensive information on state parks in Texas by writing to TPWD, 4200 Smith School Road, Austin, TX 78744; calling (800) 792–1112; or visiting the Web site at www.tpwd.state.tx.us. Camping reservations must be made by calling (512) 389–8900, regardless of the park. A complete Texas State Parks Map may be purchased by mail for $3.11 from park headquarters or $2.25 at most state parks.

MOTHER NEFF STATE PARK (ages 4 and up)

On Route 236, Moody 76557, 20 miles northwest of Temple (254–853–2389 or 512–389–8900 for camping reservations).

Mother Neff State Park—the first Texas state park—was named for former governor Pat Neff's mom, who donated the land. The park was developed by the Civilian Conservation Corps during the Depression and features tall trees, hills, ravines, and cliffs. There are hiking trails, picnic facilities, campsites, fishing spots along the Leon River, a playground, and plenty of opportunities to see such wildlife as armadillos, deer, raccoons, roadrunners, and squirrels.

THE SPJST MUSEUM OF CZECH HERITAGE (ages 6 and up)

520 North Main Street, Temple 77501 (254–773–1575). Open 8:00 A.M. to noon and 1:00 to 5:00 P.M. weekdays. **Free**.

Honors the Czech contributions to Texas. Artifacts include a 1530 Bible, an 1895 handmade dulcimer and other antique musical instruments, clocks, old-world costumes, and quilts more than 150 years old. The Slovanska Podporujici Jednota Statu Texas (Slavonic Benevolent Order of Texas) was a social group founded in the late 1800s for Czech immigrants in the state. You'll still see SPJST halls in many Texas towns.

RAILROAD AND PIONEER MUSEUM (ages 4 and up)

South Thirty-first Street at Avenue H, Temple 77501 (254–298–5172). Open Monday through Saturday 10:00 A.M. to 4:00 P.M., Sunday noon to 4:00 P.M. Adults $2.00, children $1.00.

Housed in a restored depot, the museum has exhibits devoted to pioneer farm, ranch, and home life; tools; clothing; and the early days of railroading in Texas, including an old Santa Fe steam engine.

Trains are honored in a big way at the **Texas Train Festival** in September, when the museum puts on special displays and demonstrations and Temple hosts a huge model-train show. For information call (254) 773–2185.

MILLER SPRINGS NATURAL AREA (ages 4 and up)

Northside of dam on Farm Road 2271, Temple 77501 (254–298–5720). Open dawn to dusk.

When Lake Belton overflowed its spillway in 1992, the water carved out a huge canyon and created wetlands that are being preserved as a natural area offering hiking, bird-watching, and wildlife photography. **Miracle Mile,** a fully accessible boardwalk, allows people with disabilities to view the wetlands and restored prairie below.

 TEMPLE LAKE PARK (ages 4 and up)
 On Farm Road 2305, Temple 77501, 9 miles northwest of Temple (254–773–0661).
   Cool the kids off on 172 acres along Lake Belton with a boat ramp, picnic and camping facilities, fishing, and swimming.

 LAKE BELTON (ages 4 and up)
Headquarters at the dam at the junction of Farm Road 2271 and Farm Road 439, Belton 77513 (254–939–1829).
   Lake Belton is the prime source of outdoor recreation in the area. It's noted for numerous arms and coves along its 110-mile shoreline and is surrounded by thirteen public parks offering camping, picnicking, boat ramps, marinas, fishing, and swimming. For detailed information, visit the Army Corps of Engineers headquarters at the dam.

 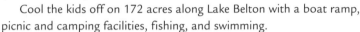

- Belton Youth Fair and PRCA Rodeo, Belton, February
- Belton Lake Water Festival, Belton, February
- Fourth of July Parade, Festival and Rodeo, Belton
- Salado Legends, Salado, July
- Central Texas State Fair, Belton, August
- Texas Early Days, Temple, October
- Holly Day Express, Temple, November
- Tablerock Festival, Salado, December

 SUMMER FUN USA (ages 4 and up)
 1410 Waco Road, Belton 77513 (254–939–0366). Open weekends beginning in mid-May, then daily Memorial Day through Labor Day. Adults $13, children $10.
   Summer Fun is a small but classic water park featuring inner-tube rides, water slides, beach volleyball, and horseshoe pits.

BELL COUNTY MUSEUM (ages 6 and up)
201 North Main Street, Belton 77513 (254–933–5243). Open Tuesday through Saturday 1:00 to 5:00 P.M. 𝐅𝐫𝐞𝐞.
    Housed in a restored 1904 library, the musum focuses on the history of the county and chronicles the life of Miriam "Ma" Ferguson, Texas's first woman governor. Other exhibits include a century-old kitchen and a post office with a working telegraph.

 CENTRAL TEXAS STAMPEDE (ages 6 and up)
301 West Loop 121, Belton 77513 (254–933–3500). Ticket prices vary.
    If you're visiting during the cooler months, and your family likes hockey, the minor league Stampede takes the ice at the Bell County Exposition Center October through March.

Where to Eat

Frank's. *2207 Lake Road, Belton 77513 (254–939–5771).* Tasty meals. $

Golden Corral Family Steakhouse. *2113 Southwest H. K. Dodgen Avenue, Temple 77501 (254–773–4064).* Steaks and all-you-can buffet with special kids' desserts. $–$$

Sorge's Italian Restaurant. *1323 South Fifty-seventh Street, Temple 77501 (254–899–1492).* Pasta and pizza. $

Where to Stay

Best Western Inn. *2625 South Thirty-first Street, Temple (254–778–5511 or 800–749–0318).* Kids stay 𝐅𝐫𝐞𝐞. $$

La Quinta. *1604 West Barton, Temple (254–771–2980 or 800–531–5900).* Pool, 𝐅𝐫𝐞𝐞 continental breakfast. $$

Salado and Killeen

Killeen is just west of Temple on Highway 190; Salado is south on I–35.
    Salado (Suh-lay-doh) was a bustling city when the Chisholm Trail ran through it back before the turn of the twentieth century, but when the railroad passed it by things got quieter. The little town is best known today for its quaint shopping area full of galleries and crafts shops and boutiques. If you're here around the first weekend in August, don't miss the annual **Salado Art Fair** in Pace Park, one of the best juried arts-and-crafts shows in the state. A

follies show and an all-you-can-eat fajita dinner are featured in the evening. Call (254) 947-5040 for more information.

The tree-shaded picnic area at **Pace Park** on Thomas Arnold Road beside Salado Creek was once a Native American campground, long before recorded history, and you can still see ruts from wagon wheels in the bedrock of the creek just north of the park.

Texas Trivia Texas celebrates both Martin Luther King's birthday and Confederate Heroes Day as official state holidays in the same week in January.

FORT HOOD (ages 6 and up)

Main Gate is on Highway 190, Killeen 76540, west of Killeen. Museums open Monday through Friday 9:00 A.M. to 3:30 P.M., Saturday and Sunday noon to 3:30 P.M., closed major holidays. Free. The gift shop closes a half hour earlier and is closed on Sunday.

Killeen is home to Fort Hood, the largest army post in the world, covering 339 square miles off Highway 190 just west of the city. The post has two museums open to the public at no charge.

The **First Cavalry Division Museum** exhibits more than 150 years of cavalry uniforms, equipment, and weapons, from swords to helicopters, artillery, tanks, and trucks. Located at Building 2218 on Headquarters Avenue; (254) 287-3626.

The **Second Armored Division Museum** features unit history from 1940 to the present and includes some of Gen. George Patton's personal items, tanks, combat photos, and dioramas. Located at Building 418 on Battalion Avenue; (254) 287-8811. Visitors should stop for directions at the Main Gate.

Where to Eat

Stagecoach Inn. *Salado exit off I–35, Salado 76571 (254–947–9400).* Known far and wide for delicious twice-baked potatoes and cornmeal biscuits. $-$$

Where to Stay

Stagecoach Inn, Salado. *Salado exit off I–35, Salado 76571 (254–947–5111 or 800–732–8994).* Texans travel hundreds of miles to stay at the place where George Armstrong Custer, Robert E. Lee, and Jesse James once slept. Today, accommodations are in a new motel. $$

For More Information

Salado Chamber of Commerce.   *(254) 947–5040. Visit the Web site at*
P.O. Box 81, Salado, TX 76571;   *www.vvm.com/salado.*

Clifton, Waco, and West

*Take Route 317 north of Killeen to Route 6 into Clifton, then return on Route 6 to Waco,
for a scenic 35-mile drive through the picturesque North Bosque River Valley.*

Waco was named after the peaceful Hueco Indians who lived on the banks
of the Brazos River here. The river valley's black soil turned the area into a cotton capital. Later, when the Chisholm Trail was blazed, the city became a cattle center. Today Waco is known as the home of Baylor University, the oldest
college in Texas and the largest Baptist university in the world.

Go Texan at Waco's **Heart o' Texas Fair and Rodeo** the first week in October. The fair showcases professional rodeo riders, livestock and horse shows,
and fine-arts exhibits. Located at the Heart o' Texas Coliseum and Fairgrounds; call (254) 752-6551.

Waco's **Old Suspension Bridge** was the nation's largest when it was built
in 1870 as a toll bridge along the Chisholm Trail. It was the model for the
Brooklyn Bridge. Today the bridge, off University Parks Drive, is still used by
pedestrians to link **Indian Spring Park** and **Martin Luther King Jr. Park** across
the Brazos River. You can enjoy 𝐅𝐫𝐞𝐞 evening concerts in the summer at
Indian Spring Park.

Just north of Waco is the tiny town of West, known for its historic Czech
cuisine and an annual festival honoring its Czech heritage. Featuring parades,
kolache contests, children's games, folk dancing, ethnic food, and an arts-and-
crafts show, **Westfest** (254-826-3188) takes places on the weekend before
Labor Day. Visit the Web site at www.westfest.com.

BOSQUE MEMORIAL MUSEUM (ages 6 and up)

*301 South Avenue, Clifton 76634 (254–675–3720). Open Friday through Sat-
urday 10:00 A.M. to 5:00 P.M., Sunday 2:00 to 5:00 P.M. Donations accepted.*
Clifton is the Norwegian Capital of Texas, and the museum displays
the largest collection of Norwegian artifacts in the South. Included are
mineral and fossil collections, guns, coins, sailing ship models, pioneer
kitchen equipment, farm tools, and Native American artifacts.

CAMERON PARK ZOO (ages 2 and up)

1701 North Fourth Street, Waco 76702 (254–750–8400 or 254–750–5980 for horseback riding; www.waco-texas.com/zoo/). Open Monday through Saturday 9:00 A.M. to 5:00 P.M., Sunday 11:00 A.M. to 5:00 P.M.; Memorial Day through Labor Day open to 6:00 P.M. Adults $4.00, children 4 through 12 $2.00.

The Cameron Park Zoo is a fifty-one-acre home near the Brazos River for antelopes, bison, giraffes, monkeys, rhinos, tigers, wolves, zebras, and other animals. The grounds are covered in native trees—cottonwoods, mesquites, pecans, and oaks—and feature a waterfall. The surrounding park on University Parks Drive at Herring has 328 acres of woods, nature walks, equestrian trails, scenic picnic areas, and a children's playground. Horseback riding is $10 an hour.

DR PEPPER MUSEUM (ages 6 and up)

300 South Fifth Street, Waco 76702 (254–757–1024; www.drpeppermuseum.com). Open Monday through Saturday 10:00 A.M. to 5:00 P.M., Sunday noon to 5:00 P.M. Adults $4.00, seniors $2.50, children 4 to 12 $2.00, preschoolers **Free***.*

The soft drink Dr Pepper was invented in Waco by Charles Curtis Alderton, and the recipe has remained unchanged since he first mixed up the concoction at the Old Corner Drug Store in 1885. The Dr Pepper Museum, in the original 1906 bottling plant, honors Alderton and the history of the unique drink. Featured are a restored soda fountain, many interactive displays for children, and a tour through the manufacturing facilities. Admission for the soda fountain or gift shop **Free**.

STRECKER MUSEUM (ages 6 and up)

In Sid Richardson Hall on the Baylor University Campus at South Fourth Street, Waco 76798; take exit 335B off I–35 (254–755–1110). Open Tuesday through Friday 9:00 A.M. to 4:00 P.M., Saturday 10:00 A.M. to noon and 1:30 to 4:00 P.M., and Sunday 2:00 to 5:00 P.M.; closed major holidays. **Free***.*

Exhibits on Native American history, geology, biology, and anthropology are the attraction for families at the Strecker Museum.

Part of the museum, but located behind Fort Fisher, is the **Governor Bill and Vara Daniel Historic Village** (254–755–1160), re-creating a century-old Texas town at 1108 University Parks Drive. Open Tuesday through Friday noon to 4:00 P.M., Saturday and Sunday 1:00 to 5:00 P.M. Adults $3.00, children $1.00.

TEXAS RANGER HALL OF FAME AND MUSEUM (ages 4 and up)

Exit 335B off I–35 in Fort Fisher Park, Waco 76702–2570 (254–750–8631; www.texasranger.org). Open daily 9:00 A.M. to 5:00 P.M. Adults $4.00, children 6 to 12 $2.00, children 5 and under **Free***.*

One of the most recognized law-enforcement agencies in the world is the Texas Rangers. The Rangers established Fort Fisher here in 1837, making the region safe for settlers. The Texas Ranger Hall of Fame and Museum is housed in a replica of that original fort at University Parks Drive on the shore of Lake Brazos. The fort serves as headquarters for Company F of the Rangers and also as a museum of the agency's colorful history. Included are an extensive firearms collection, examples of Western art, Native American artifacts, dioramas, and a slide show. Many of the docents are retired Rangers, so you can get the history from an expert. Fort Fisher is also a thirty-five-acre park with camping and picnic facilities.

Annual Waco Events

- Central Texas African-American Cultural Expo in April
- Brazos River Festival in April
- Cinco de Mayo in May
- Freedom Frolic in July
- Drag Boat Races in September
- Christmas on the Brazos in December

For more information call (254) 750–8696 or (800) 922–6386, or visit the Waco Web site at www.waco.org.

TEXAS SPORTS HALL OF FAME (ages 6 and up)

Next to Fort Fisher, 1108 South University Parks Drive, Waco 76702 (254–756–1633; www.wacocvb.com/tshof.htm). Open Monday through Saturday 10:00 A.M. to 5:00 P.M., Sunday noon to 5:00 P.M. Adults $4.00, seniors $3.50, students $2.00, children under 6 **Free***.*

If your kids don't know who Nolan Ryan, Earl Campbell, Lee Trevino, Byron Nelson, George Foreman, or Babe Didrickson Zaharias are, take them to the Texas Sports Hall of Fame, where they'll learn about these Texas heroes and more than 300 others. The museum features several different halls of fame and a video on important sporting events in the history of the state.

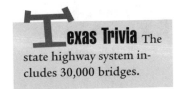

exas Trivia The state highway system includes 30,000 bridges.

 LIONS' PARK KIDDIELAND (ages 4 to 12)
1716 North Forty-second Street, Waco 76702 (254–772–4340). Open daily 10:00 A.M. to 1:00 P.M. and 5:00 to 11:30 P.M. Prices vary with activity.
The kids should like this small amusement park, which has a playground, miniature golf, tennis courts, rides for small children, a swimming pool, and a miniature train that whistles its way around the park.

 WACO WIZARDS (ages 6 and up)
4601 Bosque Boulevard, Waco 76702 (254–399–9300).
Minor league hockey is played in the Heart o' Texas Coliseum October through March.

Where to Eat

Cracker Barrel. *4275 North I–35, Waco 76702 (254–799–4729).* Wonderful southern cooking, huge gift shop in lobby. $-$$

Elite Cafe. *2132 South Valley Mills Avenue, Waco 76702 (254–754–4941).*
"Where the elite meet to eat" in Waco, specializes in chicken fried steak. $-$$

Tanglewood Farms. *221 I–35 at Second Street, Waco 76702 (254–752–7221).* Home cooking in a homey atmosphere. $-$$

Where to Stay

Best Western Motel. *215 Dutton Street, Waco 76706 (800–528–1234).* Pool, 𝓕𝓻𝓮𝓮 continental breakfast. $$

Riverplace Inn. *101 North I–35, Waco 76702 (800–792–3267).* Pool, 𝓕𝓻𝓮𝓮 continental breakfast. $$

For More Information

Waco Convention and Visitors Bureau. *P.O. Box 2570, Waco, TX 76702–2570; (800) 321–9226 or (254) 750–5810. Visit the Web site at www.wacocvb.com.*

Waco Tourist Information Center. *Exit 335B on I–35; (800) 922–6386 or (254) 750–8696.*

Mexia and Corsicana

Mexia (pronounced Meh-hay-ah) is a former oil boomtown at the intersections of Route 14 and Highway 84 with three state parks and a lake nearby for family outdoor fun.

LAKE MEXIA (ages 4 and up)

On U.S. Highway 84, Mexia 76667, 8 miles west of Mexia (254–562–5569).
Lake Mexia is a 1,200-acre impoundment of the Navasota River. You'll find facilities here for boating, camping, fishing, picnicking, swimming, and waterskiing.

CONFEDERATE REUNION GROUNDS STATE HISTORICAL PARK (ages 4 and up)

6 miles north of Mexia between Route 14 and Highway 84, 3 miles from either on Farm Road 2705, Mexia 76667 (254–562–5751).
Confederate Reunion Grounds State Historical Park is popular for picnics. On the grounds are several historic buildings, two scenic footbridges, a low dam, a cannon, and a scenic hiking trail.

FORT PARKER STATE PARK (ages 4 and up)

On Texas Highway 14, Mexia 76667, just south of Mexia (254–562–5751 or 512–389–8900 for camping reservations).
The park consists of 750-acre Lake Fort Parker and the gently rolling oak woodlands surrounding the lake. Here you can boat, camp, fish, hike, swim, or go bird-watching.

OLD FORT PARKER HISTORICAL PARK (ages 6 and up)

On Park Road 35, Groesbeck 76642, off Route 14, south of Mexia (254–729–5253).
Don't confuse the above-mentioned park with Old Fort Parker Historical Park, which is a little farther south, near the town of Groesbeck. Kids will love roaming around this reconstructed stockaded fort, a rarity in the West. The fort honors several area pioneers, especially the Parker family.

LEFTY FRIZZELL COUNTRY MUSIC MUSEUM AND PIONEER VILLAGE (ages 6 and up)

912 West Park Avenue, Corsicana 77510 (903–872–1468). Open Monday through Saturday 9:00 A.M. to 5:00 P.M., Sunday 1:00 to 5:00 P.M.

Country-music fans will want to take the family to the Lefty Frizzell Country Music Museum, located in Pioneer Village. The museum houses Frizzell's personal items, including photos, gold records, costumes, and mementos from other country singers. Outside is a life-size statue of this local boy who made it big in country music. Handprints of Merle Haggard and other singers are embedded in the sidewalk in front of the statue. Pioneer Village preserves many restored houses and buildings from the 1800s.

Cynthia Ann Parker Cynthia Parker was kidnapped from her family home at Fort Parker in 1836 by Comanches when she was nine years old. In the next twenty-five years, she forgot white ways, married Chief Peta Nocona, had three children, and repeatedly refused to return to white society. Cynthia was recaptured inadvertently by Texas Rangers when she was thirty-four during a raid on a Comanche hunting camp in which Peta Nocona was killed. She was so homesick for her Comanche family that she never settled into white society, made several unsuccessful attempts to flee, and died soon after of a broken heart.

One of her sons, Quanah Parker, became the last war chief of the Quahadi Comanche, a major figure in his tribe's resistance to white settlement and in the Comanches' adjustment to reservation life. Quanah eventually became a wealthy rancher, deputy sheriff, and close friend of Theodore Roosevelt.

For More Information

Corsicana Chamber of Commerce.
120 North Twelfth Street, Corsicana, TX 77510; (903) 874–4731. Visit the Web site at www.corsicana.org.

Ennis and Waxahachie

Ennis is an unassuming little town today, proud of its historic building preservation downtown and its annual bluebonnet crop. In the spring, the local garden club sponsors three **Bluebonnet Trails** in the area, covering a distance of 40 miles through farmlands and rolling hills. During the third weekend in April, the city hosts a **Bluebonnet Festival** featuring an arts-and-crafts show, horticultural information, Czech pastries, and wildflower seeds. For more information call the Visitors Bureau at (972) 878-4748.

Waxahachie (Walks-ah-hatchy), a small city south of Dallas, is known as the gingerbread capital of Texas because of its high number of beautifully ornate Victorian-era homes and buildings. It's worthwhile just to wander around the city streets, marveling at the amount of work it took to create these structures. The local chamber of commerce has a map available of historic buildings and locations where several movies *(Bonnie and Clyde, Tender Mercies, A Trip to Bountiful)* have been shot. Call (972) 937-2390.

Of special note is the **Ellis County Courthouse,** built in 1895. With its spires and columns of red sandstone and granite, it is perhaps the most beautiful courthouse in the state. Italian artisans were imported to carve the stone, and the building is covered with ornamental objects and faces, many said to be the face of Mabel Frame, a local woman one of the Italians fell in love with. Ask one of the shop owners around the courthouse square to tell you Mabel's story.

Texas Bluebonnets

The official state flower, bluebonnets are a member of the lupine family and have been known as wolf flower, buffalo clover, and *el conejo* (the rabbit). When Anglo settlers came to Texas, they called the flower bluebonnets because of the resemblance to the sunbonnets pioneer women wore.

The best-known legend surrounding bluebonnets says that a long time ago the Comanches were suffering from starvation and disease. Elders decided the tribe should burn their most valuable possessions as an offering to nature. A young girl overheard the council recommendation, and while everyone was asleep she took her cornhusk doll with its headdress made from blue jay feathers to a hillside, burned it, and scattered the ashes over the hill. The next morning, where the ashes had fallen, the hill was covered in beautiful blue flowers, the same shade as the blue jay feathers. These flowers, the legend says, are the bluebonnets that continue to bloom in Texas every spring.

RAILROAD AND CULTURAL HERITAGE MUSEUM (ages 6 and up)

105 Main Street, Ennis 75120 (972–875–1901). Open April through August Monday through Saturday 10:00 A.M. to 5:00 P.M. and Sunday 1:00 to 5:00 P.M.; September through April Saturday 10:00 A.M. to 5:00 P.M., Sunday 1:00 to 5:00 P.M. Adults $2.00, children under 12 Free.

Ennis was once the hub for the Houston and Texas Central Railroad, so it's only natural that it's also home to the Railroad and Cultural Heritage Museum. Artifacts include the 1897 edition of the *Book of Rules* for train operators, photos of trains that stopped in town, and a miniature replica of the train station.

TEXAS MOTORPLEX (ages 8 and up)

On Highway 287 between Ennis and Waxahachie, Ennis 75119 (800–MOTORPLEX or 972–878–2641; www.texasmotorplex.com).

If your family likes transportation a little more modern and quicker than trains, go to the Texas Motorplex, a drag-racing mecca east of Ennis. Racing is scheduled February through November, along with a number of other auto-related shows and swap meets.

SCARBOROUGH FAIRE (ages 4 and up)

On Farm Road 66, Waxahachie 75168, 2 miles west of Waxahachie, 2 miles west of I–35 East (972–938–1888).

There's nonstop fun for everyone in the family at Waxahachie's Scarborough Faire, a Renaissance festival that runs on weekends from mid-April though early June. You'll enjoy hundreds of arts-and-crafts and food booths, seven medieval entertainment stages, and wandering jugglers, wizards, jesters, royalty, and peasants, all in period costumes.

Where to Stay

Harrison Bed and Breakfast Inn. *717 West Main, Waxahachie 75168 (972–938–1922).* A wonderful place to stay, where the owners love children and have been known to keep them entertained for their parents. The rooms are sumptuous, and one has a large daybed for the kids in addition to a king-size bed for Mom and Dad. $$–$$$

For More Information

Ennis Chamber of Commerce. *2 East Ennis Avenue, P.O. Box 1237, Ennis, TX 75120; (972) 87–VISIT. Visit the Web site at www.visitennis.org.*

Waxahachie Chamber of Commerce. *102 YMCA Drive, Waxahachie, TX 75165; (972) 937–2390. Visit the Web site at www.texasusa.com/waxahachie.*

Fort Worth

Affectionately called "Cow Town," Fort Worth is where the West began, when it became one of the largest shipping points for cattle after the Civil War. This was the hub of all those cattle drives. Today it's one of Texas's largest cities and one of the anchor cities—along with Dallas to the east—of the vast Metroplex, a family vacation delight. The city may be smaller than Dallas and have a more rustic background, but thanks to wealthy patrons over the decades, Fort Worth has museums, art galleries, and fine-arts venues second to none in the state.

Now more than one hundred years old, the **Southwestern Exposition and Livestock Show and Rodeo** (817-877-2420) is a big family event in late January and early February. There's a downtown parade, livestock judging, a carnival, headliner entertainers, and a professional rodeo. Located at the Stock Show Grounds at the Will Rogers Memorial Center, 1 Amon Carter Square. Admission, $14 weekdays and Friday matinees; $16 Friday nights and weekends. Web site: www.fwstockshowrodeo.com.

 FORT WORTH ZOO (ages 2 and up)
1989 Colonial Parkway, Fort Worth 76110 (817–871–7050; www. fortworthzoo.com). Open daily 10:00 A.M. to 5:00 P.M., with extended weekend hours during the summer. Adults $7.00, children 3 to 13 $4.50, toddlers 2 and under Free.

The Fort Worth Zoo is a first-class attraction. Your family will go wild over this place, where you can get face-to-face with gorillas, orangutans, and chimpanzees at the World of Primates or watch eagles flying above and around you in Raptor Canyon. Or step back into old-time Texas at a one-room schoolhouse, ranch house, and other buildings around which the deer and the antelope do play and the buffalo do roam. Stroll tree-shaded paths that wind around the grounds so you can see more than 5,000 exotic and native animals in natural-habitat exhibits.

The kids will enjoy the **Forest Park Train Ride** (817-923-8911) at the zoo. Two ornate miniature trains carry passengers for 5 miles around Trinity and Forest Parks. Fare: $2.00.

BOTANICAL GARDENS (ages 4 and up)

3220 Botanic Drive, Fort Worth 76107 (817–871–7686). Open 8:00 A.M. to 11:00 P.M. daily. The Japanese Garden is a six-acre Oriental garden with a pagoda, moon deck, teahouse, and meditation garden. Open 10:00 A.M. to 5:00 P.M. Tuesday through Sunday.

The Botanical Gardens in Trinity Park is a showcase of 150,000 plants in both formal and natural settings. Small waterfalls, ponds, and pathways abound for a relaxing visit.

Mayfest in Trinity Park (817–332–1055) is a big gathering early in May, with hundreds of arts-and-crafts and food booths, sports activities, competitions for all ages, continuous entertainment, a special children's area, and a serenade by the city symphony.

FORT WORTH NATURE CENTER AND REFUGE (ages 4 and up)

9601 Fossil Ridge Road, Fort Worth 76135 (817–237–1111). Open Tuesday through Friday 9:00 A.M. to 5:00 P.M., Saturday 7:00 A.M. to 5:00 P.M., Sunday noon to 5:00 P.M. **Free**.

Not far from the gardens is the Fort Worth Nature Center and Refuge, just west of the Lake Worth Bridge. The 3,500-acre refuge offers an interpretive center, picnic areas, and hiking and self-guided nature trails. Some trails are wheelchair accessible. The kids will love seeing the bison herd or the white-tailed deer. There's even a prairie-dog town.

MUSEUM OF SCIENCE AND NATURAL HISTORY (ages 4 and up)

1501 Montgomery Street, Fort Worth 76107 (817–732–1631 or 817–654–1356; www.fortworthmuseum.org). Open Monday 9:00 A.M. to 5:00 P.M., Tuesday through Thursday 9:00 A.M. to 8:00 P.M., Friday and Saturday 9:00 A.M. to 9:00 P.M., Sunday noon to 8:00 P.M. Planetarium admission: $3.00, Omni admission: $6.00. Adults $6.00, children $4.00.

Have more family fun at the Museum of Science and Natural History, only this time do it in air-conditioned comfort. The huge museum complex allows kids to dig for dinosaur bones or learn about the wonders of science or history in a number of hands-on, interactive exhibits. Observe the night sky and experience other stellar phenomena at the Noble Planetarium. Then experience the ultimate in sight and sound at the Omni Theater, an 80-foot dome that envelops viewers.

MODERN ART MUSEUM (ages 6 and up)

1309 Montgomery Street, Fort Worth 76107 (817–738–9215). Open Tuesday through Friday 10:00 A.M. to 5:00 P.M., Saturday 11:00 A.M. to 5:00 P.M., Sunday noon to 5:00 P.M. **Free**.

Put a little culture into this family trip by visiting the Modern Art Museum, full of paintings and sculptures by contemporary artists and special traveling exhibits.

KIMBELL ART MUSEUM (ages 6 and up)

3333 Camp Bowie Boulevard, Fort Worth 76107 (817–332–8451 or 817–654–1034; www.kimbellart.org). Open Tuesday through Thursday and Saturday 10:00 A.M. to 5:00 P.M., Friday noon to 8:00 P.M., Sunday noon to 5:00 P.M.; closed holidays. **Free** *except for special exhibitions.*

You'll find culture galore at the Kimbell, the premier art showcase in the Southwest and recognized as one of the finest art museums in America. The collection includes eighteenth-century portraits and works by everyone from prehistoric artists to Picasso. The interior of the museum is an artwork in itself.

AMON G. CARTER MUSEUM (ages 6 and up)

3501 Camp Bowie Boulevard, Fort Worth 76107 (817–738–1933). Open Tuesday through Saturday 10:00 A.M. to 5:00 P.M., Sunday 1:00 to 5:30 P.M. **Free**.

Nearby is more fine art at the Carter Museum, which includes one of the largest collections of Western art in America, featuring works by Charles Russell and Frederic Remington. The museum also showcases traveling exhibits. Visit its Web page at www.cartermuseum.org.

CATTLEMEN'S MUSEUM (ages 4 and up)

1301 West Seventh Street, Fort Worth 76106 (817–332–7064). Open Monday through Friday 8:00 A.M. to 4:30 P.M. Donations welcomed.

Find out what Fort Worth was all about at the Cattlemen's Museum, a very kid-friendly place. The colorful history of Texas ranching is portrayed in film, photos, and cowboy artifacts.

COWTOWN RODEO (ages 4 and up)

In the Cowtown Coliseum in the Stockyards district at 121 East Exchange Avenue, Fort Worth 76106 (817–625–1025). Adults $8.00, children $5.00.

Your family is sure to enjoy a rodeo, and Fort Worth puts one on every Saturday night at the Cowtown Rodeo. In addition to regular rodeo events, **Pawnee Bill's Wild West Show** (817-647-5700) is featured.

The **Stockyards Historic Area** captures the Old West with a number of shops and restaurants along Exchange Avenue. The **Stockyards Station** is a large western festival market housed in the renovated hog and sheep pens of the original stockyards. It's the perfect place to buy souvenirs. Call (817) 626-7921 or (817) 625-5082.

To see authentic cowboys waxing poetic, make an effort to attend the annual **Red Steagall Cowboy Gathering** in October at the Stockyards. The three-day event is filled with western songs, lore, and poetry. Call (817) 884-1945.

 TARANTULA RAILROAD (ages 2 and up)
2318 Eighth Avenue, Fort Worth 76106 (817–625–7245, 817–654–0898, or 800–952–5717; www.tarantulatrain.com). Adults $10.00, children $5.50.

The Tarantula Railroad stops at Stockyards Station. The steam excursion train, pulled by a restored 1896 steam locomotive, makes a 21-mile run from the stockyards to Grapevine. The train runs through the Trinity River Valley following the route of the old Chisholm Cattle Trail and crossing an old trestle. You can purchase tickets at either the Stockyards Station or the Cotton Belt Depot in Grapevine.

Annual Fort Worth Events

- The Last Great Gunfight in February
- Main Street Arts Festival in April
- Cinco de Mayo on the last weekend in April
- Chisholm Trail Round Up in June
- Pioneer Days on Labor Day weekend
- Oktoberfest in October
- Parade of Lights on the weekend after Thanksgiving

FORT WORTH BRAHMAS (ages 6 and up)

1111 Houston Street, Fort Worth 76102 (817–336–4423). Tickets: $8.00 to $15.00.

More minor league hockey, this time at the Fort Worth Convention Center, October through March. While they may not be the stars of the National Hockey League, these skaters provide just as much action and at much more affordable prices.

 SID RICHARDSON COLLECTION OF WESTERN ART (ages 8 and up)

309 Main Street, Fort Worth 76102, in Sundance Square (817–332–6554; www.sidrmuseum.org). Open Tuesday through Friday 10:00 A.M. to 5:00 P.M., Saturday 11:00 A.M. to 6:00 P.M., Sunday 1:00 to 5:00 P.M. Closed holidays. **Free**.

The Sid Richardson Collection of Western Art is a small museum with fifty-five paintings, including works by Russell and Remington. Sundance Square was named after the Sundance Kid, who, with Butch Cassidy, once hid out in Cow Town. The most famous photograph of Cassidy's Wild Bunch was taken in the area.

 NATIONAL COWGIRL HALL OF FAME (ages 6 and up)

111 West Fourth Street, Fort Worth 76102 (817–336–4475 or 800–476–FAME; www.cowgirl.net). **Free**.

A small facility honoring the women who helped make the West great is open until the new building is completed in the museum district, across from the Museum of Science and History. The temporary office on Sundance Square has a rotating sample of exhibits and a nice gift shop.

 C. R. SMITH MUSEUM (ages 6 and up)

4601 Route 360, Fort Worth 76155, at FAA Road near the Dallas/Fort Worth Airport (817–967–1560). Open Wednesday through Saturday 10:00 A.M. to 6:00 P.M., Sunday noon to 5:00 P.M. **Free**.

You'll discover all kinds of things about passenger airplanes at the American Airlines C. R. Smith Museum. Named for the "Father of American Airlines," the museum has a number of interactive displays, films, videos, and hands-on exhibits.

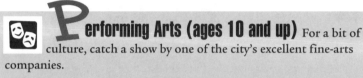

Performing Arts (ages 10 and up) For a bit of culture, catch a show by one of the city's excellent fine-arts companies.

- The Fort Worth Ballet performs at the Convention Center at 1111 Houston Street; (817) 763–0207.
- The Fort Worth Opera, the oldest in Texas, performs at the Convention Center and Scott Theatre at 3505 West Lancaster Street; (817) 737–0775.
- The Fort Worth Symphony also performs at the Convention Center; (817) 926–8831.
- The Scott Theatre puts on several Broadway shows each year; (817) 738–6509.

 BC VINTAGE FLYING MUSEUM (ages 6 and up)

In Hanger 33 at 505 Northwest Thirty-eighth Street, Fort Worth 76155 (817–624–1935). Open Saturday 10:00 A.M. to 5:00 P.M., Sunday noon to 5:00 P.M. Donation requested.

Want to see more airplanes? Go to the BC Vintage Flying Museum, where you'll see lots of World War II memorabilia and a a B-17 Flying Fortress.

 TEXAS MOTOR SPEEDWAY (ages 8 and up)

On Route 114, Fort Worth 76101, at I–35 West (817–215–8500). Call for events and prices.

A state-of-the-art track north of Fort Worth showcases NASCAR and Indy Car races on the big track, Legends Cars on the quarter-mile oval, and auto shows and concerts. Racing takes place spring through summer.

Where to Eat

Chuy's. *2006 North Main Street, Fort Worth 76106 (817–740–0602).* Popular Tex-Mex fare in a funky atmosphere. $–$$

Good Eats Grill. *1651 South University Drive, Fort Worth 76107 (817–332–9060).* Lots of good food; not for dieters. $–$$

Riscky's. *2314 Azel, 300 Main Street, or Stockyards Station, Fort Worth 76106 (817–624–8662 or 817–877–3306).* Jim Riscky is famous in these parts for his "Riscky Dust," a conglomeration of eighteen secret spices created by his grandmother that he rubs into the meat. $

Romano's Macaroni Grill. *1505 South University Drive, Fort Worth 76110 (817–336–6676).* Plentiful Italian food, and the kids get to color on the tablecloth with crayons. $-$$

Where to Stay

Clarion Hotel. *600 Commerce Street, Fort Worth 76102 (817–332–6900 or 800–252–7466).* At the performing arts center. $$$

Etta's Place. *200 West Third Street, Fort Worth 76106 (817–654–0267).* Old West feel with modern conveniences in Sundance Square. $$

Stockyards Hotel. *109 East Exchange Street, Fort Worth 76106 (817–625–6427 or 800–423–8471).* Convenient to everything in the Stockyards District. $$-$$$

For More Information

Fort Worth Convention and Visitors Bureau. *415 Throckmorton Street, Fort Worth, TX 76102–7410; (800) 433–5747 or (817) 336–8791. Visit the Web site at www.fortworth.com.*

Arlington and Mansfield

Just east of Fort Worth is Arlington, home to three of the best family attractions in all of Texas: Texas Rangers baseball, Six Flags Over Texas, and Hurricane Harbor.

TEXAS RANGERS BASEBALL (ages 4 and up)
1000 Ballpark Way, Arlington 76011, off I–30 at Route 157, (817–273–5100; www.texasrangers.com). Tickets: $2.00 to $37.50.

The American League Texas Rangers play in The Ballpark in Arlington. Many experts call this the best major-league field in the world. The Ballpark combines a very traditional look with modern comforts and conveniences, including a full-service restaurant with great views of the diamond. The architectural details are exquisite. Behind the bleacher area are several gift shops, an art gallery, and the **Legends of the Game Museum** (817-273-5099). Your children will love the Learning Center in the museum, with several interactive exhibits. A **Walk of Fame** encircles the upper promenade. The area around The Ballpark is being developed into a parks area with picnic facilities, a **Hall of Fame,** and a youth ball-park similar to the big one next door. And you get to watch baseball, too. Most games start at 7:35 P.M. Even the bleacher seats are a bargain, given the grand view of the game and park and the proximity to the museum and shops.

SIX FLAGS OVER TEXAS (ages 4 and up)

At I–30 and Route 360, Arlington 76010 (817–640–8900; www.sixflags.com). Adults $36.99, children under 48 inches $18.50. Hours vary considerably with the seasons and days of the week.

Six Flags Over Texas is the most popular tourist attraction in the state. The park is full of gravity-defying roller coasters, including the top-rated wooden Texas Giant coaster, and also features a parachute drop, a number of thrill and entertainment shows, and Looney Tune characters roaming the grounds. One of the best attractions here is called The Right Stuff, a virtual-reality ride that creates the full sensation of supersonic flight.

Six Flags Over Texas In its history, Texas has been part of six countries. The flags or seals of those nations are commemorated all over the state, from the amusement park of the same name in Arlington, to the mosaic tiles in the floor of the state capitol in Austin.

- Spain: 1519 to 1685 and 1690 to 1821
- France: 1685 to 1690
- Mexico: 1821 to 1836
- The Republic of Texas: 1836 to 1845
- The United States of America: 1845 to 1861 and 1865 to the present
- Confederate States of America: 1861 to 1865

HURRICANE HARBOR (ages 2 and up)

1800 East Lamar Boulevard, Arlington 76010, across the freeway from Six Flags, (817–265–3356). Open daily May through Labor Day, weekends only through mid-September. Adults $24.99, children $12.50.

This huge, forty-seven-acre water park (formerly Wet 'n' Wild) is one sure way to beat the Texas heat. You'll find water slides, tube rides, lagoons, and a special area for families with small children that is like a park within a park.

FUN FEST (ages 4 and up)

1801 East Lamar, Arlington 76010 (817–276–9898). Open daily during summer. Prices are pay-as-you-play, from $1.00 to $5.00.

Next door you'll find Fun Fest, with race-cart tracks, miniature golf courses, bumper boats, a video arcade, Desert Storm tanks, and a laser-tag adventure.

PUTT-PUTT GOLF AND GAMES (ages 4 and up)

1701 East Division Street, Arlington 76011 (817–277–6501). Open Monday through Thursday 9:00 A.M. to 1:00 A.M., Friday and Saturday 10:00 A.M. to 2:00 a.M., and Sunday 10:00 A.M. to 1:00 A.M.

Lots of stuff to keep the kids occupied: beautiful miniature golf course, video games, pinball, batting cages, and the top-rated go-cart track in the Metroplex area.

DYNO-ROCK INDOOR CLIMBING GYM (ages 6 and up)

608 East Front Street, Arlington 76011 (817–461–3966). Open Monday and Tuesday 3:00 to 10:00 P.M., Wednesday through Friday 11:00 A.M. to 10:00 P.M., Saturday 6:00 to 11:00 P.M., Sunday 1:00 to 9:00 P.M. Admission: $8.00 plus $6.00 for gear rental.

Now here's an unusual place where your children can be entertained and get exercise at the same time. And what kid doesn't like to climb? Here, they do so safely, in a controlled environment for all ages.

RIVER LEGACY LIVING SCIENCE CENTER (ages 6 and up)

703 Northwest Green Oaks Boulevard, Arlington 76006 (817–860–6752). Open Tuesday through Saturday 9:00 A.M. to 5:00 P.M. Adults $2.00, children $1.00.

You'll find a wide range of interactive environmental education exhibits here, including a simulated raft ride down the Trinity River.

KOW BELL INDOOR RODEO (ages 4 and up)

On Route 157, Mansfield 76063, 8 miles south of I–20, (817–477–3092). Two-hour rodeos are held every Saturday and Sunday beginning at 8:00 P.M., while bull-riding practices are every Monday and Friday evening. Adults $6.00, children $3.00.

How can you visit Texas and not see a rodeo? Your family will have plenty of opportunities in the Metroplex area, including the weekly Kow Bell Indoor Rodeo in Mansfield.

Where to Eat

Chuck E. Cheese. *3200 Justiss Drive, Arlington 76011 (817–633–7366).* Food and fun with pizza and video games. $-$$

Cracker Barrel. *1251 North Watson Road, Arlington 76011 (817–633–5477).* Great southern cooking, huge gift shop in lobby. $-$$

Friday's Front Row Sports Grill. *1000 Ballpark Way (inside The Ballpark), Arlington 76011 (817–265–5192).* Food is good, but the view is spectacular when it's game day. $$

Outback Steakhouse. *2101 North Collins Avenue,* Arlington *76011 (817–265–9381).* People rave about the flavorful steaks, pasta dishes, shrimp, and Bloomin' Onions. $$

Where to Stay

La Quinta Inn. *825 North Watson Road, Arlington 76011 (800–NU–ROOMS).* Pool, **Free** continental breakfast. $$

Lexington Hotel Suites. *1607 North Watson Road, Arlington 76011 (817–640–4444 or 800–640–4445).* Close to all the attractions, but out of the flow of the main traffic. Shuttles to most area attractions. Pool, whirlpool/spa, full gym, spacious rooms, **Free** all-you-can-eat full breakfast buffet. Children under thirteen stay **Free**. $$

Marriott. *1500 Convention Center Drive, Arlington 76011 (817–261–8200 or 800–442–7275).* A little pricey, but it's directly adjacent to The Ballpark and close to Six Flags and Hurricane Harbor. $$$

For More Information

Arlington Visitors Center. *1905 East Randol Road, Arlington, TX 76011; (800) 433–5374 or (817) 265–7721. Visit the Web site at www.arlington.org.*

Texas Trivia The state nickname is the Lone Star State, from the solitary star on the state flag.

Duncanville, Grand Prairie, Irving, and Grapevine

Whatever you do, don't miss the annual **Championship American Indian Pow-Wow** if you're in Grand Prairie in early September. Dancers from tribes across the country gather to compete for money and trophies. Try the fry bread or Navajo tacos. Call (972) 647-2331.

KIDSVILLE (ages 4 and up)

206 James Collins Boulevard, Duncanville 75116 (972–780–5070).

Kidsville has been rated the top children's playground in the Metroplex by *Dallas Child* magazine. The huge mazelike facility was built by volunteers and offers children an almost endless variety of slides, swings, and places to climb on or up or around or through, with a swimming pool next door.

CEDAR HILL STATE PARK (ages 4 and up)

On Farm Road 1382, Grand Prairie 75106, 4 miles southeast of (972–291–3900 or 512–389–8900 for camping reservations).

Surrounded by the largest urban area in Texas, Cedar Hill offers a quiet, rustic respite. Here you'll find wooded campsite sand picnic areas. On Joe Pool Lake you can boat, fish, or swim. Or you can visit the pioneer homestead at the Penn Farm Complex.

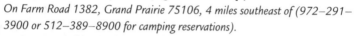

PALACE OF WAX AND RIPLEY'S BELIEVE IT OR NOT! MUSEUM (ages 4 and up)

601 East Safari Parkway, Grand Prairie 75050 (972–263–2391). Open April through Labor Day 10:00 A.M. to 9:00 P.M. daily; during the remainder of the year open 10:00 A.M. to 6:00 P.M. daily. Adults $9.95, children $6.95.

That castle you see off I-30 at Beltline is the Palace of Wax and Ripley's Believe It or Not! Your family will find their favorite movie stars and historical figures portrayed in lifelike detail at the wax museum, while over at Ripley's they'll be amazed at the oddities and curiosities collected there.

LAS COLINAS

6301 North O'Connor Road, Irving 75060 (972–869–3456; www.studiosatlascolinas.com). Studio tours 10:30 A.M. and 12:30, 2:30, and 4:00 P.M. daily (Sunday tours start at 12:30 P.M.). Adults $12.95, children $7.95.

Las Colinas at is a complex of shops and restaurants in Irving that will fascinate your family with its active movie studio. The studio tour will give you a look behind the scenes at a film and television sound stage. *JFK* and *Robocop,* among others, were filmed here. The **National Museum of Communications** showcases memorabilia from pens to satellites. The **Las Colinas Flower Clock,** at Route 114 and O'Connor Road, is a beautifully landscaped area perfect for pictures of the kids. Another great photo spot is at the fountain with the sculpture of galloping horses.

DALLAS COWBOYS FOOTBALL (ages 6 and up)

Loop 12 at Carpenter Expressway, Irving 75060 (972–579–5000 or 214–373–8000 for tickets; www.dallascowboys.com). Tour the hole-in-the-roof stadium Monday through Friday at 10:00 A.M., noon, and 2:00 P.M.; Saturday 11:00 A.M. and 1:00 P.M., except on Saturday before a game. Game tickets are $36 to $61.

The Dallas Cowboys call Texas Stadium in Irving home. No team has won more Super Bowls than the Cowboys, long called America's Team in football. The Cowboys play from September to January, and, given the popularity of the team, you'd be well advised to buy tickets many weeks, even months, in advance. The Cowboys also offer special packages that include hotel rooms, tickets for better seats than you can buy through an agent, and transportation to the stadium.

> **Texas Trivia** The most famous resident of the Studios at Los Colinas is Barney the purple dinosaur. The PBS TV series *Barney & Friends* is filmed there. Barney was created by Texan Sheryl Leach when she couldn't find a good video for her two-year-old son.

GRAPEVINE HERITAGE CENTER (ages 4 and up)

701 South Main Street, Grapevine 76051 (817–329–2438). Open Sunday through Friday 1:00 to 5:00 P.M., Saturday 10:00 A.M. to 5:00 P.M. **Free**.

See railroad memorabilia housed in the restored 1901 Cotton Belt Railroad train station. The depot has several exhibits on the history of Grapevine and casts of dinosaur tracks found nearby. The **Tarantula Railroad** from Fort Worth makes its turnaround at the 1927 Santa Fe Turntable nearby.

For More Information

Duncanville Convention and Visitors Bureau. *203 West Wheatland Drive, Duncanville, TX 75116; (214) 780–5099.*

Grand Prairie Chamber of Commerce. *605 Safari Parkway, Suite A-6, Grand Prairie, TX 75050; (800) 2888–FUN or (214) 263–9588.*

Grapevine Chamber of Commerce. *701 South Main Street, Grapevine, TX 76051; (817) 329–2438.*

Irving Chamber of Commerce. *3333 North MacArthur Boulevard, Irving, TX 75060; (800) 2–IRVING. Visit the Web site at www.irvingtexas.com.*

Plano, Garland, and Mesquite

Plano has become known as the "Balloon Capital of Texas." On most calm mornings you'll see a colorful balloon or two floating over the city, and hot-air balloon races are scheduled the last weekend in September. The festival features hundreds of balloons wafting through the air, an arts-and-crafts fair, and balloon rides for the adventurous. Also, the Balloonport at 1791 Millard Drive will take up to four passengers at sunrise and sunset every day, weather permitting. Call (972) 422-0212.

 INTERURBAN RAILWAY STATION MUSEUM (ages 4 and up)
901 East Fifteenth Street, Plano 75086 (972–461–7250). Open Saturday 10:00 A.M. to 6:00 P.M. **Free.**

Railroad memorabilia and historic artifacts are preserved at this museum, housed in the restored train station in the midst of historic downtown. The surrounding downtown area has several nice shops, boutiques, and cafes.

 MOUNTASIA FANTASY GOLF (ages 4 and up)
2400 Premier Drive off Highway 75 at Parker Road, Plano 75074 (972–424–9940). Open Monday through Saturday 10:00 A.M. to midnight, Sunday noon to 11:00 P.M. Admission, $3.00 to $5.00.

This fifty-four-hole course takes golfers through caves, waterfalls, and other obstacles. There's also a video arcade and bumper boats.

Top Texas Rodeos

- Southwestern Exposition and Fat Stock Show, Fort Worth, in January
- San Antonio Livestock Exposition and Rodeo, San Antonio, in early February
- Houston Livestock Show and Rodeo, Houston, in late February
- Pecos Rodeo, the world's first rodeo, Pecos, on July 4
- Cowtown Rodeo, Fort Worth, weekends
- Kow Bell Rodeo, Mansfield, Saturday evenings
- Mesquite Rodeo, Mesquite, Friday and Saturday April through September
- All-Girl Rodeo, Fort Worth, in October

SOUTHFORK RANCH (ages 6 and up)

3700 Hogge Road (Farm Road 2551), Plano 75002 (972–442–7800 or 800–989–7800; www.foreverresorts.com). Open daily 9:00 A.M. to 5:00 P.M. Adults $7.95 plus tax, children $5.95 plus tax.

If anyone in your family was a fan of the TV show *Dallas*, then don't miss a tour of Southfork, made famous by the program. You can tour the mansion and grounds and a museum dedicated to the show and see herds of horses and longhorn cattle. You can eat at Miss Ellie's Deli or buy Western stuff at the Lincolns and Longhorns gift shop, which features the Continental that Jock Ewing drove in the show.

SURF AND SWIM (ages 4 and up)

440 Oates Drive, Garland 75040 (972–686–1237). Open daily June through September.

Surf and Swim is a city park with a wave-action pool, grass beaches, and picnic areas in the pecan groves.

LANDMARK MUSEUM (ages 6 and up)

Fourth and State Streets in Heritage Park, Garland 75040 (972–205–2749 or 972–272–9160). Open Monday through Friday 9:00 A.M. to 4:30 P.M. **Free**.

The Landmark Museum, a restored Santa Fe train depot, houses area historic artifacts, including an antique railcar. It's also a great place for photos of the children.

CELEBRATION STATION (ages 4 and up)

4040 Towne Crossing Boulevard, Mesquite 75185 (972–279–7888). Open 10:00 A.M. daily Memorial Day through Labor Day; otherwise Monday through Thursday 2:00 to 9:00 P.M., Friday 2:00 P.M. to midnight, Saturday 10:00 A.M. to midnight, Sunday 11:00 A.M. to midnight. Each activity priced separately.

A challenging miniature golf course, bumper boats, go-carts, and a video arcade are just a few of the things that will entertain your family here.

MESQUITE CHAMPIONSHIP RODEO (ages 4 and up)

Military Parkway at I–635, Mesquite 75185 (972–222–BULL or 800–833–9339). Adults $10.00, children $4.00.

You don't have to wait for an annual event to see top-notch rodeo-ing. Just take the family to the Mesquite Championship for performances every Friday and Saturday night April through September. The facility has a restaurant, pony rides, and a Kiddie Korral for youngsters.

SAMUELL FARM (ages 4 and up)

 Beltline Road at U.S. Highway 80, Mesquite 75185 (214–670–7866 or 800–
 670–FARM). Open Monday through Saturday 9:00 A.M. to 5:00 P.M. Adults
$3.00, children 3 through 11 $2.00.

     Your kids can experience a working pioneer farm here. The 340 acres
features a variety of animals, a petting zoo, farm machinery, fishing
ponds, picnic tables, a playground, pony rides, hayrides, and hiking and
horse trails.

DEVIL'S BOWL SPEEDWAY (ages 6 and up)

Lawson Road at U.S. Highway 80, Mesquite 75185 (972–222–2421). Every
Friday and Saturday evening March through November. Adults $10.00, children
12 through 15 $5.00, children 5 through 11 $2.00.

    The Devil's Bowl Speedway features car and motorcycle racing on its
half-mile oval track.

Where to Eat

Luby's Cafeteria. *811 North Central Expressway (U.S. Highway 75), Plano 75075 (972–423–9120). A favorite among longtime Texans.* $

Romano's Macaroni Grill. *5005 West Park Boulevard, Plano 75093 (972–964–6676). Plentiful Italian food, and the kids get to color on the tablecloth with crayons.* $–$$

Where to Stay

Fairfield Inn. *4020 Towne Crossing Boulevard, Mesquite 75150 (972–686–8286).* $$$

La Quinta. *1820 North Central Expressway (U.S. Highway 75), Plano 75075 (972–423–1300 or 800–531–5900).* $$

For More Information

Garland Chamber of Commerce. *914 South Garland Avenue, Garland, TX 75040; (972) 272–7551. Visit the Web site at www.garlandchamber.org.*

Mesquite Visitors Bureau. *617 North Ebrite Street, Mesquite, TX 75185; (972) 285–0211 or (800)*

541–2355. Visit the Web site at www.mesquitechamber.com.

Plano Convention and Visitors Bureau. *2000 East Spring Creek Parkway, Plano, TX 75086–0358; (800) 81–PLANO or (972) 422–0296. Visit the Web site at www.ci.plano.tx.us.*

Dallas

Dallas is Texas's third largest city, having just been edged out for second place by San Antonio, but it's still the most metropolitan of them all. It's the leader in the Southwest for banking and wholesale business and headquarters to many of the nation's top companies. Wholesalers flock to the Dallas Market Center complex, where items at the Home Furnishings Mart, Info-mart, World Trade Center, Trade Mart, Apparel Mart, Decorative Center District, and Menswear Mart set the standards for what you'll be buying in the future. The complex isn't open to the public, but you'll notice its futuristic buildings on the north side of I-35 just before you get to downtown.

Texas Trivia

The smallest county is Rockwall County, just east of Dallas, with 128 square miles.

The city loves sports and culture and hosts the annual **State Fair of Texas,** one of the largest such extravaganzas in the country. Restaurants, shops, and boutiques in Dallas are second to none. You just can't be bored here.

FRONTIERS OF FLIGHT MUSEUM (ages 6 and up)

Love Field Lobby on Cedar Springs at Mockingbird Lane, Dallas 75235 (214–350–3600). Open Monday through Saturday 10:00 A.M. to 5:00 P.M., Sunday 1:00 to 5:00 P.M. Adults $2.00, children $1.00.

The Frontiers of Flight Museum chronicles the history of aviation from early balloon flights to the space program through a number of exhibits and displays.

CAVANAUGH FLIGHT MUSEUM (ages 6 and up)

4571 Claire Chennault Drive at Addison Airport, Dallas 75248 (972–380–8800). Open Monday through Saturday 9:00 A.M. to 5:00 P.M., Sunday 11:00 A.M. to 5:00 P.M. Adults $5.50, children $2.75, under 5 **Free.**

More than thirty planes from both World Wars, Korea, and Vietnam are displayed, along with an aviation art gallery and gift shop.

OLD CITY PARK (ages 4 and up)

1717 Gano Street, Dallas 75215 (214–421–5141). For special events informa-tion visit the home page at www.oldcitypark.org. Open Tuesday through Saturday 10:00 A.M. to 4:00 P.M., Sunday 1:30 to 4:30 P.M. Adults $6.00, children $3.00.

Take a quick step back in time into furnished log cabins, century-old shops, a Victorian bandstand, a drummer's hotel, and southern mansions.

DALLAS WORLD AQUARIUM (ages 2 and up)

1801 North Griffin Street, Dallas 75202 (214–720–2224). Open Monday through Friday 11:00 A.M. to 6:00 P.M., Saturday 10:00 A.M. to 6:00 P.M., Sunday noon to 6:00 P.M. Adults $10.95, children $6.00.

The Dallas World Aquarium is one of two nice aquariums in Dallas. This one features sea life from the world's oceans, including corals, giant clams, sharks, and stingrays.

DALLAS ZOO (ages 2 and up)

621 East Clarendon Drive, Dallas 75201 (214–670–5656; www.dallas-zoo.org). Open daily 9:00 A.M. to 5:00 P.M. Adults $6.00, seniors $4.00, children $3.00.

Your family can see thousands of animals, including the world's largest rattlesnake collection, at the Dallas Zoo. Among the highlights are the twenty-five-acre Wilds of Africa exhibit and a monorail that will take you on a bird's-eye tour. The facility also has picnic areas and a miniature train.

DALLAS NATURE CENTER (ages 4 and up)

7171 Mountain Creek Parkway, Dallas 75203 (972–296–1955; www.
dallasnaturecenter.org). Open daily 7:00 A.M. to 7:00 P.M. **Free**.

The Dallas Nature Center is a 360-acre park with picnic areas, a butterfly garden, and 7 miles of hiking trails around Joe Pool Lake. The area is the habitat for many animals and birds, including some rare ones like the black-capped vireo. The visitors center has a number of educational exhibits.

MALIBU SPEEDZONE (ages 6 and up)

11130 Malibu Drive, Dallas 75229 (972–247–RACE; www.speedzone.com). Open Monday through Thursday 10:00 A.M. to 11:00 P.M., Friday and Saturday 10:00 A.M. to 11:00 P.M., Sunday 11:00 A.M. to 11:00 P.M. From $3.00 per lap to $12.00 per lap, with multilap packages and group rates available.

See who's fastest in your family at Malibu Speedzone. The facility has differently powered race cars for children or adults, including a two-seater. Or play the video games.

REUNION TOWER (ages 2 and up)

Houston and Reunion Streets, Dallas 75207, downtown (214–712–7145). Observation deck open Sunday through Thursday 10:00 A.M. to 10:00 P.M., Friday and Saturday 10:00 A.M. to midnight. Adults $3.00, children $2.00.

Reunion Tower is a fifty-story tower with an observation deck and revolving restaurant at the top. Admission is **Free** with restaurant receipt. The view of Dallas, especially at night, is tremendous. The restaurant is open for lunch 11:30 A.M. to 2:00 P.M. and dinner from 6:00 to 11:00 P.M. This is a popular place to eat, so make reservations well in advance.

REUNION ARENA (ages 6 and up)

Next door is Reunion Arena, where professional sports, circuses, and concerts are in order. Although getting up in age, Reunion is one of the best indoor sports arenas.

- The National Basketball Association **Dallas Mavericks** seat prices are in the $8.00 to $70.00 range. Call (972) 988–3865 or visit the Web site at www.nba.com/mavericks/ for information.

- The National Hockey League **Dallas Stars** seats are in the $20 to $250 range. Call (214) GO–STARS or visit the Web site at /www.dallasstars.com for ticket information.

- **Dallas Sidekicks** indoor soccer seats cost $5.00 to $25.00. Call (214) 653–0200 or check out the Web site at www.sidekicks.com.

SIXTH FLOOR MUSEUM (ages 10 and up)

411 Elm Street, Dallas 75202 (214–747–6660; www.jfk.org). Open Daily 10:00 A.M. to 6:00 P.M. Closed Christmas. Adults $6.00, seniors and students $5.00, children under 6 **Free**.

Unfortunately, one of the things Dallas is best known for is being the place where President John F. Kennedy was killed. The Sixth Floor Museum honors JFK with exhibits on his life and death, including photographs, artifacts, and a film. The museum is housed on the sixth floor of the former Texas Schoolbook Depository Building at Houston and Elm Streets, where Lee Harvey Oswald allegedly fired his fatal shots. Nearby, at Main and Market Streets, are a cenotaph and memorial park dedicated to Kennedy.

CONSPIRACY MUSEUM (ages 10 and up)

110 South Market Street, Dallas 75202 (214–741–3040). Open daily 10:00 A.M. to 6:00 P.M. Adults $7.00, children $3.00.

Of course, some folks don't believe Oswald killed Kennedy. You'll find their museum a couple blocks away. The Conspiracy Museum has several exhibits and displays revealing many assassination conspiracy theories, from Lincoln to Kennedy.

FAIR PARK (ages 2 and up)

Cullum Boulevard at Fitzhugh Avenue, Dallas 75210 (214–670–8400).

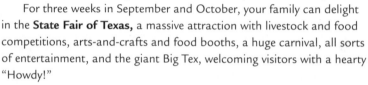

For three weeks in September and October, your family can delight in the **State Fair of Texas,** a massive attraction with livestock and food competitions, arts-and-crafts and food booths, a huge carnival, all sorts of entertainment, and the giant Big Tex, welcoming visitors with a hearty "Howdy!"

In addition, the park hosts the **Dallas Burn** professional soccer team (214-979-0303) and musicals nightly Tuesday through Saturday from June through August.

Recognized as a National Historic Landmark for its Art Deco architecture, Fair Park features year-round attractions, including the following:

- The **Age of Steam Museum** preserves old locomotives, cars, and memorabilia. The gift shop is housed in the restored 1905 Houston and Texas Central Depot. Open Wednesday through Sunday 10:00 A.M. to 5:00 P.M. Admission $4.00 adults, $2.00 children. Call (214) 428-0101.

- Your kids should love the daily (except Monday) shark and piranha feedings at the **Dallas Aquarium,** which also features more than 375 species of marine and freshwater fish, reptiles, and amphibians. Open daily 9:00 A.M. to 4:30 P.M. Admission $3.00 adults, $1.50 children. Call (214) 670-8443, or visit the Web site at www.dallaszoo.org.

- The **Dallas Horticulture Center** has a seven-acre garden area, botanical collections, and a special Garden for the Blind, featuring plants noted for their textures or scents. Open Tuesday through Saturday 10:00 A.M. to 5:00 P.M., Sunday 1:00 to 5:00 P.M. Call (214) 428-7476. 𝓕ree admission.

- The **Museum of Natural History** displays a collection on native animal life in authentic habitats. Open daily 10:00 A.M. to 5:00 P.M. Admission $5.00 adults, $3.00 students. Call (214) 421-3466.

- The **Science Place and TI Founders IMAX Theater** has hundreds of hands-on exhibits and displays about science, energy, and health, as well as a planetarium show and a 79-foot domed IMAX theater. Open Tuesday through Sunday 9:30 A.M. to 5:30 P.M. Exhibit admission is $6.00 for adults, $3.00 for children. Planetarium admission is $3.00 for all. IMAX shows are $6.00 for adults, $5.00 for children. An all-inclusive pass is $13.00 for adults, $9.00 for children. Call (214) 428-7200.

MUSEUM OF AFRICAN-AMERICAN LIFE AND CULTURE (ages 6 and up)

3536 Grand Avenue, Dallas 75210, near Fair Park (214–565–9026). Open Tuesday through Thursday noon to 5:00 P.M., Friday noon to 9:00 P.M., Saturday 10:00 A.M. to 5:00 P.M., Sunday noon to 5:00 P.M. Free.

The Museum of African-American Life and Culture has one of the largest—and best—collections of African-American folk art in the country, as well as cultural and historical exhibits. The interior of the building is also impressive.

DALLAS FIREFIGHTERS MUSEUM (ages 4 and up)

3801 Parry Avenue, Dallas 75210, near Fair Park (214–821–1500). Open Monday through Friday 9:00 A.M. to 4:00 P.M. Free.

Everyone is fascinated with firefighters. You can see more than one hundred years of city history at the Dallas Firefighters Museum, also near Fair Park. The museum is housed in a restored 1907 fire station that includes an 1884 horse-drawn steamer and a 1936 ladder truck among the many historical displays and exhibits.

BIBLICAL ARTS CENTER (ages 4 and up)

7500 Park Lane, Dallas 75225 (214–691–4661). Open Tuesday through Saturday 10:00 A.M. to 5:00 P.M., to 9:00 P.M. on Thursday, and Sunday 1:00 to 5:00 P.M. Free.

A nondenominational showcase of biblical arts in an inspirational building. The galleries house religious art from around the world, a replica of the tomb of Christ, and St. Paul's Gate at Damascus.

DALLAS MUSEUM OF ART (ages 10 and up)

1717 North Harwood Street, Dallas 75201 (214–922–1200). Open Tuesday, Wednesday, and Friday 11:00 A.M. to 4:00 P.M., Thursday 11:00 A.M. to 9:00 P.M., Saturday and Sunday 11:00 A.M. to 5:00 P.M. **Free.**

The Dallas Museum of Art features an extensive collection of pre-Columbian art along with American and European masters and traveling exhibits.

DALLAS ARBORETUM AND BOTANICAL GARDENS (ages 2 and up)

8525 Garland Road, Dallas 75218 (214–327–8263). Open daily 10:00 A.M. to 6:00 P.M. Adults $6.00, children $3.00.

Relax in sixty-six acres of natural beauty at the Dallas Arboretum and Botanical Gardens. The gardens have more than 2,000 varieties of azaleas among the thousands of blooming plants and ferns. Two historic mansions and White Rock Lake are also on the grounds.

INTERNATIONAL MUSEUM OF CULTURES (ages 4 and up)

7500 West Camp Wisdom Road, Dallas 75236 (972–708–7406). Open Tuesday through Friday 10:00 A.M. to 5:00 P.M., Saturday and Sunday 1:30 to 5:00 P.M. Donation requested.

Through life-size and miniature exhibits, the museum portrays cultures from around the world. The diversity here is almost overwhelming.

THE PERFORMING ARTS (ages 10 and up)

Dallas is renowned for its performing-arts companies, so try to make a performance or two part of your visit. For information on concerts and other events around the city, call the Artsline at (214) 522-2659.

- The **Dallas Black Dance Theatre** performs September through May at the Majestic Theater, 1925 Elm Street; (214) 871–2376.

- The **Dallas Opera** performs November to February at the Centrum, 3102 Oak Lawn Street; (214) 443–1000.

- The **Dallas Symphony** plays in the Morton H. Meyerson Symphony Center, 2301 Flora Street; (214) 692–0203.

- The **Dallas Theatre Center** performs at the only theater Frank Lloyd Wright designed, the Kalita Humphreys Theater, at 3636 Turtle Creek Boulevard; (214) 526–8857. The company presents several plays specifically for children and teenagers during the summer.

Where to Eat

Baby Doe's. *3305 Harry Hines Boulevard, Dallas 75210 (214–871–7310).* Rustic elegance and good eats in an old mine replica. $$

Traildust Steak House. *10841 Composite Drive, Dallas 75235 (214–357–3862).* Texas-style food and fun with live country music nightly. $$

Medieval Times. *2021 North Stemmons Street, Dallas 75207 (214–761–1800 or 800–229–9900).* Food and fun with displays of falconry, horsemanship, and sorcery, and a jousting tournament. $$$

Sonny Bryan's Smokehouse. *2202 Inwood Avenue, Dallas 75235 (214–357–7120).* Sure the food is good, but the funky atmosphere, featuring tables made of car hoods with school-desk chairs, is what's fun. $

Where to Stay

Howard Johnson. *9386 LBJ Freeway, Dallas 75234 (972–690–1220).* $$

La Quinta. *10001 North Central Expressway, Dallas 75231 (214–361–8200).* $$–$$$

Lexington Hotel Suites. *4150 Independence Drive, Dallas 75237 (972–298–7014).* $$

For More Information

Dallas Convention and Visitors Bureau. *1201 Elm Street, Dallas, TX 75270; (800) C–DALLAS or (214) 746–6677. Visit the Web site at www. dallascvb.com.*

Texas Trivia When 39 miles of Highways 81 and 287 south of Ringgold were paved in 1936, sand taken from a pit in the area was mixed with paving material. The sand was found to contain gold in very small amounts. So when you drive down the road here, you're on a highway paved with gold.

Lewisville, Denton, and Gainesville

For a nice scenic drive with panoramic views of the rolling hills, travel on Farm Roads 372, 678, and 902 east and south of Gainesville.

LAKE LEWISVILLE (ages 4 and up)

Hackberry Road off Farm Road 423, Lewisville 75067 (972–434–1666 or 800–657–9571).

Lake Lewisville is very popular in the Metroplex area for outdoor recreation. The 23,000-acre lake is surrounded by seventeen parks, most of them administered by the Army Corps of Engineers. You'll find marinas, boat ramps, fishing supplies, and rentals. At some of the parks you'll find campsites, screened shelters, fish-cleaning stations, picnic areas, and playgrounds.

DAUGHTERS OF THE AMERICAN REPUBLIC MUSEUM (ages 6 and up)

117 Gell Avenue, Denton 76201 (940–898–3201). Open Monday through Friday 8:00 A.M. to 5:00 P.M. during fall and spring semesters, Monday through Thursday during summer semester. **Free***.*

The DAR Museum on the campus of Texas Women's University is a unique collection of all the inaugural gowns worn by the First Ladies of Texas, either wives of presidents of the republic, wives of governors, or wives of Texans who served as U.S. president.

RAY ROBERTS LAKE STATE PARK (ages 4 and up)

Farm Road 445 off I–35, Denton 76201 (940–686–2148 Isle du Bois or 940–637–2294 Johnson Branch; for camping reservations call 512–389–8900).

You'll find plenty of splashing and fishing at Ray Roberts Lake State Park. The park is comprised of two units, Isle du Bois and Johnson Branch, and several satellite parks border the 30,000-acre Ray Roberts Lake. The facilities have campsites, picnic areas, boat ramps, more than 20 miles of hiking and biking trails, and plenty of places to swim or fish.

FRANK BUCK ZOO (ages 4 and up)

Leonard Park off California Street, Gainesville 76240 (940–668–4530). Open November through March 9:00 A.M. to 5:00 P.M.; April through August 9:00 A.M. to 6:00 P.M.; September through October 9:30 A.M. to 6:00 P.M. **Free.**

Unless you're traveling with your grandparents, no one in your family is likely to remember who Frank Buck was. The famous adventurer of the 1930s and 1940s made the phrase "Bring 'em back alive" a household saying as he captured hundreds of wild animals for zoos. The Frank Buck Zoo is named to honor Gainesville's famous son. The zoo is home to monkeys, zebras, flamingos, bears, elephants, and more. The facility also has shaded picnic areas.

Annual Area Events

- North Texas Farm Toy Show, Gainesville, February
- Spring Arts and Crafts Fair, Lewisville, March
- Depot Days, Gainesville, May
- Chamber of Commerce Rodeo Week, Gainesville, July
- Labor Day Rodeo, Lewisville, September
- Victorian Christmas and Teddy Bear Parade, Denton, December
- Children's Christmas Party, Gainesville, December
- Old Town Christmas Stroll, Lewisville, December

For More Information

Denton Convention and Visitors Bureau. *5800 North I–35, Denton, TX 76201; (888) 381–1818 or (940) 382–7895. Visit the Web site at www.denton-chamber.org.*

Gainesville Chamber of Commerce. *101 South Culbertson Street, Gainesville, TX 76240; (940) 665–2831. Visit the Web site at www.gainesville.tx.us.*

Lewisville Visitors Bureau. *233 West Main Street, Lewisville, TX 75067; (800) 657–9571 or (972) 436–9571.*

Denison, Sherman, and McKinney

This area, near the Texas-Oklahoma border, is a great place if you just want to relax. Small towns and lots of outdoor recreation are the order of the day here.

Dwight Eisenhower—who was born in Denison shortly before his parents moved to Kansas—was the first native Texan to become president, and two state parks in the area commemorate the World War II hero.

  EISENHOWER BIRTHPLACE STATE HISTORIC PARK (ages 10 and up)

208 East Day Street, Denison 75020 (903–465–8908). Open daily 9:00 A.M. to 5:00 P.M.

The two-story, gabled house Ike was born in has been restored to its appearance in 1890, the year Eisenhower was born. You'll see family possessions, period antiques, and hundreds of items relating to Eisenhower and his place in history. The ten-acre park also has a hiking trail following an abandoned railroad track.

 RED RIVER RAILROAD MUSEUM (ages 4 and up)

101 East Main Street, Denison 75021 (903–463–6238). Open Monday through Saturday 10:00 A.M. to 1:00 P.M. and 2:00 to 4:00 P.M. **Free.**

Denison was founded in 1872 because of the railroad, specifically the Missouri, Kansas, and Texas line. That pioneer heritage has been preserved here with artifacts, pictures, MKT railroad equipment, and rolling stock.

  GRAYSON COUNTY FRONTIER VILLAGE (ages 4 and up)

Loy Park at the Frontier Village exit off U.S. Highway 75, Denison 75020 (903–463–2487). Open mid-May to mid-October, Wednesday through Sunday 1:00 to 4:00 P.M.

The Grayson County Frontier Village in Denison is not a typical county museum, it's a collection of eighteen rustic buildings dating from 1840 to 1900, all restored and furnished. The museum exhibits household items, clothing, and tools from pioneer days.

EISENHOWER STATE PARK (ages 4 and up)

Park Road 20 off Farm Road 1310, Denison 75020, 5 miles north of Denison (903–465–1956 or 512–389–8900 for camping reservations).

This park is distinctly different from the Eisenhower Birthplace. Perched on rocky cliffs above Lake Texoma, the 450-acre park has a modern marina, campsites, boat rentals, screened shelters, picnic areas, hiking and biking trails, and, of course, swimming and fishing.

LAKE TEXOMA (ages 4 and up)

North of U.S. Highway 82, Denison 75020, west of Denison (903–465–4990).

Lake Texoma is a huge, 89,000-acre reservoir, impounding the Red River in Texas and Oklahoma. It's one of the most popular places for outdoor recreation in the state. The surrounding Army Corps of Engineers parks have more than fifty campgrounds, dozens of trailer parks, more than a hundred picnic areas, more than a hundred screened shelters, and more than eighty boat ramps. Some piers even have enclosed areas where you can fish in air-conditioned comfort. Modern marinas and

Texas Trivia Lake Texoma is one of 6,736 reservoirs in Texas. The Red River, at 1,360 miles, is the second longest river in the state; the Rio Grande is longest.

resorts dot the 580 miles of shoreline. The Cross Timbers Hiking Trail winds through 14 miles of woods around the lake. Fishing is considered some of the best in either state. Maps, detailed information, and exhibits on the building of Denison Dam can be found at the dam headquarters on Highway 75A, a few miles north of Denison.

HAGERMAN WILDLIFE REFUGE (ages 4 and up)

On Farm Road 1417, Sherman 75090, 4 miles north of Sherman (903–786–2826).

Hagerman Wildlife Refuge surrounds the Big Mineral Arm of Lake Texoma with 12,000 acres of habitat—including 3,000 acres of marshland—that are home to 280 species of migratory waterfowl and other birds. A variety of geese calls Hagerman its winter home. The refuge has a 4-mile auto tour with roadside exhibits providing information on the area and wildlife, several hiking and biking trails, three picnic areas, an observation tower, wildlife blinds, a visitors center, and a historical exhibit depicting the old town of Hagerman that was removed before the flooding of Lake Texoma. Camping and swimming are not permitted.

HEARD NATURAL SCIENCE MUSEUM AND WILDLIFE SANCTUARY (ages 4 and up)

On Farm Road 1378, McKinney 75070, 5 miles south of McKinney (972–562–5566; www.heardmuseum.org). Open Tuesday through Saturday 9:00 A.M. to 5:00 P.M., Sunday 1:00 to 5:00 P.M. **Free.**

Your family can see more wildlife at the Heard Natural Science Museum and Wildlife Sanctuary. The facility is a little more visitor friendly than Hagerman. Exhibits include fossils, archaeology, seashells, rocks, and live animals; there are also several nature trails through the 274-acre sanctuary

Annual Area Events

- Livestock Show, Sherman, March
- Texoma Lakefest, Denison, April
- U.S. National Aerobatic Competition, Denison, September
- Red River Valley Arts Festival, Sherman, September
- Grayson County Fair, Sherman, October
- Main Street Fall Festival, Denison, October

and a paved trail for wheelchairs. The gift shop has nature books, specimens, and other nature-related items.

Where to Eat

Catfish King. *3301 Highway 75 North, Sherman 75090 (903–868–2953).* A local favorite, huge portions. $

Golden Corral. *2811 Loy Lake Road, Sherman 75090 (903–892–3366).* All-you-can-eat buffet. $–$$

Showboat Pizza & BBQ. *At Grandpappy Point Marina on Farm Road 84, Denison 75020 (903–465–9496).* Good food and a good view. $–$$

Where to Stay

Grandpappy Point Marina Cabins. *On Farm Road 84, Denison 75020 (903–465–6330 or 888–855–1972).* On Lake Texoma, full marina. $$

Grayson House. *2105 Texoma Parkway, Sherman 79090 (903–892–2161).* Pool, Jacuzzi, **Free** continental breakfast. $$

Ramada Inn. *1600 South Austin Avenue, Denison 75020 (903–465–6800).* **Free** full breakfast. $$

For More Information

Denison Chamber of Commerce.
313 West Woodard Street, P.O. Box 325, Denison, TX 75021–0325; (903) 465–1551. Visit the Web site at www.denisontexas.com.

McKinney Chamber of Commerce.
1801 West Louisiana Street, P. O. Box 621, McKinney, TX 75070; (972) 542–0163. Visit the Web site at www.mckinneytx.org.

Sherman Chamber of Commerce.
307 West Washington Street, Sherman, TX 75090; (888) 893–1188 or (903) 893–1184. Visit the Web site at www. shermantexas.com.

Wichita Falls and Jacksboro

The original falls on the Wichita River were destroyed by a flood in 1886, but the city has re-created them in a beautifully landscaped park in the middle of the city.

The Wichita Falls Waterfall is off I-44 at Highway 277. More than 3,500 gallons of water a minute are recirculated through the 54-foot-high waterfall that drops in a series of steps over rocks; a stairway next to the falls goes from top to bottom. The park is cooling, relaxing, and a great place for photographs. Call (940) 723-9988 or visit the Web site at www.wichitafalls.org. for area information.

LUCY PARK (ages 4 and up)
Sunset Drive at U.S. Highway 277, Wichita Falls 76301. Open 6:00 A.M. to midnight.

Near the falls is Lucy Park, a nice place for picnics and just playing around. The park has a log cabin, swimming pool, duck pond, paved nature trail, and children's playground. The **River Walk** trail connects the park to the falls.

RAILROAD MUSEUM (ages 4 and up)
501 Eighth Street, Wichita Falls 76301 (940–723–2661). Open Saturday noon to 4:00 P.M. Free.

A nice collection of railroad cars—including a diesel engine, a Pullman car, two World War II troop sleepers, a baggage car, a post office car, a coach and several cabooses—are preserved at the museum.

THE PLEX ENTERTAINMENT CENTER (ages 4 and up)

4131 Southwest Parkway, Wichita Falls 76309 (940–696–1222). Open Sunday through Thursday 11:00 A.M. to 10:00 P.M., Friday 11:00 A.M. to midnight, Saturday 10:00 A.M. to midnight. Prices vary by activity.

The classic kid place full of go-carts, bumper boats, video games, miniature golf courses, and more.

LAND OF LEGENDS (ages 4 and up)

4800 Sisk Road, Wichita Falls 76310 (940–691–0682). Open Monday through Saturday 10:00 A.M. to 4:00 P.M. **Free**.

Land of Legends is a living-history museum in Fort Wakan Tanka Trading Post. The facility has a replica of a trapper's cabin, carpenter and blacksmith shops, and a functioning general store. Costumed characters often roam the grounds, dressed as mountain men or Native Americans. You can camp out or fish at Legends Lake. Staying in a tepee overnight will cost you just $10.

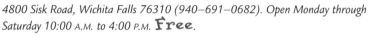

WICHITA FALLS MUSEUM AND ART CENTER (ages 6 and up)

2 Eureka Circle, Wichita Falls 76308 (940–692–0923). Open Tuesday through Saturday 10:00 A.M. to 5:00 P.M., Sunday 1:00 to 5:00 P.M. Adults $4.00, children $3.00, planetarium $2.00 additional.

The Wichita Falls Museum and Art Center is a fascinating family outing, full of science, art, and history exhibits, with planetarium shows on weekends.

LAKE ARROWHEAD STATE PARK (ages 4 and up)

On Farm Road 1954 off U.S. Highway 281, Wichita Falls 76301, 14 miles south of Wichita Falls (940–528–2211 or 512–389–8900 for camping reservations).

Water recreation is the attraction at Lake Arrowhead State Park. You'll find campsites, rest rooms with showers, a grocery store, and boat ramps. A nice place to spend the day fishing, swimming, or water-skiing. Tip: The lake is dotted with steel oil derricks, and the waters around these structures are usually great for fishing.

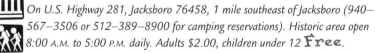

FORT RICHARDSON STATE HISTORIC SITE (ages 6 and up)

On U.S. Highway 281, Jacksboro 76458, 1 mile southeast of Jacksboro (940–567–3506 or 512–389–8900 for camping reservations). Historic area open 8:00 A.M. to 5:00 P.M. daily. Adults $2.00, children under 12 **Free**.

You can visit another historic fort in Jacksboro. Fort Richardson has a couple of restored buildings, including an officer's quarters that serves as a visitors center, and several ruins. In addition to soaking up nineteenth-century military history, the family can enjoy camping, picnicking, fishing in the old quarry pond (stocked with rainbow trout in the winter), or hiking along the three nature trails.

Where to Eat

Casa Mañana. *609 Eighth Street, Wichita Falls 76301(940–723–5661).* Tasty Mexican food. $

Chuck E. Cheese. *2935 Southwest Parkway, Wichita Falls 76309 (940–692–*

7882). Fun and pasta, with video games, music. $–$$

Luby's Cafeteria. *1801 Ninth Street, Wichita Falls 76301(940–723–6022).* A favorite among Texans for decades. $

Where to Stay

La Quinta. *1128 Central Freeway, Wichita Falls 76305 (940–322–6971).* Pool, ℱree continental breakfast. $$

Trade Winds. *1212 Broad Street, Wichita Falls 76306 (940–723–8008).* Pool. $$

For More Information

Wichita Falls Convention and Visitors Bureau. *1000 Fifth Street, Wichita Falls, TX 76307–0630; (800) 799–MPEC*

or (940) 723–MPEC. Visit the Web site at www.wichitafalls.org.

Mineral Wells and Weatherford

You're in a very rural area of Texas now, and the nearby Brazos River offers the perfect chance for your family to get away from it all, enjoying beautiful scenery on a relatively calm and quiet river. Several companies rent canoes for float trips.

The area is the birthplace of the Loving-Goodnight cattle drives of the Old West, and Oliver Loving—the man Larry McMurtry based the character of Gus McCrae on in *Lonesome Dove*—is buried in Weatherford. Water from the Crazy Well in Mineral Wells was all the rage in the nineteenth century.

By the way, that huge castle-looking structure you're bound to see at 1825 Bankhead Drive in Weatherford is the **Pythian Home,** built by the Knights of

Pythias in 1907. It's private, but if you want a tour, one can be arranged through the chamber of commerce at (940) 596-3801.

FAMOUS MINERAL WATER COMPANY (ages 6 and up)

209 Northwest Sixth Street, Mineral Wells 76067 (940–325–8870). Tours Tuesday through Saturday 8:00 A.M. to 1:00 P.M. **Free.**

Mineral Wells was famous in the nineteenth century for water that was said to cure just about anything, including mental illness. Only one of those companies that bottled the well water is operating today, the Famous Mineral Water Company. The company no longer makes outrageous claims for the water, however. Tours take you to the drinking pavilion, well, and bottling plant.

MINERAL WELLS STATE PARK (ages 4 and up)

On U.S. Highway 80, 3 miles east of Mineral Wells 76067 (940–328–1171 or 512–389–8900 for camping reservations).

Find more outdoor recreation at Lake Mineral Wells State Park. This is another of the many parks built by the Civilian Conservation Corps in the 1930s. The chances for your kids to see wildlife like white-tailed deer and wild turkeys are excellent in this heavily wooded park surrounding Lake Mineral Wells. Facilities include boat ramps, campsites with water, picnic areas, five fishing piers, a swimming area, a recreation hall, screened shelters, and showers. More than 20 miles of hiking and equestrian trails wind through the park.

POSSUM KINGDOM STATE PARK (ages 4 and up)

Park Road 33, Caddo 76429, 17 miles north of Caddo (940–549–1803 or 512–389–8900 for camping reservations).

Possum Kingdom State Park is one of the premier outdoor-recreation havens in Texas, tucked away in the rugged Palo Pinto Mountains. The 20,000-acre lake has the clearest, bluest water you'll find anywhere in the state. The kids will enjoy watching the cliff swallows, the almost-tame deer strolling through the grounds, the cattle that are part of the official State Longhorn Herd, or the opossums after which the lake is named. The park has boat ramps, campsites, picnic tables, and grills. The swimming and the fishing are both great. To get there, take U.S. Highway 180 east of Mineral Wells for about 40 miles to Caddo, then go north 17 miles on Park Road 33 to the lake.

HOLLAND LAKE PARK (ages 4 and up)

 On Clear Lake Road, Weatherford 76086, off exit 409 from I–20, (940–594–3801).

Holland Lake Park is a ten-acre living museum of nature with marked trails that explore three distinct ecosystems. The park also has a playground and picnic facilities.

 LAKE WEATHERFORD (ages 4 and up)

 On Farm Road 730, Weatherford 76086, off U.S. Highway 180, 7 miles east of Weatherford (940–594–3801).

 Lake Weatherford is another city-owned park on the Clear Fork of the Trinity River. The area has many public and commercial swimming and fishing areas.

 PETER PAN (ages 6 and up)

1214 Charles Street, Weatherford 76086 (940–598–4150). Library open Monday, Wednesday, Friday, and Saturday 10:00 A.M. to 6:00 P.M.; Tuesday and Thursday 1:00 to 9:00 P.M. **Free**.

The kids might wonder why there's a statue of Peter Pan in front of the Weatherford city library. You can explain to them that Weatherford was the home of Mary Martin, who created the role on Broadway. The library has some costumes, music scores, and other Martin memorabilia.

Annual Area Events

- Palo Pinto County Livestock Show and Fair, Mineral Wells, March
- Crazy Water Festival, Mineral Wells, June
- Peach Festival, Weatherford, July
- Parker County Frontier Days, Livestock Show and Rodeo, Weatherford, July
- Best Little Balloonfest in Texas, Possum Kingdom, October

For More Information

Mineral Wells Chamber of Commerce. *511 East Hubbard Street, P.O. Box 1408, Mineral Wells, TX 76068–1408; (940) 325–2557.*

Weatherford Visitors Center. *401 Fort Worth Street, Weatherford, TX 76086; (940) 596–3801.*

Granbury, Glen Rose, Cleburne, Meridian, and Whitney

You'll find a fair amount of history in Granbury, one of the best small cities in Texas. For example, Davy Crockett's wife and son are buried here, and you can also visit the grave of Jesse James at the city cemetery, North Crockett and Moore Streets. Well, his family claims it's Jesse, who, they say, survived his wounds to retire here. Call (817) 573-5548 or (800) 950-2212 for information on the man who claimed to be James and another who claimed to be Lincoln assassin John Wilkes Booth.

Texas Trivia Acton State Park, near Granbury, is the smallest state park in the United States with just .006 acre.

You'll find a number of nice shops and restaurants around the courthouse square. You should find ample **free** parking in the lot inside the square. The attractive courthouse itself is a little unusual: Its tower clock still functions.

ACTON STATE HISTORICAL PARK (ages 4 and up)
On Farm Road 167, Granbury 76031, about 6 miles east of Granbury (817–645–4215).

Davy Crockett's widow, Elizabeth, and son, Robert, are buried here. After Crockett died at the Alamo, the new Republic of Texas gave his family land nearby, so they moved from Tennessee. The entire park encompasses just the graves and monument.

BRAZOS OLD FASHIONED DRIVE-IN (ages 4 and up)
1800 West Pearl Street, Granbury 76048 (817–573–1311). Movies at 9:00 P.M. Friday through Tuesday during daylight savings time, otherwise 7:45 P.M. $10 per carload.

The Brazos Old Fashioned Drive-In is one of the few remaining drive-in theaters in the nation. Fewer than a dozen remain in Texas. Drive in, tune your radio to the movie sound, enjoy some popcorn, and relax.

THE GULCH (ages 4 and up)
5100 Highway 377 East, Granbury 76048 (817–579–1515). Golf is $5.50 for adults, $4.50 for children 9 and under.

The Gulch is a family entertainment park that claims to be the world's largest miniature golf course—on three rolling, shady acres. It's certainly the most beautiful. You'll play through a naturally landscaped area of creeks and waterfalls and wildflowers. You'll also find batting cages, a picnic area, two sand volleyball courts, and a video arcade.

THE GREAT RACE AUTOMOTIVE HALL OF FAME
(ages 6 and up)

*114 North Crockett Street, Granbury 76048 (817–573–5200). Open Saturday
10:00 A.M. to 5:00 P.M., Sunday noon to 5:00 P.M. Donations requested.*

Historic cars from the beginning of the twentieth century are preserved here, and the exhibits rotate periodically.

LAKE GRANBURY

*Contact the visitors center at (817) 573–5548 or www.granburytx.com for infor-
mation.*

Lake Granbury is almost everywhere you look when you're in town.
Public and commercial facilities are all along the 100 miles of shoreline,
so you won't
have any prob-
lem finding a
place to picnic,
swim, fish, or
water-ski.

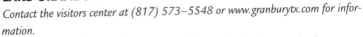 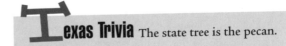

Texas Trivia The state tree is the pecan.

THE PROMISE (ages 6 and up)

*On Bo Gibbs Drive off U.S. Highway 67, Glen Rose 76043 (254–897–4341 or
800–687–2661; www.thepromise.org). Performances are Friday and
Saturday evenings June through October. Adults $12.00 to $19.00, children
$8.00 to $15.00.*

Glen Rose is home to *The Promise,* a historical reenactment of the life
of Jesus of Nazareth. The musical drama is presented in the open-air
Texas Amphitheater just north of downtown (you'll see the flashing sign).

FOSSIL RIM WILDLIFE CENTER (ages 4 and up)

*Off U.S. Highway 67, Glen Rose 76043, 3 miles west of Glen Rose
(254–897–2960; www.fossilrim.com). Adults $12.95, children $9.95.*

Discover some the world's most endangered animals at Fossil Rim.
White rhinos, zebras, and cheetahs roam free on the 2,900 acres of valleys and savannas. Facilities include a petting pasture for children, picnic
areas, a restaurant, nature trails, and an educational center. If your family is athletically inclined, take a guided tour of the park on mountain
bikes for $30.

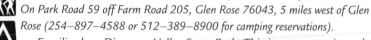

DINOSAUR VALLEY STATE PARK (ages 4 and up)

On Park Road 59 off Farm Road 205, Glen Rose 76043, 5 miles west of Glen Rose (254–897–4588 or 512–389–8900 for camping reservations).

Families love Dinosaur Valley State Park. This is a very scenic park on the banks of the Paluxy River, where you can camp, have a picnic, or roam over one of the many hiking trails. But you'll also be fascinated by the dinosaurs. A couple of giant replicas overlook the grounds near the park entrance. And real footprints can be seen in the riverbed. These are the best-preserved tracks in the state, and among the best in the country.

***S*cenic Drive** Follow Farm Road 205 to U.S. Highway 67 to Farm Road 200, traveling from Dinosaur Valley State Park to Cleburne State Park for a quiet drive through rolling hills covered with wildflowers in the spring.

Interpretive exhibits at the visitors center will give you an idea of what this area looked like a hundred million years ago.

CLEBURNE STATE PARK (ages 4 and up)

On Park Road 21 off Farm Road 200, Cleburne 76031, about 12 miles west of Cleburne (817–645–4215 or 512–389–8900 for camping reservations).

A real out-of-the-way place, Cleburne is a 528-acre park surrounded by white rock hills where oak, elm, mesquite, cedar, and redbud trees are almost jungle thick, and in spring bluebonnets carpet the open spaces. Your family can fish, swim, or boat on the lake that flows from three natural springs, picnic; or camp out. And you've got a good chance to see deer, wild turkey, ducks, geese, and armadillos.

MERIDIAN STATE PARK (ages 4 and up)

On Texas Highway 22, Meridian 76665, 3 miles southwest of Meridian (254–435–2536 or 512–389–8900 for camping reservations).

Meridian State Park is a quiet spot with 500 wooded acres and abundant plants, wildflowers, animals, and birds. Facilities include campsites, swimming, fishing, boating, 5 miles of scenic bike trails, and 6 miles of hiking trails.

LAKE WHITNEY STATE PARK (ages 4 and up)

On Farm Road 1244, Whitney 76692, 3 miles west of Whitney (254–694–3793 or 512–389–8900 for camping reservations).

Lake Whitney is the fourth largest lake in Texas, extending 45 miles along the Brazos River. The park itself has scattered oak groves, and in the spring bluebonnets and Indian paintbrushes cover the landscape. You can swim, ski, or fish on the lake, renowned for its trophy-size bass, or take a hike along the nature trail.

Annual Area Events

- Old Fashioned Fourth of July, Granbury
- Bluegrass Festival, Tres Rios Park, Glen Rose, September
- Granbury Civil War Re-enactment, Granbury, September
- Comanche County Pow-Wow, Comanche, September
- Harvest Moon Festival, Granbury, October

Where to Eat

Hennington's Texas Cafe. *121 East Bridge Street, Granbury 76048 (817–573–5612).* Texas-style food on the square. $–$$

Irby's Burgers & Catfish. *801 East Pearl Street, Granbury 76048 (817–573–7311).* $

Pearl Street Pasta House. *101 East Pearl Street, Granbury 76048 (817–279–7719).* Italian restaurant where you can mix and match your own pasta and sauces. $–$$

Where to Stay

Arbor House Bed and Breakfast. *530 East Pearl Street, Granbury 76048 (817–573–0073 or 800–641–0073).* The best place to stay in town, overlooking the lake and close to the square. Accommodations are modern, and the owners let you have the run of a large refrigerator downstairs and always put out cookies, brownies, or other sweet treats for their guests. Visit the Web site at www2.itexas.net/~arbor for complete information and a virtual tour of the inn. $$

Days Inn. *1339 North Plaza Drive, Granbury 76048 (800–858–8607).* $$

Inn on the River. *205 Southwest Barnard Street, Glen Rose 76043 (800–575–2101).* $$

For More Information

Granbury Convention and Visitors Bureau. *100 North Crockett Street, Granbury, TX 76048; (800) 950–2212 or* *(817) 573–5548. Visit the Web site at www.granbury.org.*

The Panhandle

The Panhandle is also known as the *Llano Estacado* (yawn-oh es-tah-cah-doe), Spanish for "staked plains." Historians believe the name originated with the famous Coronado expedition, whose members staked their route across the featureless sea of grass so they could find their way back. When you drive through the Panhandle, across many miles of almost absolutely level agricultural lands with no landmarks on any horizon, you'll see how easily a person could get lost without road signs.

But these plains are broken up, rather abruptly in places, by the Caprock Escarpment, which marks the edge of the High Plains. This escarpment creates many of the best scenic wonders in the Panhandle, like Palo Duro Canyon, Caprock Canyon, and the Red River Valley.

Getting around is remarkably easy since many of the main highways—I-27 and I-40; U.S. Highways 385, 380, 87, 84, 70, and 60; and Texas Highway 70—travel in almost straight lines from place to place.

Brownfield and Lubbock

Several famous musicians have called Lubbock home, including rock and roll pioneer Buddy Holly. You can relax a while at the **Buddy Holly Statue and Walk of Fame** at Eighth Street and Avenue Q, near the Civic Center. The monument pays tribute to the many celebrities raised here. The centerpiece is a statue of Holly, guitar in hand. Plaques around the base of the statue honor Holly and his band, The Crickets; Waylon Jennings; Bob Wills; Mac Davis; Roy Orbison; Tanya Tucker; actor Barry Corbin; and others. It's a favorite place for locals to have lunch. For general information about Lubbock, visit the Web site www.lubbock.org.

THE PANHANDLE

Allan's Top Annual Family Fun Events

- Arts Festival, Lubbock, April (806-744-2787)
- FunFest, Amarillo, May (806-374-0802)
- Sheriff's Posse Rodeo, Brownfield, July (806-637-2564)
- Old West Days, Amarillo, July (806-378-4297)
- XIT Rodeo and Reunion, Dalhart, August (806-249-5646)
- National Cowboy Symposium, Lubbock, September (806-795-2455)
- Tri-State Fair, Amarillo, September (806-376-7767)
- Texas Tech Intercollegiate Rodeo, Lubbock, October (806-742-3351)
- World Championship Ranch Rodeo, Amarillo, November (806-358-7382)
- Old Fashioned Christmas, Panhandle-Plains Museum in Canyon, December (806-655-2244)

COLEMAN PARK (ages 4 and up)

South of Brownfield on U.S. Highway 385, Brownfield 79316 (806–637–2564).

Coleman Park is a forty-four-acre recreation site with picnic areas, trailer campsites, a playground, and a swimming pool. This is one of the best values in the state because your family can camp here for up to four days for **Free.**

TERRY COUNTY HISTORICAL MUSEUM (ages 6 and up)

600 East Cardwell Street, Brownfield 79316 (806–637–2467). Open 10:00 A.M. to noon and 1:00 P.M. to 3:00 P.M. Tuesday through Friday, noon to 4:00 P.M. Saturday. Adults 50 cents, children 25 cents.

In town, stop by the Terry County Historical Museum. The small museum, once the home of A. M. Brownfield, has displays on area history, with an emphasis on pioneer artifacts. The first county jail and a 1917 vintage Santa Fe Railway Depot are on the grounds.

MUSEUM OF TEXAS TECH AND MOODY PLANETARIUM (ages 6 and up)

Fourth Street at Indiana Avenue on the Texas Tech campus, Lubbock 79401 (806–742–2490). The museum is open Tuesday, Wednesday, Friday, and Saturday 10:00 A.M. to 5:00 P.M.; Thursday 10:00 A.M. to 8:30 P.M.; Sunday 1:00 to 5:00 P.M. Planetarium programs are offered Tuesday, Wednesday, and Friday at 3:30 P.M.; Thursday at 7:30 P.M.; Saturday and Sunday at 2:00 and 3:30 P.M. Museum Free; planetarium $1.00 adults, 50 cents students.

Lubbock is home to Texas Tech University, which could be the center of any visit. Your family could spend all day at the Museum of Texas Tech University. Museum exhibits cover the arts and humanities and the social and natural sciences, with an emphasis on area pioneer history and natural history. It's also the home of Moody Planetarium, featuring astronomy programs and space exhibits, which the kids should love.

RANCHING HERITAGE CENTER (ages 4 and up)

Fourth Street at Indiana Avenue, Lubbock 79401 (806–742–2482). Open Monday through Saturday 10:00 A.M. to 5:00 P.M., Sunday 1:00 to 5:00 P.M. (except November 1 through March 31, when it is closed on Monday). Donations welcomed.

Adjacent to the university museum is the Ranching Heritage Center. This fourteen-acre site will give the kids a good idea about what pioneer life was like on the Llano Estacado as you wander around thirty-three structures that have been restored or relocated here. Buildings include a cowboy bunkhouse, windmills, barns, a school, and several homes.

Texas Two-Lane Etiquette

Some Texans are in a hurry and some aren't. Remarkably, those who aren't always seem to respect those who are by moving over toward the shoulder of the road to let the speeder zip by. If the shoulder is paved, as many are, this is actually legal under highway rules. So if you're not in a hurry and you're in front of a Texan who is, don't be surprised if he or she gets upset with you if you don't move off to the right to let the faster driver pass by. And if you're the one who is in a hurry and a slower driver lets you pass, don't forget to say thanks by touching the brim of your hat or giving a quick wave of your hand as you pass.

LUBBOCK CRICKETS BASEBALL (ages 4 and up)

Sixth Street at Flint on Texas Tech University campus, Lubbock 79401 (806–749–2255). Tickets: $5.00 to $8.50.

If you happen to be in town during baseball season, May through Labor Day, don't miss the Lubbock Crickets at Dan Law Field. You can't find more family-oriented entertainment than a minor-league baseball game.

MACKENZIE PARK AND PRAIRIE DOG TOWN (ages 2 and up)

Fourth Street at I–27, Lubbock 79401 (806–767–2687). Open daily. Joyland is open mid-March through mid-October 7:00 to 10:00 P.M. Monday through Friday, 2:00 to 10:00 P.M. Saturday and Sunday. Call (806) 765–6679 for golf course tee times and (806) 763–2719 for Joyland details.

Frolicking prairie dogs are the main attraction at Mackenzie Park and Prairie Dog Town. These pint-size rodents love to entertain children. The day-use park also includes a thirty-six-hole golf course, a sports complex where you're likely to see a softball game almost anytime, and **Joyland Amusement Park,** with twenty-three kiddie rides. **Yellow House Canyon,** site of the region's last Native American fight in 1877, is also part of the park.

SCIENCE SPECTRUM AND OMNIMAX THEATER (ages 2 and up)

2579 South Loop 289, Lubbock 79423 (806–745–2525 or 806–745–MAXX for film times). Open Monday through Friday 10:00 A.M. to 5:30 P.M., Saturday 10:00 A.M. to 7:00 P.M., Sunday 1:00 to 5:30 P.M. Museum: $5.50 adults, $4.50 children. Omnimax: $6.50 adults, $5.50 children.

If you want the kids to learn something and be entertained at the same time, visit the Science Spectrum/Omnimax at 2579 South Loop 289. It's difficult to tell who has more fun at this place, children rushing from exhibit to exhibit or their parents watching them with delight. Unlike most museums, with warnings not to touch, the Science Spectrum is a hands-on place with more than seventy exhibits on three floors encouraging children to learn about science, technology, and music. And in the Omnimax Theater you can watch films much larger than life projected on the interior 58-foot dome, imparting a very real feeling of being in the film.

LUBBOCK LAKE LANDMARK (ages 4 and up)

2200 North Landmark Drive, Lubbock 79408 (806–741–0306 or 806–742–2490). Open Tuesday through Saturday 9:00 A.M. to 5:00 P.M., Sunday 1:00 to 5:00 P.M.

On the edge of the city at U.S. Highway 84 (Clovis Road) and Loop 289, you'll find Lubbock Lake Landmark, where your family can relax, have a picnic, and learn about America from the beginning of human occupation. Scientists have discovered evidence in Yellow House Canyon indicating this site has been occupied since 12,000 B.C. It's the only known site in North America that contains deposits related to all of the cultures that have occupied the Southern Plains. Excavations have also revealed mammoths, extinct American camels and horses, giant bison, and a 6-foot-long armadillo. An interpretive center displays fossils and artifacts from the site and features a children's learning center. The day-use area includes picnic tables and interpretive trails.

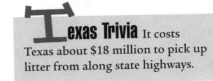

Texas Trivia It costs Texas about $18 million to pick up litter from along state highways.

TEXAS WATER RAMPAGE (ages 2 and up)

6600 Brownfield Highway, Lubbock 79407, on U.S. Highway 62, about a mile west of Loop 289 (806–796–0701). Admission: $12.75 adults, $5.00 children under 4 feet. Hours vary with the season.

Need to cool off? Drive to Texas Water Rampage, a water park with swimming pools, tube slides, toddler splash pool, volleyball courts, picnic tables, and go-carts.

BUFFALO SPRINGS LAKE (ages 2 and up)

5 miles south of Lubbock on Farm Road 835, Lubbock 79404 (806–747–3353).

If your family likes to get wet at a more relaxed pace, head to Buffalo Springs Lake. At this spring-fed oasis in Yellow House Canyon, you can relax on the beach, camp out, or just have a picnic. You can swim, fish, rent a paddleboat, or sharpen your skill on the archery range.

Where to Eat

Cattle Baron Steak and Seafood Grill. *8201 Quaker Avenue, Lubbock* 79424 (806–798–7033). Steaks and seafood done up right. $$

County Line Smokehouse. *Half mile west of I–27 on Farm Road 2641, Lubbock 79401 (806–763–6001).* Famous Texas barbecue and homemade desserts. Has a special children's menu, and kids will enjoy the adjacent lake with ducks, geese, and peacocks. $$

La Amistad. *1636 Thirteenth Street, Lubbock 79401 (806–765–0296).* The top Tex-Mex food in town. $-$$

Where to Stay

Comfort Suites. *5113 South Loop 289, Lubbock 79424 (806–798–0002).* Pool, **Free** continental breakfast, children under 13 stay **Free**. $$

Lubbock Inn. *3901 Nineteenth Street, Lubbock 79410 (806–792–5181).* Children under 12 stay **Free**. $$-$$$

For More Information

Lubbock Convention and Tourist Bureau. *Fourteenth Street and Avenue K, Lubbock, TX 79408; (806) 747–5232. Visit the Web site at www.lubbock.org.*

Plainview, Muleshoe, and Hereford

You'd expect to find a memorial to mules in a town called Muleshoe, wouldn't you? You won't be disappointed. The **National Mule Memorial** is at the intersection of U.S. Highways 70 and 84 downtown and is a popular spot to take photos of the kids.

LLANO ESTACADO MUSEUM (ages 6 and up)
1900 West Eighth Street, Plainview 79072 (806–296–4735). Open weekdays 9:00 A.M. to 5:00 P.M. year-round, also weekends March through November 1:00 to 5:00 P.M. **Free**.

The Llano Estacado Museum, on the campus of Wayland Baptist University, is full of intriguing items, including prehistoric artifacts dating from 8000 B.C., a gem and mineral collection, and a prehistoric elephant skull and tusks.

MULESHOE NATIONAL WILDLIFE REFUGE (ages 4 and up)
20 miles south of Muleshoe on Texas Highway 214, Muleshoe 79347 (806–946–3341). Open during daylight hours.

If you want to see live animals, head south of town to the Muleshoe Wildlife Refuge. Your children will delight in the prairie-dog town, located along the entrance road. The refuge's three lakes attract a number of birds, including rare sandhill cranes. As many as 100,000 cranes nest here at one time. Eagles can be seen during fall and winter months.

Texas Tunes

Texas has an incredible diversity of music, and to capture the state's true flavor you should play its music as you drive its roads, which you'll have ample opportunity for in the Panhandle. Here's a sampling of the best Texas traveling tunes:

- *After Awhile* by Jimmie Dale Gilmore (lyrical traveling music)
- *Buddy Holly: The Original Master Tapes* by Buddy Holly (no one sang it better)
- *Conjunto Aztlan* by Conjunto Aztlan (a history of Tex-Mex sounds on one disc)
- *Corridos De La Frontera* by Santiago Jimenez Jr. (authentic border music)
- *Desert Dreams* by Ben Tavera King (music meant for Big Bend)
- *Destiny's Gate* by Tish Hinojosa (folk rock with a Latina accent)
- *Ernest Tubb Live* by Ernest Tubb (no-frills country by the master)
- *Fathers and Sons* by Asleep at the Wheel (the ultimate road music)
- *Little Love Affairs* by Nanci Griffith (sweetness)

DEAF SMITH COUNTY HISTORICAL MUSEUM (ages 6 and up)

400 Sampson, Hereford 79045 (806–364–4338). Open Monday through Saturday 10:00 A.M. to 5:00 P.M., Sunday by appointment. **Free**.

At the Deaf Smith Museum is about as accurate a look at the region one hundred years ago as you can get without actually going back in time. The museum is housed in a pioneer schoolhouse. There are other restored frontier buildings on the grounds, along with a railroad caboose and an old dugout home.

Umbarger and Canyon

Head north on U.S. Highway 87 to Canyon, then west on Farm Road 1714 to Umbarger.

Canyon is a small town with some pretty big attractions, such as the impressive Palo Duro Canyon just outside of town, and is home to West Texas State University. The town figured heavily in the history of the Texas cattle business, originating as the headquarters of the huge T Anchor Ranch in 1878, and famed cattleman Charles Goodnight lived nearby. Several Native American battles also took place in the area, including the final battle that Col. Ranald Mackenzie led against the Comanche, crushing the tribe as a serious threat to white settlers in the state.

 ### BUFFALO LAKE NATIONAL WILDLIFE REFUGE (ages 4 and up)

 3 miles south of Umbarger on Farm Road 168, Umbarger 79091 (806–499–3382). Open daily from 8:00 A.M. to 10:00 P.M.

Buffalo Lake is a 7,677-acre haven for ducks and geese, as well as bobcats, deer, porcupines, badgers, hawks, and owls. It's also one of the best places to see prairie dogs. Your family can enjoy either the interpretive walking trail or a 5-mile interpretive auto route. Picnic areas and campsites are available.

Allan's Top Family Fun Ideas

1. Palo Duro Canyon State Park, Canyon
2. Don Harrington Discovery Center, Amarillo
3. Wonderland Amusement Park, Amarillo
4. Science Spectrum, Lubbock
5. Lubbock Crickets baseball, Lubbock
6. Bar H Dude Ranch, Clarendon
7. The Panhandle-Plains Historical Museum, Canyon
8. Cowboy Mornings and Evenings, Canyon
9. The Texas Tech museum complex, Lubbock
10. Square House Museum, Panhandle

PANHANDLE-PLAINS HISTORICAL MUSEUM (ages 4 and up)
2401 Fourth Avenue, Canyon 79016, on the campus of West Texas State University (806–656–2244; /www.wtamu.edu/museum). Open Monday through Saturday 9:00 A.M. to 5:00 P.M. (to 6:00 P.M. during the summer), Sunday 2:00 to 6:00 P.M. Adults $4.00, seniors $3.00, children 13 and over $4.00 and children 4–12 $1.00, children 3 and under Free.

The first place to visit in Canyon has to be the Panhandle-Plains Historical Museum. This is Texas's oldest and largest state museum and is the best place in the state to learn all about the Panhandle. Your family will learn about regional ranching and petroleum-mining history and enjoy impressive natural-history exhibits. Walk through an authentic pioneer town rebuilt inside the museum. See an extensive gun collection and prehistoric fossils. If your children like dinosaurs or cowboys and Indians, they're going to love this place.

The museum puts on an **Old Fashioned Christmas** in early December that takes advantage of its pioneer village to reenact a holiday of a hundred years ago, complete with demonstrations of pioneer crafts and skills, Santa in an antique sleigh, vintage Christmas cards, and a special Storyteller's Corner for children.

 PALO DURO CANYON STATE PARK (ages 4 and up)
12 miles east of Canyon on Texas Highway 217, Canyon 79015 (806–488–2227 or 512–389–8900 for camping reservations; www.paloducanyon.com). Open June through August 6:00 A.M. to 10:00 P.M.; September through October 7:00 A.M. to 10:00 P.M.; November through May 8:00 A.M. to 10:00 P.M.

In terms of size and grandeur, Palo Duro Canyon is second in the United States only to Arizona's Grand Canyon. Carved by the Prairie Dog Fork of the Red River, the canyon is 20 miles across at its widest point, 1,100 feet down at its deepest. Palo Duro means "hard wood," referring to the junipers in the canyon. Rock formations here date back more than 900 million years, and it's easy to find dinosaur fossils in the canyon, but leave them where you find them so others can enjoy them as well. You can rent horses or mountain bikes or drive around. You might also want to hike some of the park's many trails, the most famous of which is the **Lighthouse Trail,** a half-day trip that passes through delightful scenery but can be quite hot in summer. The park has an interpretive center, picnic and camping areas, a concession stand, and a store full of kitschy souvenirs.

TEXAS (ages 4 and up)

At Pioneer Amphitheater in Palo Duro Canyon State Park, Canyon 79015 (806–655–2181). Performances are six nights a week (Monday through Saturday) at 8:30 P.M. June through August. Adults $8.00 to $17.00 Monday through Thursday, $10.00 to $19.00 Friday and Saturday. Children under 12 $4.00 to $17.00. Friday and Saturday, adults $10.00 to $21.00, children $5.00 to $21.00.

Here's a play even the children will be thrilled to see. Thunder and lightning, horsemen carrying flags atop the 600-foot canyon wall that serves as a backdrop to the stage, and singers and dancers in Western and Native American garb bring back the 1880s at the outdoor musical *Texas*. The play is presented in the 1,742-seat Pioneer Amphitheater and was written by Pulitzer Prize–winning author Paul Green. There is a ticket office located at 1514 Fifth Avenue in downtown Canyon where you can get tickets and also pick up information on hundreds of area attractions.

The First Thanksgiving

One claim to the first Thanksgiving on what is now American soil is the one for Palo Duro Canyon on May 29, 1541, several decades before the Pilgrims broke bread with Native Americans in New England. This was a day of Thanksgiving ordered by Spanish explorer Francisco Vasquez de Coronado after leading his men up from Mexico in search of gold. Instead, nearly out of food, Coronado found the canyon oasis and a tribe of Native Americans living on the canyon floor.

COWBOY MORNINGS AND EVENINGS

Palo Duro Canyon, Canyon 79015 (800–658–2613 or 806–944–5562). Open April through October (daily June through August). Morning: $19.00 adults, $14.50 children 4 to 12. Evening: $25.00 adults, $14.50 children.

From April through October you can do breakfast or dinner as the cowpokes did, with a mesquite fire on the open range on the rim of Palo Duro Canyon, thanks to Cowboy Mornings and Evenings. A picturesque twenty-minute ride on mule-drawn wagons ends at the campsite where, at the 8:30 A.M. breakfast, your family will chow down on real ranch chuck: Panhandle-size eggs, sausage, sourdough biscuits with country gravy, and cowboy coffee. At the 6:30 P.M. dinner you'll be treated to more of those great biscuits, huge steaks, beans, salad, and a campfire cobbler. Then sit back and watch the hands brand cattle, rope, or toss cowchips.

Where to Eat

Railroad Crossing Steakhouse. *Fourteenth Avenue at U.S. Highway 87, Canyon 79015 (806–655–7701).* Large portions; friendly folks serving tender steaks, chicken, and seafood. Specials are usually true bargains. $-$$

Where to Stay

Hudspeth House Bed and Breakfast Inn. *1905 Fourth Avenue, Canyon 79015 (800–655–9809 or 806–655–9800).* Restored old boardinghouse with antique furnishings. Visit the Web site at www.hudspethinn.com for a tour. $$

For More Information

Canyon Chamber of Commerce. *1518 Fifth Avenue, P.O. Box 8, Canyon, TX 79015; (806) 655–7815. Visit the Web site at www. iitexas.com/gpages/canyon.htm.*

Amarillo

Before you do anything else in Amarillo, drive a little out of your way west on I-40 to **Cadillac Ranch,** located in a field on the south side of the highway. During your stay, people will ask if you've seen this sight, so you might as well get it out of the way first. What you'll see here is Stanley Marsh 3's outdoor sculpture of ten Cadillacs (from 1949 to 1963) planted nose down into the ground at the same angle as Cheops's pyramid. Your children might ask the inevitable question why, but no one really knows why Marsh did it, and he's never explained. It's just there. At regular intervals, Marsh invites anyone to come out and paint graffiti all over the Caddys. To see what you're going to see, visit the Web site at users.online.be/~gruwez/cadillacranch/crmain.htm.

Texas Trivia Famed area rancher and former Texas Ranger Charles Goodnight not only pioneered cattle drives, he invented the chuckwagon.

AMARILLO MUSEUM OF ART (ages 6 and up)

2200 South Van Buren Street, Amarillo 79190 (806–371–5050). Open Tuesday through Friday 10:00 A.M. to 5:00 P.M., Saturday and Sunday 1:00 to 5:00 P.M. **Free***.*

More conventional art can be seen at the Amarillo Museum of Art, on the campus of Amarillo College. The museum houses a permanent exhibit of paintings and sculptures and hosts other exhibits during the year. Fine-arts performances, classes, and lectures are also featured.

DON HARRINGTON DISCOVERY CENTER (ages 4 and up)

1200 Streit Drive, Amarillo 79106 (806–355–9548). Open Tuesday through Saturday 10:00 A.M. to 5:00 P.M., Sunday 1:00 to 5:00 P.M. Museum **Free***, planetarium shows $3.00.*

The Don Harrington Discovery Center can be an exhaustive experience. There's something to delight everyone in your family here. Located in the Harrington Medical Center, in the center of a fifty-one-acre park with a lake and picnic areas, the museum's hands-on exhibits let your children learn about a wide range of natural phenomena, from the depths of the sea to outer space. A planetarium features star shows and 360-degree films.

AMARILLO ZOO (ages 4 and up)

Twenty-fourth Street at U.S. Highway 287, Amarillo 79109 (806–381–7911). Open 9:30 A.M. to 5:30 P.M. Tuesday through Sunday. **Free***.*

A good place for the children to watch animals is the Amarillo Zoo, in Thompson Park near Wonderland. This is a nice little zoo with animals that appeal to youngsters, such as monkeys, bears, and big cats. There's also an emphasis on animals of the High Plains, including a herd of buffalo. You haven't lived until you've been licked by a buffalo with a tongue larger than a ten-year-old's leg.

WONDERLAND AMUSEMENT PARK (ages 4 and up)

River Road exit off U.S. Highway 287 North, Amarillo 79107 (806–383–4712). Open daily Memorial Day through Labor Day, weekends April and May. Hours vary with the seasons. Admission $2.00; ride tickets are $1.50 each, $3.50 for miniature golf. All-day, all-inclusive tickets $9.95 weekdays, $15.95 weekends.

Typical kid fare is available at Wonderland Amusement Park, the largest theme park in Texas after the Six Flags behemoths in Houston, Dallas, and San Antonio. Your brood will find more than twenty rides, including the kind you expect at the more famous parks: fancy roller coasters, a log ride, and a white-water ride, along with miniature golf, video arcades, bumper cars, and a spook house.

  ## AMERICAN QUARTER HORSE HERITAGE CENTER (ages 6 and up)

2601 I–40, Amarillo 79104 (806–376–5181). The center is open May through August, Monday through Saturday 9:00 A.M. to 5:00 P.M., Sunday noon to 5:00 P.M.; open September through April, Tuesday through Saturday 10:00 A.M. to 5:00 P.M., Sunday noon to 5:00 P.M. Adults $4.00, children $2.50, children under 5 ᖴree.

If you have any horse lovers in your family, don't miss the American Quarter Horse Heritage Center. Discover the breed's history as both a Western ranch favorite and racehorse, the first American horse breed. The center features displays, videos, hands-on exhibits, and a gift shop. One area the kids are sure to love allows children to get on the back of a fake horse in a race starting gate, giving them a jockey's-eye view. They can also listen to Fella, the talking horse.

 ## AMARILLO DILLAS BASEBALL (ages 4 and up)

Third and Grand Streets, Amarillo 79104 (806–342–3455). Prices: $5.00 to $7.00.

For baseball lovers in the family, drive over to Dick Bivins Stadium on the Tri-State Fairgrounds to watch the Amarillo Dillas play minor-league ball in the Texas-Louisiana League from May through August. Baseball is a great family entertainment bargain.

 ## AMARILLO RATTLERS HOCKEY (ages 4 and up)

401 South Buchanan Street, Amarillo 79107 (806–378–3096). Prices: $8.50 to $13.00.

The minor-league Rattlers play in the Western Professional Hockey League. They take to the ice October through March at the Amarillo Civic Center.

Ｔexas Trivia
Amarillo is the largest meat-producing area in the nation; 25 percent of all beef consumed in the United States and 88 percent of all beef consumed in Texas is produced in this city.

Texas Trivia In 1893, Amarillo's population was listed as "between 500 and 600 humans and 50,000 head of cattle."

Where to Eat

Big Texan Steak Ranch. *7701 I–40, Amarillo 79160 (800–657–7177 or 806–372–7000).* If you can eat a monster seventy-two-ounce steak with all the trimmings in an hour, you get it **Free.** Kids might be tempted to try some of the more exotic items on the menu, like rattlesnake or rabbit. Maybe not. Try to visit on a Tuesday when the restaurant features a wide variety of western entertainment. $–$$

Cracker Barrel Old Country Store. *2323 I–40, Amarillo 79104 (806–372–2034).* Great southern cooking; huge gift shop in lobby. $–$$

Ruby Tequila's Mexican Kitchen. *2108 Paramount, Amarillo 79109 (806–358–7829).* Real fine Tex-Mex fare. $

Where to Stay

Best Western. *1610 Coulter, Amarillo 79106 (806–358–7861 or 800–528–1234).* Indoor atrium, pool, and hot tub. Children stay **Free.** $$

Big Texan Steak Ranch Motel. *7701 I–40, Amarillo 79160 (806–372–5000 or 800–657–7177).* Features a heated Texas-shaped pool. $$

Comfort Inn. *2100 South Coulter, Amarillo 79106 (806–358–6141 or 800–228–5150).* **Free** breakfast and an indoor pool. $$

For More Information

Amarillo Convention and Visitors Bureau. *7703-A I–40 East, Amarillo, TX 79104; (800) 692–1338 or (803)* 374–1497. *Visit the Web site at www.amarillo-cvb.org.*

Tascosa and Dalhart

Head north on U.S. Highway 385 from I–40 after you leave Amarillo.
As you pass by the town of Tascosa on your way to Dalhart, don't blink—you might miss it. Tascosa was one of the roughest, toughest towns in Texas in the late 1800s, but it's gone now. Only ruins and a museum remain. Dalhart was, and continues to be, a center for the cattle business.

OLD TASCOSA AND CAL FARLEY'S BOYS RANCH (ages 4 and up)

36 miles northwest of Amarillo on U.S. Highway 385 at Spur 233, Boys Ranch 79010 (806–372–2341 or 800–687–3722). Museum open daily 10:00 A.M. to 5:00 P.M. Free.

If you're traveling to the ghost town of Tascosa from Amarillo, take Farm Road 1061 to Highway 385, the most scenic drive in the area. Built by settlers in the 1870s, Tascosa was a shipping point for Panhandle farms and ranches, including the famous XIT Ranch near Dalhart. Your children will be able to walk in the footsteps of Billy the Kid and Kit Carson, who once strode along Tascosa's boardwalks. But, just like in the movies, the railroad bypassed old Tascosa,

Texas Trivia At its largest, the XIT Ranch encompassed 3,047,975 acres—roughly the size of Connecticut. In 1886, the ranch ran 150,000 head of cattle.

and the town up and died during the Depression. The Boot Hill Cemetery is maintained by youths from Cal Farley's Boys Ranch, a 10,000-acre home for troubled youth founded in 1939.

The ranch also runs the **Julian Bivins Museum,** in the old county courthouse at Tascosa. It houses pioneer, Native American, and prehistoric artifacts.

The ranch has a renowned rodeo, The Boys Ranch Rodeo, in September. It is held in the afternoons with a barbecue lunch served at noon.

DALLAM-HARTLEY COUNTIES XIT MUSEUM (ages 6 and up)

108 East Fifth Street, Dalhart 79022 (806–249–5390). Open Monday through Saturday 9:00 A.M. to 5:00 P.M., with an art show and educational program the first Sunday of each month from 2:00 to 5:00 P.M. Donations requested.

In the 1880s, the XIT Ranch was the largest ranch in the world, with three million acres. The north fence was 200 miles from the south fence. That impressive range has been subdivided over the years, but the XIT still operates. The XIT Ranch Museum preserves the ranch's history along with Indian artifacts.

In August the ranch and the city host the annual **XIT Rodeo and Reunion** to honor all those who have ever worked on the ranch. The festival features a rodeo, of course, an antique car show, a fun run, a parade, and **Free** barbecue and watermelon. Call (806) 249-5646.

 ### LAKE RITA BLANCA WILDLIFE MANAGEMENT AREA (ages 4 and up)

 1.5 miles south of Dalhart on Farm Road 281, Dalhart 79022 (806–353–0486). For wildlife viewing, head to Lake Rita Blanca, where your family can see all sorts of waterfowl and maybe a few eagles during winter months.

 ### RITA BLANCA NATIONAL GRASSLAND (ages 4 and up)

12 miles east of Dalhart on Texas Highway 296, Dalhart 79022 (806–362–4254).

 For more of a wilderness experience, visit the Rita Blanca National Grassland, where your family will discover a network of hiking, biking, and wildlife-watching trails where you're likely to see pronghorn antelope, coyotes, foxes, prairie dogs, owls, and hawks.

For More Information

Dalhart Chamber of Commerce.
102 East Seventh Street, Dalhart, TX 79022; (806) 249–5646.

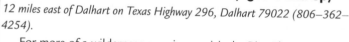

Fritch and Panhandle

Traveling east on U.S. Highway 87, take Texas Highway 152 east and Texas Highway 207 south to loop around Lake Meredith.
Fritch is the gateway town for Lake Meredith and the Alibates Flint Quarries, while Panhandle is a center for wheat farming, cattle ranching, and some petroleum production.

LAKE MEREDITH NATIONAL RECREATION AREA (ages 4 and up)

1 mile east of Fritch on Texas Highway 136, Fritch 79036 (806–857–3151).

Lake Meredith was formed by damming the Canadian River, producing 100 miles of shoreline, and if you're looking for outdoor recreation of any type, this is the place. Recreation areas surround the lake and include off-road vehicle trails, picnic and camping areas, shelters, boat ramps and docks, marinas, and fishing and swimming areas.

LAKE MEREDITH AQUATIC AND WILDLIFE MUSEUM (ages 4 and up)

104 North Rob, Fritch 79036 (806–857–2458). Open Monday through Saturday 8:30 A.M. to 5:00 P.M., Sunday 2:00 to 5:00 P.M. **Free.**

The Lake Meredith Museum has more than sixteen species of fish from the lake displayed in aquariums. There are also exhibits on Alibates flint and arrowhead making.

ALIBATES NATIONAL MONUMENT (ages 6 and up)

7.5 miles south of Fritch on Texas Highway 136, Fritch 79036 (806–857–3151). Tours are by reservation daily Memorial Day through Labor Day at 10:00 A.M. and 2:00 P.M. and end with brief instructions on how to chip your own flint into points. **Free.**

Alibates National Monument overlooks Lake Meredith and preserves the quarries where Native peoples mined and flaked flint for more than 12,000 years. An ancient Native American village, pictographs, and giant pits full of buffalo bones have been found here. Off-season tours are by reservation, so call ahead.

Texas Trivia Don't spend too much time trying to figure out what language "Alibates" is or what it means. The area was named for nearby Allie Bates Creek. The creek was named for a local cowboy, Allen (Allie) Bates. The word *Alibates* was a recording mistake made by a geologist in 1907.

SQUARE HOUSE MUSEUM (ages 6 and up)

Fifth Street and Elsie Avenue, Panhandle 79068 (806–537–3524). Open Monday through Saturday 9:00 A.M. to 5:30 P.M., Sunday 1:00 to 5:30 P.M. Donations welcomed.

You might be little surprised that such a small town has such a big museum as Panhandle's Square House Museum. The eight-structure complex in Pioneer Park chronicles Panhandle history from the first Native peoples to modern industries. The main building, the Square House, was built in the 1880s with wood brought from Dodge City, Kansas. In addition to the usual

Thomas Cree's Little Tree

On the south side of U.S. Highway 60, about 5 miles southwest of the city of Panhandle, is the very first tree planted in the entire Panhandle region of Texas. Immense plains were once a sea of grass from horizon to horizon here. In 1888, pioneer settler Thomas Cree hauled a sapling of bois d'arc from beyond the Caprock area and planted it by his dugout home. Cree is long gone, but the tree thrived until 1969, when it was killed by an agricultural chemical. Natural seedlings from the original tree are growing at the site today.

ranch and farming exhibits, you will find a railroad exhibit, a wildlife hall, a Texas flags exhibit, a pioneer windmill, a blacksmith shop, and two art galleries. Many of the exhibits are hands-on for children.

Claude and Quitaque

Continue south on Texas Highway 207 to Claude, then on Texas Highway 86 east to Quitaque.

Like many Texas towns, Claude was established as a railroad stop. Today you'll see grain elevators and stockyards all around, with a few antiques shops in town. Quitaque (pronounced Kitty-kway) has a more romantic background. It started as the site of a Native American trading post, was a major stagecoach stop, and now serves the area's farms and ranches.

 ARMSTRONG COUNTY MUSEUM (ages 6 and up)
   120 North Trice Street, Claude 79017 (806–226–2187; www.searchtexas.com/gem-theatre/). Open Tuesday through Friday from 10:00 A.M. to 4:00 P.M., Saturday and Sunday from 1:00 to 5:00 P.M. Free.

Have a Boy Scout in your little troop? Then don't miss the Armstrong County Museum. Unlike other Panhandle museums, this one doesn't concentrate just on ranching history. It focuses on Boy Scouts since the town has one of the oldest Boy Scout troops west of the Mississippi. It's a half block north of U.S. Highway 287. The adjacent Gem Theatre is used for educational and entertainment programs.

CAPROCK CANYONS STATE PARK (ages 4 and up)

3 miles north of Quitaque on County Road 1065, Quitaque 79255 (806–455–1492).

Almost a companion piece to Palo Duro Canyon State Park, Caprock Canyons State Park near Quitaque covers 13,960 scenic acres of colorful cliffs and canyons and is loaded with wildlife and birds. You can take the kids hiking or mountain biking or hire a horse and trot off on several trails. You'll find

Scenic Drive When you leave town, take Route 207 south for a nice scenic drive that'll surprise you. For miles agricultural riches spread from horizon to horizon, then the highway plunges into spectacular Palo Duro and Tule Canyons, revealing several sheer buttes and a rampage of colors.

picnic areas, campsites, fishing, and swimming at Lake Theo, where you can also rent canoes.

You can access the **Caprock Canyon Trailway** here as well. This is a 65-mile-long system of trails that runs through three counties, across the plains, through rugged canyons, and into the Red River Valley. One of the features is an abandoned railway tunnel, one of very few in Texas.

For More Information

Quitaque Chamber of Commerce.
(806) 455–1456. Visit the Web site at www.traveltex.com.

Clarendon

Head north on Texas Highway 70.
Farming and ranching remain the focus in the Clarendon area, one of the oldest towns in the Panhandle. The city was founded by the Reverend L. H. Carhart in 1878 as a refuge for cowboys who weren't rowdy drinkers.

SAINTS' ROOST MUSEUM (ages 6 and up)

On Texas Highway 70, Clarendon 79226 (806–874–2746). Open weekends during the summer from 1:00 to 5:00 P.M. **Free**.

Clarendon was founded by a Methodist minister as a "sobriety settlement" to counteract the wide-open ways common in other cow towns. For that reason cowboys nicknamed the place "Saints' Roost," and you can find out all about its history at the Saints' Roost Museum on the main road downtown. The museum is housed in the former Adair Hospital, founded in 1910 for local cowboys, and features heirlooms from area ranches, farms, and businesses.

The city holds an annual **Saints' Roost Celebration** over the July Fourth weekend, with three nights of rodeoing, a parade, an arts-and-crafts show, country music, an old-timer's reunion, children's contests and games, and a barbecue cookout. Great family fun. Call (806) 874-2421.

BAR H DUDE RANCH (ages 4 and up)

5 miles west of Clarendon on Farm Road 3257, Clarendon 79226, off Highway 287 (806–874–2634). Rates, including horseback riding and all meals: $63.00 for adults, $52.50 for children 13 to 16, $42.00 for children 6 to 12, $26.25 for children 2 to 5.

For a taste of real ranch life, check into the Bar H Dude Ranch for a night or two. Here the kids can watch cowboys work cattle, feed livestock, mend fences, move the herd, and do dozens of other ranch chores. You can climb into the saddle and join in, too, if you want. Or you can just relax on the porch, pitch horseshoes, take a stroll, try some fishing, or splash around in the pool. Mesquite-grilled food awaits at the chuck wagon when the sun comes up and when it goes down.

Texas Trivia The lowest temperature ever recorded in Texas was minus twenty-three degrees in Tulia on February 12, 1899, and in Seminole on February 8, 1933.

McLean

It might be difficult to explain to your children the almost mythical lure of old Route 66, but maybe a trip to McLean will help. In town are a restored Phillips 66 gas station dating from the 1930s and re-creations of an old Route 66 cafe and typical tourist court. You can't miss them; they're on Route 66 right in town.

DEVIL'S ROPE MUSEUM (ages 6 and up)

Kingsley Street at Old Route 66, McLean 79057 (806–779–2225). Open May through October, Tuesday through Saturday 10:00 A.M. to 4:00 P.M., Sunday 1:00 to 4:00 P.M.; November through April, Friday and Saturday 10:00 A.M. to 4:00 P.M., Sunday 1:00 P.M. to 4:00 P.M. Donations requested.

Make a stop at the Devil's Rope Museum, home not only to the world's largest collection of barbed wire ("the devil's rope" to ranchers favoring open ranges) and related artifacts, but to the largest display of old Route 66 memorabilia along old Route 66.

 ### ALANREED-MCLEAN AREA MUSEUM (ages 6 and up)

117 North Main Street, McLean 79057 (806–779–2731). Open Wednesday through Saturday 10:00 A.M. to 4:00 P.M., Sunday 1:00 to 4:00 P.M. Donations welcomed.

More traditional artifacts tracing the history of area pioneers can be found at the Alanreed-McLean Area Museum. This museum also contains exhibits and records on the German prisoner-of-war camp that was located here during World War II.

> **Texas Trivia** The highest temperature ever recorded in Texas was 120 degrees in Seymour on August 12, 1936.

Shamrock and Quanah

Traveling east on I–40 will take you to Shamrock, near the Oklahoma border. To get to Quanah, head south on U.S. Highway 83, then east on U.S. Highway 287, following near the border.

Shamrock was named by its founder, George Nichels, an Irish sheep rancher, and ranching was the primary business in town until oil was struck in 1926. Today agriculture, tourism, and oil and gas production are what keep the city bustling. Quanah was named for Quanah Parker, last war chief of the Comanches. Today the city is a central shipping point for cotton, dairy, and meat products.

BLARNEY STONE (ages 4 and up)

400 East Second Street in Elmore Park, Shamrock 79079 (806–256–2501). **Free**.

You say you'd like to kiss the Blarney Stone but don't want to travel all the way to Ireland to do it? Go to Shamrock. A fragment of genuine Blarney Stone from the ruins of Blarney Castle in County Cork is displayed in **Elmore Park**. As befits a town with this name, there's a big festival on the weekend closest to St. Patrick's Day (March 17), with barrel racing, team roping, a beard-growing contest, fun runs, water polo, a chili cook-off, dancing, and a carnival.

 ## PIONEER WEST MUSEUM (ages 6 and up)

206 North Madden Street, Shamrock 79079 (806–256–3941). Open Monday through Friday 10:00 A.M. to noon and 1:00 to 3:00 P.M. **Free**.

Before you leave Shamrock, wander though the Pioneer West Museum, housed in the old Reynolds Hotel, where twenty rooms are filled with an eclectic blend of exhibits on topics ranging from NASA space missions to Native American culture.

   ## COPPER BREAKS STATE PARK (ages 4 and up)

8 miles south of Quanah on Texas Highway 6, Quanah 79252 (940–839–4331).

In these canyons and plains, you'll find a fascinating blend of natural and cultural history. The Comanche and Kiowa hunted buffalo here, and Cynthia Ann Parker was recaptured nearby. Your kids are likely to spy deer, hawks, coyotes, jackrabbits, and roadrunners all over the area. And when they tire of looking for wildlife, they can cool off in the sixty-acre lake, go fishing, or hike along one of the scenic trails.

For More Information

Quanah Chamber of Commerce. *220 South Main Street, P.O. Box 158, Quanah, TX 79252; (940) 663–2222.*

Shamrock Chamber of Commerce. *207 North Main Street, Shamrock, TX 79079; (806) 256–2501. Visit the Web site at www.iitexas.com/gpages/shamrock.htm.*

West Texas and Big Bend

West Texas and the Big Bend country are what most non-Texans think of when they picture Texas: vast, beautiful badlands covered in cactus with an occasional mountain lurching up like a ship from the desert sea. This area west of the Pecos River is so rugged that Apache and Comanche Indians never stayed; they just passed through. Early Spanish explorers labeled this place *el despoblado,* the uninhabited land. It remains remarkably the same today, except for the sprawling metropolis of El Paso, the twin cities of Midland and Odessa in the Permian Basin, and a few other smaller towns that grew up to support ranching and oil businesses in the nineteenth century.

The major thoroughfares here are I-10, I-20, and U.S. Highway 90, running east and west. Be prepared to drive long distances in this region, even if you fly into a major population center. Cities are few and very far between, as are gas stations, so plan ahead for meals and lodging. And be prepared to have something for the kids to do in the car as you dodge tumbleweeds driving over these vast landscapes.

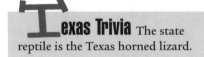

Texas Trivia The state reptile is the Texas horned lizard.

Junction and Fort McKavett

Driving west from Junction, I-10 becomes pretty bleak and stays that way for 450 miles until you reach the New Mexico border around El Paso. The rugged plains and hills are broken by a few buttes off in the distance. If you want variety, you'll find it only off the interstate.

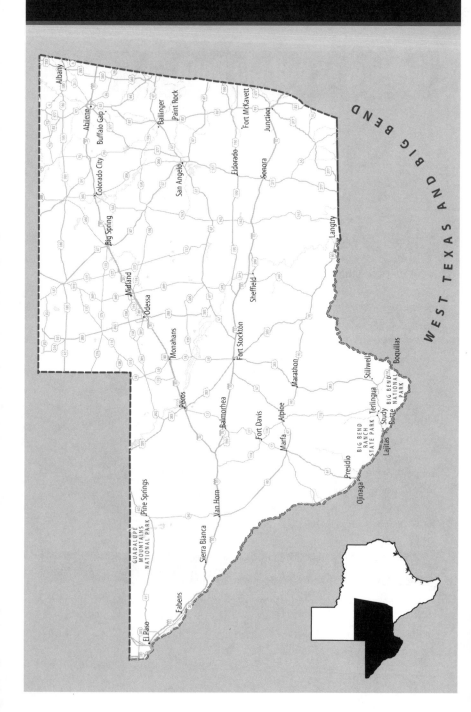

WEST TEXAS AND BIG BEND

Allan's Top Annual Family Fun Events

- Cowboy Poetry Gathering, Alpine, March (915-837-2326 or 915-837-8191)
- Juan de Oñate First Thanksgiving Festival, El Paso, April (915-592-5252)
- Sabers, Saddles, and Spurs, San Angelo, May (915-657-4441)
- Western Heritage Classic Rodeo, Abilene, May (915-676-2556 or 800-727-7704)
- Odessa Shakespere Festival, Odessa, during summer (915-332-1586)
- West of the Pecos Rodeo, Pecos, July (915-445-2406 or 800-588-7326)
- Border Folk Festival, El Paso, October (915-532-7273)
- Confederate Air Force Airsho, Midland, October (915-683-3381 or 915-563-1000)
- World Championship Chili Cook-off, Terlingua, November (915-371-2234)
- Christmas at Old Fort Concho, San Angelo, December (915-481-2646)

SOUTH LLANO RIVER STATE PARK (ages 4 and up)

5 miles south of Junction off U.S. Highway 377, Junction 76849 (915–446–3994).

Right where the Texas Hill Country ends and west Texas begins is Junction, a small town that is home to South Llano River State Park. The quiet, cool river is perfect for family canoeing, tubing, and swimming. Three miles of hiking trails also wind through the park's pecan bottom, where you're likely to see white-tailed deer and wild turkeys. Trails from the park also lead into the adjoining 2,123-acre **Walter Buck Wildlife Management Area,** where a 2-mile hiking trail circles the oxbow lakes and the kids should be able to spot a lot of wildlife.

FORT MCKAVETT STATE HISTORICAL PARK (ages 6 and up)

About 35 miles north of Junction on Farm Road 864, off Farm Road 1674, Fort McKavett 76841 (915–396–2358). Open Wednesday through Sunday 8:00 A.M. to 5:00 P.M.

Fort McKavett, founded in 1852, has been relatively untouched by time. Constant use by civilians after the fort was closed have kept many of the old post structures in near original condition. The park, overlooking the San Saba River, has fifteen restored buildings and the ruins of many others. Interpretive exhibits in the 1870 hospital ward trace the history of the region, and a self-guided trail leads to the lime kiln and Government Springs. At its peak, the fort housed 400 soldiers, most of them members of the famed Buffalo Soldiers regiments.

> **Texas Trivia** Although Gen. Phillip Sheridan opined that he'd prefer living in hell to Texas, his colleague Gen. William T. Sherman called Fort McKavett "the prettiest post in Texas."

For More Information

Kimble County Chamber of Commerce. *402 Main Street, Junction, TX 76849; (800) KIMBLE–4.*

Sonora and Eldorado

CAVERNS OF SONORA (ages 4 and up)

8 miles west of Sonora exit 392 to Ranch Road 1989 (915–387–3105 or 915–387–6507). Open daily from 8:00 A.M. to 6:00 P.M. March through September; 9:00 A.M. to 5:00 P.M. October through February. Adults $9.00 to $17.00, children $7.00 to $13.00, depending on tour.

About 60 miles west of Junction is a nice little oasis, the city of Sonora. Eight miles farther you'll find the Caverns of Sonora. This isn't the biggest cave in Texas, but it's certainly the prettiest. The 1.5-mile walk winds down around some of the most delicate and brilliant formations found anywhere in the world, including a crystalline butterfly. On the surface, the kids will enjoy the sluice, where they can pan for unusual minerals.

ELDORADO WOOLENS (ages 6 and up)

409 Southwest Main Street, Eldorado 76936 (915–853–2541). Open Monday through Friday 8:00 A.M. to 5:00 P.M., Saturday 8:00 A.M. to 4:00 P.M. **Free**.

Along U.S. Highway 277 you'll find the only working woolen mill in the southwest. You can tour the mill and stroll along the village's Historic Walking Tour to see some old architecture.

San Angelo

San Angelo is a little town full of big surprises. The biggest surprise is probably the Concho River Pearls. Lustrous pearls in colors ranging from pink to purple are produced by one of twelve varieties of freshwater mussels in the river. (The word *concha* means "shell" in Spanish.) Various shops in town sell items made from the pearls. If your family wants to gather their own, and kids love to try this, you need a permit from the Texas Parks and Wildlife Department. The pearls are celebrated with *Pearl of the Conchos,* a bronze mermaid statue grasping a huge pearl at Celebration Bridge in the historic area of the city. The visitors bureau can give you more information on the permits at (915) 655-4136 or (800) 375-1206, or get more details on the Web site www.sanangelotx.com.

FORT CONCHO NATIONAL HISTORIC LANDMARK (ages 4 and up)

213 East Avenue D, San Angelo 76903 (915–481–2646 or 915–657–4441 for special events; www.fortconcho.com). The Fort Concho Museum and the three other museums also housed at the fort are open 10:00 A.M. to 5:00 P.M. Tuesday through Saturday and 1:00 to 5:00 P.M. Sunday. Donations welcomed.

Fort Concho National Historic Landmark is one of the best-preserved Indian Wars forts in the country. Situated on forty acres in the heart of downtown, several of the fort's twenty-three buildings are furnished with original antiques and replicas of the furnishings used when the fort was active in the late 1800s. A number of infantry and cavalry units were stationed here between 1867 and 1889, including all four regiments of the Buffalo Soldiers. Children will love seeing the staff and volunteers, who dress in period uniforms to lend authenticity.

One of the more fascinating museums on the Fort Concho grounds is the **E. H. Danner Museum of Telephony,** which displays telephone equipment used in the region from the invention of the device to modern days. Call (915) 653-0756.

The **San Angelo Museum of Fine Arts,** also housed in Fort Concho, blends historic and contemporary art, featuring a wide variety of special exhibits throughout the year. Call (915) 658-4084.

Appropriately housed in the Fort Concho Post Hospital is the **Robert Wood Johnson Museum of Frontier Medicine,** tracing medical treatment from the founding of the fort in 1867 into the twentieth century. Your children will appreciate your family doctor more when they see some of these items from the nineteenth century.

If you're in town in May, the kids will love **Sabers, Saddles, and Spurs,** a cavalry review held on the Fort Concho grounds. The fort's living-history troops and other costumed and uniformed riders take you into the nineteenth century with precision drills, contests, and cowboy polo competitions. Call (915) 657-4441.

In early December the fort does something similar with a Christmas theme: **Christmas at Old Fort Concho.** Dancers, singers, and living-history performers bring a typical 1800s holiday season to life, with an emphasis on different cultures. In addition, your family can enjoy wagon rides, cowboy poets, campfire entertainment, an arts-and-crafts show, food booths, and a special children's area with interactive programs and craft instruction. Call (915) 481-2646.

 CHILDREN'S ART MUSEUM (ages 6 and up)

36 East Twohig Street, San Angelo 76903 (915–655–5000). Open Tuesday through Friday from 10:00 A.M. to 6:00 P.M., Saturday and Sunday from 1:00 to 5:00 P.M. Admission: $2.00.

One of the more unusual museums in the state is the Children's Art Museum, on the first floor of the Cactus Hotel downtown. The museum not only features children's art and a picture-book library but has a variety of programs designed to inspire kids' creativity.

The Cactus Hotel was one of the first Hiltons ever constructed and was the most ornate when it was built in 1929. In addition to the Children's Art Museum, the hotel also houses a restaurant and a coffee shop and plays host to the locally popular Cactus Jazz Concerts.

 ANGELO STATE UNIVERSITY PLANETARIUM (ages 6 and up)

Pierce and Vanderventer Streets, San Angelo 76903 (915–942–2136; www.angelo.edu/). Shows are at 8:00 P.M. Thursday and 2:00 P.M. Saturday when classes are in session. Admission: $3.00 for adults, $1.50 for students.

Another surprise in tiny San Angelo is Angelo State University Planetarium, the fourth largest university planetarium in the nation. You'll find it in the Nursing and Physical Sciences Building on the ASU campus.

RIVER WALK AND NEFF'S AMUSEUMENT PARK (ages 4 and up)

At Celebration Bridge, San Angelo 76903 (915–653–1206 for River Walk; 915–653–3014 for Neff's Amusement Park). Children's park opens at 1:30 P.M. weekends, 6:30 P.M. weekdays during the summer. River Walk is Free*; prices vary for activities.*

If the family is looking for a little exercise, along with nice views, try the San Angelo River Walk, a 4.5-mile lighted trail that wanders through landscaped parks and gardens, by huge pecan trees and beautiful homes, near fountains and waterfalls, and to a nine-hole city golf course, a miniature golf course, and Neff's Amusement Park. The River Walk ends at the RiverStage, where outdoor performances are regularly held. The big date here is the Fourth of July, when the San Angelo Symphony performs before a fireworks display.

SAN ANGELO NATURE CENTER (ages 4 and up)

7409 Knickerbocker Road, San Angelo 76904, off Highway 87 south of town (915–942–0121). Open Wednesday and Thursday from 9:00 A.M. to 3:00 P.M., Saturday and Sunday from noon to 4:00 P.M. Admission: $2.00 per person for ages 3 and up.

Another facility dedicated to children is the San Angelo Nature Center, on the shores of Lake Nasworthy at Mary Lee Park. The center provides interactive programs, a nature trail, and a museum.

SAN ANGELO STATE PARK (ages 4 and up)

West of downtown San Angelo, off U.S. Highway 87, on Farm Road 2288, San Angelo 76901 (915–949–4757).

On the shores of O. C. Fisher Reservoir are the 7,000 acres of San Angelo State Park. You can boat on the lake, fish, swim, camp, hike along developed and undeveloped trails, or watch abundant wildlife.

Where to Eat

Cattleman's Steak House and Chocolate Factory. *441 Rio Concho Drive, San Angelo 76903 (915–658–2828).* Excellent Angus beef steaks; watch chocolate being made. $-$$

Harlow's Restaurant. *532 West Beauregard, San Angelo 76903 (915–657–2771).* Buffet-style barbecue, wonderful mesquite fried steaks. $$

Mejor Que Nada. *1911 South Bryant, San Angelo 76903 (915–655–3553).* Children's magic show Wednesday nights; mariachi music Wednesday through Saturday. $

Where to Stay

Cactus Hotel. *36 East Twohig Street, San Angelo 76903 (915–655–5000).* Historic, downtown. $$

Howard Johnson Hotel. *333 Rio Concho Drive , San Angelo 76903 (915–659–0717).* Indoor pool and family recreation center. $$

Inn of the West. *415 West Beauregard, San Angelo 76903 (915–653–2995 or 800–582–9668).* Indoor pool; children under 12 stay **free**. $$

For More Information

San Angelo Chamber of Commerce. *500 Rio Concho Drive, San Angelo, TX 76903; (800) 375–1206 or (915)* *655–4136. Visit the Web site at www.sanangelo-tx.com.*

Paint Rock, Ballinger, and Buffalo Gap

PAINT ROCK EXCURSIONS (ages 4 and up)

32 miles southeast of San Angelo on Ranch Road 380, Paint Rock 76866 (915–732–4418 or 915–732–4376). Tours June through August from 9:00 A.M. to 5:00 P.M. Monday through Saturday and from 1:00 to 5:00 P.M. Sunday. Other months by appointment only. Adults $6.00, children $3.00.

Tiny Paint Rock is one of the largest prehistoric Native American pictograph sites in the United States. More than 1,500 paintings line a limestone bluff just north of the Concho River. Weekend tours include a boat ride down the river, where you can see all sorts of wildlife.

O. H. IVIE RESERVOIR (ages 4 and up)

20 miles southeast of Ballinger on Farm Road 1929, Ballinger 76821 (915–365–2333).

Stop at Lake Ivie to cool the family off in its 25,000 acres of boating and fishing opportunities. The lake, created in 1992, also has several campsites.

Texas Critters

- **Armadillos**—A favorite of children, the nine-banded armadillo is the state mammal and the critter you're most likely to see squished on the pavement since it's slow, blind, and rather stupid. Don't allow your kids to play with them; many carry serious diseases.

- **Coyotes**—The wild dogs of Texas are almost a symbol of the Old West since they always seem to be howling in the distance whenever cowpokes build a campfire in the movies. You, too, might hear them if you're camped out in an isolated area, but they are the least commonly seen of all the critters listed here.

- **Fire Ants**—They are the reason you don't want to go barefoot on a picnic. These nasty insects are everywhere, and when they bite you'll know why they call them fire ants. Watch your kids carefully because these ants will swarm up an offending foot in a flash.

- **Horny Toads**—Some folks also call them Horned Frogs, especially students at Texas Christian University, where they are the school mascot, but they're neither frogs nor toads despite their flat, fat appearance. They're actually lizards, as befitting the state reptile, and look quite prehistoric.

- **Jackrabbits**—You'll know one when you see one: They have huge ears, usually held bolt upright, and large, powerful hind feet. Some oldsters swear they've seen jackrabbits outrun locomotives. But then, they also say they've seen jackalopes, a rare cross between a white-tailed deer and jackrabbit.

- **Longhorns**—A tough, lean breed of cattle that thrived on the Texas range and were able to withstand the withering trail drives of the late 1800s. Today they are mostly trophy cattle as modern ranchers have turned to better money-making breeds. Some horn spans can reach 8 feet across.

- **Roadrunners**—In west Texas you'll hear this bird called *paisano*, which means "little buddy" in Mexican slang. You'll find them racing alongside your car all over the back roads. But only your car can go "beep-beep."

ABILENE STATE PARK (ages 4 and up)

4 miles southwest of Buffalo Gap on Farm Road 89, Tuscola 79562 (915–572–3204).

Take a short detour down to Abilene State Park, where you'll find overnight camping facilities ranging from tent sites to screened shelters with electricity. Or your family can picnic under giant pecan trees or swim at the pool (open Memorial Day through Labor Day). Most of the park's 490 acres have been left in their natural, semiarid state of prairie grass and wooded stream valleys. Bordering the park on the west is Lake Abilene, the water supply for Abilene, where you can fish.

BUFFALO GAP HISTORIC VILLAGE (ages 4 and up)

Farm Road 89, Buffalo Gap 79508 (915–572–3365; www.mem.edu/academic/depts/grady/bgap.html). Open March 15 through November 15 from 10:00 A.M. to 6:00 P.M. Monday through Saturday and noon to 6:00 P.M. Sunday; from November 16 through March 14 it's open 10:00 A.M. to 5:00 P.M. Friday and Saturday and noon to 5:00 P.M. Sunday. Adults $4.00, students $1.75.

About 4 miles north of Abilene State Park is Buffalo Gap Historic Village, where an entire frontier town is preserved, including many original buildings, most of them more than one hundred years old. You'll find a museum depicting the history of the Abilene area in the courthouse and jail building. The current town has several restaurants and unusual shops.

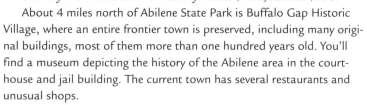

Allan's Top Family Fun Ideas

1. Big Bend National Park, Big Bend
2. Rio Grande Raft Trip, Lajitas
3. Wet 'n' Wild Water World, El Paso
4. McDonald Observatory, Fort Davis
5. Caverns of Sonora, Sonora
6. Abilene Zoological Gardens and Discovery Center, Abilene
7. Indian Cliffs Ranch/Cattlemen's Steak House, Fabens
8. Monahans Sandhills State Park, Monahans
9. El Paso Saddleblanket Co., El Paso
10. Woodward Agate Ranch, Alpine

Texas Trivia In April, most of Texas is experiencing weather much of the rest of the nation would call summer, not spring. But on April 5, 1996, Sweetwater received 18 inches of snow. The same storm dropped a record-breaking 9.3 inches of snow on Abilene.

Abilene

Abilene is at the junction of several major highways in west Texas: I–20 and U.S. Highways 83, 84, and 277.

Founded as a shipping point for cattle, Abilene was named for Abilene, Kansas, another great cattle town. Once oil was discovered, it gave the city a double economic punch. While reveling in its past, the city also looks to its future with three universities—Abilene Christian, Hardin-Simmons, and McMurry—as well as Cisco Junior College and Texas State Technical College.

Your family is certain to enjoy the **Western Heritage Classic Rodeo** in mid-May. Unlike many rodeos, this one features working cowboys competing in ranch events, campfire cook-offs, horse racing, and a western art show. Call (915) 676-2556 or (800) 727-7724.

ABILENE ZOOLOGICAL GARDENS AND DISCOVERY CENTER (ages 4 and up)

Texas Highway 36 at Loop 322, Abilene 79601 (915–676–6085 or 915–672–9771; www.abilene.com/visitors/zoo.html). Open Memorial Day to Labor Day from 9:00 A.M. to 5:00 P.M. Monday through Friday and 9:00 A.M. to 7:00 P.M. weekends and holidays, and during the rest of the year from 9:00 A.M. to 5:00 P.M. daily. Adults $3.00, children 3 through 12 $2.00, children in strollers $1.00.

The primary family attraction in Abilene is the Abilene Zoological Gardens and Discovery Center, an award-winning zoo that features more than 500 species of birds, mammals, reptiles, and amphibians. The thirteen-acre complex compares plants and animals of the American Southwest with similar regions in Africa, comparing the Texas plains to the African veldt. Large open areas allow different species to live together as they would in the wild. The Discovery Center features aquariums, a tropical aviary, and a trail that is home to lemurs, mongooses, and ringtails. Adjacent **Nelson Park** has a nice children's playground.

GRACE CULTURAL CENTER (ages 4 and up)

102 Cypress Street, Abilene 79601 (915–673–4587; www.abilene.com/grace). Open Tuesday, Wednesday, Friday, and Saturday from 10:00 A.M. to 5:00 P.M., Thursday from 10:00 A.M. to 8:30 P.M. Adults $3.00, children $1.00.

The Grace Cultural Center, in the historic Grace Hotel, is now home to three museums. The **Abilene Children's Museum** has hands-on activities that let your youngsters experience art, science, and technology. The **Historical Museum** uses re-created rooms and memorabilia to showcase Abilene's history. The **Art Museum** displays permanent and special exhibits of folk art, sculpture, Western art, and photography.

LAKE FORT PHANTOM HILL (ages 4 and up)

14 miles north of Abilene on Farm Road 600, Abilene 79601 (915–676–2556 or 800–727–7704).

Here's a place to relax, cool off in the lake, and maybe fish a little. Near the lake is **Fort Phantom Hill,** built in 1851 with three buildings and a dozen chimneys, which remain from the days it protected area settlers and travelers on the Butterfield Trail.

For More Information

Abilene Chamber of Commerce.
1101 North First Street, Abilene, TX 79601; (800) 727–7704. Visit the Web site at www.abilene.com/visitors.

Albany, Colorado City, and Big Spring

Albany is on Texas Highway 6 east of Abilene, while Colorado City and Big Spring are on I–20 west of Abilene.

Founded as a cattle shipping point on the Western Trail to Dodge City, Albany remains a major cattle supply center, along with its oil interests. Oil is a big thing in Colorado City as well. The big spring that Big Spring is named for bubbles up in the middle of the city. The spring attracted buffalo herds, antelope, wild horses, Comanches and Shawnees, and early Texas Rangers. Today, a city park surrounds the spring.

OLD JAIL ART CENTER (ages 6 and up)

211 South Second Street, Albany (915–762–2269). Open Tuesday through Saturday from 10:00 A.M. to 5:00 P.M., Sunday from 2:00 to 5:00 P.M., closed holidays. **Free**.

Head northeast on Texas Highway 351 to Albany, another of those small Texas towns with several interesting sights. The most famous is the Old Jail Art Center, on Second Street, a block from the courthouse. The Jail has an exceptional permanent art collection that includes the work of Picasso and Modigliani.

  FORT GRIFFIN STATE PARK (ages 4 and up)

15 miles north of Albany on U.S. Highway 283, Albany 76430 (915–762–3592).

At the Clear Fork of the Brazos River is Fort Griffin State Park. The fort was a primary center for trail-herd cowboys and buffalo hunters. This is where Wyatt Earp met Doc Holliday. You can walk on the sidewalks they walked on and wander around the ruins of many of the buildings, seeing three restored structures and a small museum. You can also camp, fish, have a picnic, play horseshoes, or go on a nature walk. The park also has campsites, hiking trails, picnic areas, and a playground for kids.

 HEART OF TEXAS MUSEUM (ages 6 and up)

340 East Third Street, Colorado City 79512 (915–728–8285). Open 2:00 to 5:00 P.M. daily except Monday. Donations welcomed.

Colorado (Cawl-oh-ray-doh) City, on I-20, was one of the fastest growing cities in Texas before the turn of the twentieth century, but a severe drought and competition from other shipping points turned the boom into a bust from which the town has never fully recovered. The Heart of Texas Museum preserves artifacts not only from pioneer days but from modern times as well, such as the display on Desert Storm.

Nearby, at Second and Chestnut Streets, is the **Branding Wall** in Kiwanis Park, where you can see more than 230 cattle brands that are or have been used in the county, making for a good backdrop in photos of the kids.

 LAKE COLORADO CITY STATE PARK (ages 4 and up)

12 miles southwest of Colorado City, take the Farm Road 2836 exit off I–20, Colorado City 79512 (915–728–3931).

This is a 500-acre park along the banks of a 1,600-acre lake, where your family can camp, picnic, swim, water-ski, or fish.

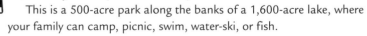

COMANCHE TRAIL PARK (ages 4 and up)

On U.S. Highway 87, Big Spring 79721 (915–263–8311).

The spring for which the city of Big Spring is named is in Comanche Trail Park. The park, just south of town, has a golf course and tennis courts, hiking and biking trails, overnight camping, sailing on Comanche Trail Lake, and the Comanche Trail Amphitheater, built of hand-cut native limestone.

HERITAGE MUSEUM (ages 6 and up)

510 Scurry Street, Big Spring 79720 (915–267–8255). Open Tuesday through Friday 10:00 A.M. to 5:30 P.M., Saturday 10:00 A.M. to 5:00 P.M. Donations requested.

The Heritage Museum houses the world's largest collection of Texas Longhorn steer horns and an exhibit of forty-six rare and unusual phonographs.

BIG SPRING STATE PARK (ages 4 and up)

About 4 miles west of Big Spring on Farm Road 700, Big Spring 79720 (915–263–4931). Open daily April through October from 8:00 A.M. to 10:00 P.M., November through March from 8:00 A.M. to 8:00 P.M.

Big Spring State Park is the closest thing this area of west Texas has to a mountain. A 200-foot mesa that overlooks the city west of downtown, the park has a children's playground, picnic areas, a prairie-dog town, and nature trails. Camping is available on top of Scenic Mountain.

For More Information

Big Spring Convention and Visitors Bureau. *215 West Third Street, Big Spring, TX 79721–1391; (800) 734–7641 or (915) 263–7641.*

Midland

Midway between Dallas and El Paso, but only about 40 miles west of Big Spring.

PERMIAN BASIN PETROLEUM MUSEUM (ages 6 and up)

1500 I–20 West, Midland 79701 (915–683–4403). Open 9:00 A.M. to 5:00 P.M. Monday through Saturday and 2:00 to 5:00 P.M. Sunday, the museum closes on Thanksgiving Day, Christmas Eve, and Christmas. Adults $5.00, students $4.00, children 6–11 $3.00, children under 6 **Free**.

Midland and its twin city, Odessa, are the center for oil exploration in Texas, so it's appropriate that the Permian Basin Petroleum Museum is here. You can see the museum from the interstate. It's that red building at the Route 349 exit with the dozens of oil-field derricks beside it. Here your family will explore 500 million years of history, walk under a vast sea to view the Permian Basin as it was 230 million years ago, stroll down a typical boomtown, examine rock samples, learn how wells are drilled, and feel the force of an underground explosion. You'll see everything from old cable tool rigs to modern pump jacks. The kids can even play the Oil Game and might hit a gusher. In addition to the

Texas Trivia By 1928, Texas was the nation's leading oil producing state, a position it has never relinquished. Today the state pumps out around 650 million barrels of crude and gas a year from more than 240,000 wells.

petroleum paraphernalia, the museum also focuses on the Comanche War Trail, which passed through the heart of Midland, site of the last Comanche raid in Texas.

MIDLAND ROCKHOUNDS BASEBALL (ages 4 and up)

4300 North Lamesa Road, Midland 79705 (915–683–4251; www. midlandrockhounds.org). Tickets: $5.00 to $7.00 adults, $2.50 children.

The Midland Rockhounds, a farm team of the Oakland A's, play AA minor-league ball at Christensen Stadium. Concessions here aren't limited to just peanuts and hot dogs; you can also get pizza, nachos, and Frito pies. The ballpark also has a special family section where beer sales aren't allowed. The Rockhounds play April through August.

MUSEUM OF THE SOUTHWEST (ages 4 and up)

1705 West Missouri Street, Midland 79701 (915–683–2882). Open Tuesday through Saturday from 10:00 A.M. to 5:00 P.M., Sunday 2:00 to 5:00 P.M. Closed major holidays. **Free**.

The Museum of the Southwest complex covers an entire city block. Exhibits feature Southwestern painting, sculpture, and ceramics, with a crafts fair the first weekend following Labor Day. In the complex are two other museums. The **Fredda Turner Durham Children's Museum** gives kids an interactive environment for exploration and learning, including a computer area. **The Marion West Blakemore Planetarium,** (915) 683-2882, holds public shows at 2:00 and 3:30 P.M. on the first weekend of every month.

CONFEDERATE AIR FORCE AMERICAN AIRPOWER HERITAGE MUSEUM (ages 4 and up)

9600 Wright Drive, Midland 79711 8 miles west of the city, off I–20 next to the Midland International Airport (915–563–1000; www.confederateairforce.org). Open Monday through Saturday 9:00 A.M. to 5:00 P.M., Sunday and holidays noon to 5:00 P.M. Adults $7.00, teens $6.00, children 6–12 $5.00, children 5 and under **Free**.

The Confederate Air Force Flying Museum is one place that will fascinate both children and parents, showcasing a large number of antique aircraft. Contrary to its name, the Confederate Air Force has nothing to do with the Civil War. Its World War II vintage planes fly at air shows here and around the country. About 20 of the 135 aircraft in the CAF's Ghost Squadron are on display here at any one time, and the headquarters is home to the annual Airsho in October. The museum preserves authentic World War II artifacts and memorabilia, opening new exhibits each year. If your child is a model builder, he or she will love the gift shop, which has the largest collection of model airplanes for sale in one place.

 HERO'S WATER WORLD (ages 4 and up)

12300 East Business Loop 20, Midland 79711 (915–563–1933). Open noon to 7:00 P.M. Monday through Friday and Sunday, an hour earlier on Saturday. Adults $12.50, children $7.50, children 5 and under **Free**.

Go a couple of miles farther down I-20 to cool off at Hero's Water World, a place any family desperately needs in the hot Texas summers. This is one of the largest water parks in Texas, and there's something here for every adult or child, from water slides to white-water streams to ocean waves. One nice family touch: If you just want to watch your kids get wet, you can get a **Free** spectator pass with a refundable $10 deposit.

Where to Eat

See Odessa listings for more nearby dining and lodging options.

Golden Corral. *4709 North Midkiff (915–689–7706), and 4037 East Forty-second Street, Midland 79705 (915–363–8705).* Good steaks and all-you-can-eat buffet give the family plenty of choices. $–$$

Luigi's. *111 Big Spring Street, Midland 79701 (915–683–6363).* Family-owned, family-oriented, and great Italian food. $–$$

Where to Stay

Best Western. *3100 West Wall Street, Midland 79701 (915–699–4144).* Pool, **Free** continental breakfast. $$

Lexington Hotel Suites. *1003 South Midkiff, Midland 79701 (915–697– 3155).* Pool, **Free** breakfast, children under 16 stay **Free**. $$

For More Information

Midland Convention and Visitors Bureau. *109 North Main Street, Midland, TX 79702; (800) 624–6435 or (915) 683–3381.*

Odessa

PRESIDENTIAL MUSEUM (ages 6 and up)

622 North Lee Street, Odessa 79761 (915–332–7123). Open Tuesday through Saturday from 10:00 A.M. to 5:00 P.M. Adults $2.00, children under 17 **Free**.

The middle of nowhere in Texas may seem like a strange place for the Presidential Museum, but it's in Odessa nonetheless. The museum houses an impressive collection of items relating to the U.S. presidency. The Hall of Presidents displays objects related to individual presidents, the Dishong Collection displays replicas of First Lady inaugural gowns, and one exhibit focuses on campaigns.

GLOBE THEATER (ages 6 and up)

2308 Shakespeare Road, Odessa 79761 (915–332–1586).

If the idea of a Presidential Museum in Odessa isn't odd enough for you, how about a replica of Shakespeare's Globe Theatre along with a full Shakespearean library in a replica of Anne Hathaway's cottage, and a summer Shakespeare festival? Call the theater for show times and special events, from Broadway musicals to country-and-western revues.

ART INSTITUTE FOR THE PERMIAN BASIN (ages 6 and up)

4909 East University Boulevard, Odessa 79762 (915–368–7222 or 915– 550–3811). Open Tuesday through Saturday from 10:00 A.M. to 5:00 P.M., Sunday from 2:00 to 5:00 P.M. **Free**.

If art is your thing, check out the Art Institute for the Permian Basin, on the campus of the University of Texas–Permian Basin, for exhibits of historic and contemporary art and photography, a sculpture garden, and art education programs.

Texas Tunes
Here are some more recommendations for good Texas traveling music:

- *Live at the Old Quarter* by Townes Van Zandt (one of the great songwriters)
- *Loco Gringo's Lament* by Ray Wylie Hubbard (the quintessential Texas outlaw matured)
- *Navajo Rug* by Jerry Jeff Walker (a country folk highlight)
- *Ocean Front Property* by George Strait (straight country)
- *The Original Texas Playboys* by Bob Wills and the Texas Playboys (they created Texas swing)
- *Piano Rags* by Scott Joplin (the ragtime master)
- *Red-Headed Stranger* by Willie Nelson (the album that made Willie a legend)
- *Road to Ensenada* by Lyle Lovett (funny and poignant; the best of the best)
- *Selena Live* by Selena (capture a moment of her magic)
- *Texas Blues* by Lightnin' Hopkins (the blues master)
- *This Is My Home* by Chris and Judy (songs written for children that adults will enjoy as well)
- *22 All-Time Favorites* by Gene Autry (the original singing cowboy, still unmatched)
- *The Wind Knows My Name* by Tim Henderson (music that's pure Texas poetry)

ODESSA JACKALOPES HOCKEY (ages 6 and up)
4201 Andrews Highway, Odessa 79762 (915–552–7825). Tickets: $6.00 to $12.00.

The minor-league Jackalopes play in the Ector County Coliseum during the winter months.

MIDESSA PORCELAIN DOLL FACTORY (ages 2 and up)

4209 South County Road 1290, Odessa 79765 (915–563–1522). Open Monday through Saturday 9:00 A.M. to 5:00 P.M. **Free**.

You'll discover a wonderland of dolls at the Midessa Porcelain Doll Factory. Your children can marvel at dolls being made and buy all kinds of dolls, doll furniture and houses, kits, and supplies.

WORLD'S LARGEST JACK RABBIT (ages 2 and up)

802 North Sam Houston Avenue, Odessa 79761.

Odessa calls it *The World's Largest Jack Rabbit.* So what if it's just a statue? The 10-foot bunny in the parking lot of the Ector County Independent School District's administration building is a popular place to take photos of the kids.

ODESSA METEOR CRATER (ages 4 and up)

About 10 miles west of the city off I–20 at the Farm Road 1936 exit, Odessa 79760.

At 550 feet in diameter and 6 feet deep, the Odessa Meteor Crater is said to be the second largest known meteor crater in the United States, but wind erosion has taken a heavy toll on its shape, and it really doesn't look like much. At least your family can say "been there, done that" if you go. A chunk of the meteor that crashed here is at the Permian Basin Petroleum Museum. The site has picnic tables and a barbecue grill.

Where to Eat

Luby's Cafeteria. *4101 East Forty-second Street, Odessa 79762 (915–367–0723).* Legendary in Texas for its quality and selection. $–$$

Rosa's Cafe and Tortilla Factory. *4945 East Forty-second Street, Odessa 79762 (915–550–2204).* Good, homemade Mexican food. $

Where to Stay

K-Bar Ranch. *15448-A South Jasper, Odessa 79763 (915–580–4046 or 915–580–5880).* Delight in a two-story mountain covered in stuffed animals right in the middle of the living room.

Two bed-and-breakfast rooms in the main lodge cater to families. Take excursions onto the ranch to see a number of the exotic animals. $$–$$$

For More Information

Odessa Chamber of Commerce.
*700 North Grant Street, Odessa, TX
79760; (800) 780–HOST or (915)*

*332–9111. Visit the Web site at
www.odessachamber.com.*

Monahans

MONAHANS SANDHILLS STATE PARK (ages 4 and up)
*6 miles northeast of Monahans off I–20 on Park Road 41, Monahans 79756
(915–943–2092).*
   This is where kids love to surf the sand. Rent a sand-surfing disk and
fly down the smooth, cream-colored sand dunes. The park
is 4,000 acres of always-changing, wind-sculpted
dunes that look more like the Sahara Desert than Texas. In
addition to sand sliding, the park has horseback rides, hiking trails, camping and picnic
sites, interpretive rides in a utility vehicle, and a museum.

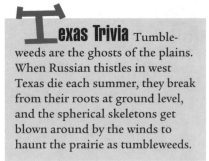

Texas Trivia Tumbleweeds are the ghosts of the plains. When Russian thistles in west Texas die each summer, they break from their roots at ground level, and the spherical skeletons get blown around by the winds to haunt the prairie as tumbleweeds.

MILLION BARREL MUSEUM (ages 6 and up)
*2 miles east of Monahans on U.S. Highway 80, Monahans 79756 (915–
943–8401). Open Tuesday through Saturday 10:00 A.M. to 8:00 P.M., Sunday
2:00 to 8:00 P.M.* **Free.**
   The Million Barrel Museum surrounds a big hole in the ground that
was once a Shell Oil tank. The museum complex includes a historic hotel,
the first jail in the county, oil-field equipment, and an amphitheater.

For More Information

Monahans Chamber of Commerce.
401 South Dwight Street, Monahans, TX

*79756; (915) 943–2187. Visit the
Web site at www.monahans.org.*

Texas Trivia The deepest well in Texas was a 29,670-foot dry hole in Pecos County.

Pecos

Pecos is where rodeos all began, when several cowboys from neighboring ranches got together to prove once and for all who was best at their occupation. That was back in 1883, and the town still holds a rodeo every July Fourth. The **West of the Pecos Rodeo** is a four-day event that also features a parade, old-timers' reunion, and western art show. Call (915) 445-2406.

WEST OF THE PECOS MUSEUM AND PARK (ages 4 and up)
120 East First Street, Pecos 79772 (915–445–5076). Open Monday through Saturday 9:00 A.M. to 5:00 P.M., Sunday 1:00 to 5:00 P.M. Adults $4.00, children 6–18 $1.00, children under 5 **Free**.

The West of the Pecos Museum and Park occupies an old saloon and two floors of a historic hotel, full of artifacts. An adjacent park contains the first building in Pecos; the grave of Clay Allison, the "Gentleman Gunfighter"; and a replica of Judge Roy Bean's saloon (you can see the real Jersey Lilly in Langtry).

MAXEY PARK AND ZOO (ages 4 and up)
Off I–20 between U.S. Highway 285 and Texas Highway 17, Pecos 79772 (915–445–2406). **Free**.

The kids will enjoy seeing animals indigenous to west Texas: antelope, buffalo, deer, javelina, long-horns, mountain lions, and prairie dogs. Another feature of the park is **Kid's City,** a large playground that can occupy children for hours.

Texas Trivia The county with the smallest population is Loving County in west Texas, with ninety-six people.

For More Information

Pecos Chamber of Commerce. *111 South Cedar Street, Pecos, TX 79772;* *(915) 445–2406. Visit the Web site at www.texasusa.com/pecos.*

Balmorhea and Van Horn

Head south on Route 17 about 40 miles from Pecos to the small town of Balmorhea (Bal-moh-ray), a literal oasis in the parched west Texas landscape.

BALMORHEA STATE PARK (ages 4 and up)

On Route 17 just south of I–10, Toyahvale 79786 (915–375–2370). Open daily from 8:00 A.M. to dark.

Families in the area flock to this park, where historic San Solomon Springs form the world's largest spring-fed swimming pool, more than an acre large. In addition to campsites, the park features San Solomon Springs Court, a moderately priced eighteen-unit motel.

Where to Eat

Papa Chuy's. *1200 West Broadway, Van Horn 7986 (915–283–2066).* Mexican food and John Madden's "Haul of Fame," which displays plaques and photos of the winners of the famed football announcer's annual All-Madden Team. $–$$

Smokehouse Restaurant. *905 West Broadway, Van Horn 79855 (915–283–2453).* Steaks, smoked meats, and even seafood. Also houses a classic auto museum. $–$$

Pine Springs

GUADALUPE MOUNTAINS NATIONAL PARK (ages 8 and up)

On U.S. Highway 62, Salt Flat 79847, at the New Mexico border (915–828–3251; www.nps.gov/gumo/). Frijole Information Center and Museum open 8:00 A.M. to 4:30 P.M. daily except Christmas.

Head north on Texas Highway 54 from Van Horn for a nice scenic drive to Guadalupe Mountains National Park, home to Guadalupe Peak, Texas's tallest mountain at 8,749 feet. The park has majestic vistas all around and some of the best hiking in the state, especially the trail into McKittrick Canyon, which blazes with color in the fall. The rugged Guadalupe Peak trail provides breathtaking panoramas at the summit. The park is maintained as a primitive wilderness, so it has no accommodations beyond a few campsites. The closest motels, restaurants, and grocery stores are in New Mexico. If you do decide to explore some of the trails, make sure you and your family are in good shape and carry lots of water. The hikes here are long and often grueling, so they're not recommended for small children. The only paved road cuts through a tiny portion of the park at its southeastern boundary.

El Paso

El Paso sprawls at the foot of the Franklin Mountains, presenting an unusual vista with rocky hills and mountains to the north and the Rio Grande plain and Chihuahuan Desert to the south. The Mexican metropolis of Juarez is just across the river. West of the city, the borders of Texas, New Mexico, and old Mexico swirl together as easily as American and Mexican cultures do here. The family attractions in El Paso are numerous, and that doesn't even include the shopping possibilities, from small arts-and-crafts boutiques to several new malls.

If Mexico fascinates you, head across the border into Juarez, where you'll find several shopping centers, many small boutiques, parks and museums, old missions, and a variety of restaurants. Four international bridges cross from El Paso into Juarez. For more detailed visitor information, contact the Juarez Tourist Service at (011) 52-16-11-37-07.

The best-known park area across the border is **Juarez Chamizal Park,** at the Cordova Bridge. The park has replicas of several famous sites in Mexico, such as Chichén Itzá and Teotihuacan. Adjacent to this park, on the U.S. side, are **Chamizal National Monument,** (915) 532-7273, and **Chamizal National Park.** All three commemorate settlement of a land dispute between the two countries.

The **Border Folk Festival** in mid-October will give your family a heavy dose of what El Paso is all about. The Chamizal area boasts plentiful food and arts-and-crafts booths, and American, Mexican, and other international singers and dancers all day long and into the night. Call (915) 532-7273.

Texas Trivia Although many people think of Texas as either flat desert or beaches, the state has ninety-one mountains that are a mile or more high, all of them in west Texas. The top seven:

- Guadalupe Peak, at 8,749 feet, is the state's highest mountain.
- Bush Mountain is 8,631 feet.
- Sumard Peak is 8,615 feet.
- Bartlett Mountain is 8,508 feet.
- Mount Livermore is 8,378 feet.
- Pine Top Mountain is 8,368 feet.
- El Capitan Peak is 8,085 feet.

HUECO TANKS STATE HISTORICAL PARK (ages 4 and up)

32 miles east of El Paso; go north on Ranch Road 2775 to Park Road 68, El Paso 79938 (915–857–1135).

Taking U.S. Highway 180 west from the Guadalupe mountains provides a view of the salt flats before you arrive at Hueco Tanks State Historical Park, east of El Paso. *Hueco* (pronounced Way-co) means "hollow" in Spanish. It refers to a large number of depressions in the mountain rock that collect water, providing refreshment to travelers for hundreds of years. The area was the site of a Butterfield Stage station and has numerous prehistoric Native American pictographs. In recent years, the rugged faces of the mountains have attracted rock climbers from around the world, and you're likely to see some spidering up the walls on any weekend. The park has picnic areas and a few campsites.

Texas Trivia The longest river in the state is the Rio Grande (the second longest in the United States), which forms the international boundary between Texas and Mexico, extending 1,270 miles from El Paso to Brownsville. Other principal rivers are the Brazos, Colorado, Guadalupe, Neches, Nueces, Pecos, Red, Trinity, and Sabine.

EL PASO TROLLEYS (ages 4 and up)

All the trolleys leave from the Civic Center Plaza at Santa Fe and San Antonio Streets, although you can board the city trolley anywhere along its route. See the following for telephone numbers and fares.

A nice way for your family to forget about traffic and still get around town, and into Juarez, is via the El Paso Trolleys. The El Paso routes cover the main downtown area and two of the city's international crossings for just a quarter. Call (915) 533-3333.

The **Trolley on a Mission,** (915) 544-0062, will take your family on a tour of **Mission Corpus Christi, Ysleta del Sur Pueblo, Mission Socorro,** and **Mission San Elizario.** The El Paso–Juarez Trolley makes a loop into Mexico near several of the best shopping areas in Juarez. Fares are $10.00 adults, $8.00 children. Schedules are subject to change, so call (915) 544-0061. A travel tip: The trolley ticket office at the Civic Center is full of brochures from area attractions and accommodations.

FORT BLISS MUSEUMS (ages 6 and up)

Wilson Road at Texas Highway 54, El Paso 79903. 𝐅𝐫𝐞𝐞.

Fort Bliss, bordering the El Paso airport, has been an active army base since 1848. On the base are several 𝐅𝐫𝐞𝐞 museums:

- The **Fort Bliss Museum** is a replica of the original adobe fort, with several displays on frontier military life. It's at Pleasanton Road and Sheridan Drive in Building 5051. Open daily 9:00 A.M. to 4:30 P.M. Call (915) 568-2804.

- The **Air Defense and Artillery Museum,** in Building 5000 on Pleasanton Road, is the only one of its kind in the country, with hands-on displays and dioramas. Open Wednesday through Sunday from 9:00 A.M. to 4:30 P.M. Call (915) 568-4518.

- The **Museum of the Noncommissioned Officer** is in Building 11331 at Barksdale and Thirty-fifth Streets. It traces the history of the NCO from the Revolutionary War to the present. Open Monday through Friday 9:00 A.M. to 4:00 P.M., Saturday and Sunday noon to 4:00 P.M. Call (915) 568-8646.

- The **Third Armored Cavalry Museum,** in Building 2407 at Forrest Road, honors the Third Cavalry that fought in the Mexican and Indian Wars. Open Monday through Friday 7:30 A.M. to 4:30 P.M. Call (915) 568-1922.

BORDER PATROL MUSEUM (ages 6 and up)

4315 Woodrow Bean Transmountain Road on Loop 375, El Paso 79924, off Route 54 (915–759–6060). Open Tuesday through Saturday 9:00 A.M. to 5:00 P.M., closed holidays. 𝐅𝐫𝐞𝐞.

The museum chronicles the U.S. Border Patrol from its beginnings in the Old West to the high-tech world of the present.

WILDERNESS PARK MUSEUM (ages 4 and up)

4301 Woodrow Bean Transmountain Road, El Paso 79924 (915–755–4332). Open Tuesday through Saturday from 9:00 A.M. to 5:00 P.M. Adults $1.00, children 50 cents.

Next door to the Border Patrol Museum is the Wilderness Park Museum, the perfect place for your kids to get acquainted with west Texas history, geology, and plants. The museum displays collections of pottery and other prehistoric artifacts, along with several life-size dioramas, and offers a self-guided nature trail where your family can learn all about the region's plant life.

FRANKLIN MOUNTAINS STATE PARK (ages 4 and up)

Along Texas Highway 375, Canutillo 79835 (915–566–6441).

Continue northward on the Transmountain Road (Loop 375), the highest state highway in Texas, for some nice views of the area. Several scenic overlooks are by the side of the road. You'll also notice some parking areas that are jumping-off points for trails into Franklin Mountains State Park, which you happen to be driving through. The park is undeveloped, so only day-use activities are allowed. A side road off the main route will take you into the picnic areas of the park.

WET 'N' WILD WATER WORLD (ages 4 and up)

At exit 0 on I–10, Anthony 79821 (915–886–2222; www.wetwild.com). Open daily May through mid-August, weekends in early May through September. Hours vary widely throughout the season. Adults $17, children $15, nonswimmers $12.

To cool off the kids during the hot months, continue west on the interstate just a couple of miles to the last exit in Texas, and Wet 'n' Wild Water World is on the south side of the freeway.

EL PASO CENTENNIAL MUSEUM (ages 6 and up)

University Avenue at Wiggins Road, El Paso 79902 (915–747–5565; www.utep.edu/museum). Open Tuesday through Friday from 10:00 A.M. to 3:00 P.M., Sunday from 1:30 to 5:30 P.M. **Free**.

The Centennial Museum, on the University of Texas–El Paso campus, features photos and maps, pottery and jewelry, and other displays of the area's history and geology.

EL PASO MUSEUM OF ART (ages 6 and up)

Main and Santa Fe Streets, El Paso 79901 (915–532–1707; www. elpasoartmuseum.org). Open Tuesday through Saturday 10:00 A.M. to 5:00 P.M., Sunday 1:00 to 5:00 P.M. Adults $1.00, students 50 cents. **Free** *on Sunday.*

The Museum of Art is renowned for its frequent exhibits of classical and contemporary Mexican and Southwestern art. The new facility tripled the museum's space, so you'll now see more of its permanent collection, which used to rotate.

EL PASO MUSEUM OF HISTORY (ages 6 and up)

I–10 at the Avenue of the Americas, El Paso 79901 (915–858–1928). Open Tuesday through Sunday from 9:00 A.M. to 4:50 P.M., closed some holidays. Adults $1.00, children 50 cents.

The Museum of History focuses on U.S. Cavalry mementos and Southwestern history from the conquistadors to Pancho Villa. Museum volunteers hold special programs for children.

The First Thanksgiving

The First Thanksgiving The first Thanksgiving in the United States was held in El Paso, twenty-three years before the Pilgrims's day of thanks we now celebrate nationally. In April 1598, explorer Don Juan de Oñate and his expedition reached the area after a grueling 200-mile march across the Chihuahuan Desert. Many of his men and livestock were near death. Nearby Native Americans visited Oñate's camp, shared food, and were entertained by a play written by one of the expedition captains as thanks for being delivered from their ordeal. It's said to be the first drama performed by Europeans on what would become U.S. soil.

The account of this first Thanksgiving was not translated into English until 1933, many decades after President Lincoln designated the fourth Thursday in November to commemorate the Pilgrim Thanksgiving.

INSIGHTS, EL PASO SCIENCE CENTER (ages 4 and up)
505 North Santa Fe Avenue, El Paso 79901 (915–534–0000). Open Tuesday through Saturday from 9:00 A.M. to 5:00 P.M., except major holidays. Adults $5.00, children $2.00.

All the exhibits at Insights, El Paso Science Center, are designed to make learning about science and technology an active experience for children and interested parents. Virtually everything is hands-on.

MAGOFFIN HOME STATE HISTORICAL PARK (ages 8 and up)
1120 Magoffin Avenue, El Paso 79901 (915–533–5147).

The Magoffin Home is a perfectly preserved territorial hacienda built in 1875 by one of the prominent pioneer families in the area. Inside are many of the family's original furnishings, paintings, and artifacts.

EL PASO SADDLEBLANKET CO. (ages 4 and up)
601 North Oregon Avenue, El Paso, 79901 (915–544–1000). Open Monday through Friday 9:00 A.M. to 5:00 P.M., Saturday 10:00 A.M. to 4:00 P.M.

The El Paso Saddleblanket Co. is a wonderland. You'll find great bargains on everything from, yes, saddle blankets to pottery and leather goods. Your children, meanwhile, will be running from one end of the 36,000-square-foot showroom to the other, trying out bullwhips or playing with freeze-dried piranhas. There's something for everyone here.

EL PASO ZOO (ages 4 and up)
4001 East Paisano Drive at Evergreen, El Paso 79905 (915–544–1928; www. elpasozoo.org). Open daily 9:30 A.M. to late afternoon. Adults $4.00, children $2.00.

Seems like every city of any size in Texas has a zoo, and El Paso is no exception. The El Paso Zoo is home to more than 400 exotic animals on eighteen acres. Your family will love the shaded walkways as they watch the birds, fish, mammals, and reptiles.

EL PASO BUZZARDS HOCKEY (ages 6 and up)
100 East Paisano Drive, El Paso 79901 (915–533–9899 or 915–534–7825). Ticket prices vary.

The minor-league Buzzards take to the ice in the El Paso County Coliseum.

EL PASO DIABLOS BASEBALL (ages 4 and up)
9700 Gateway North, El Paso 79924 (915–755–2000; www.diablos.com). Tickets $4.00 to $6.00.

It's hard to beat a night at the ballpark for good, affordable family entertainment, and it's difficult to beat the El Paso Diablos for minor-league baseball fun. The AA Texas League Diablos play at Cohen Stadium from April through August. One of the great family attractions is the **Hard Ball Cafe,** where you and the kids get seats at a game, special recognition on the scoreboard, souvenir drink cups, and all you can eat for two hours for just $12 per person.

WESTERN PLAYLAND (ages 4 and up)
6900 Delta Drive, El Paso 79905; take the Trowbridge exit off I–10 about 6 miles from downtown (915–772–3914; www.WesternPlayland.com). Open weekends March through October, daily June through August. Admission $14.75 for all rides or $3.00 general admission with each ride costing $2.00.

Western Playland at Ascarate Park is a typical amusement park that will keep your kids occupied all day with twenty-eight rides and various games, arcades, entertainment pavilions, and even a volleyball court.

TIGUA CULTURAL CENTER (ages 4 and up)

305 Yaya Lane, El Paso 79907; take the Zaragosa exit from I–10 and go south (915–859–5287). Open Tuesday through Sunday from 8:30 A.M. to 5:00 P.M. Free.

A lovely way for the family to spend part of the day is at the Tigua Cultural Center. It's the showcase for the Ysleta del Sur Pueblo, the oldest existing community in Texas, founded by Tigua Indians in 1680. The Tigua Cultural Center has a central courtyard where Tiguas demonstrate tribal dances at 11:00 A.M., 1:00 P.M., and 3:00 P.M. on weekends. The courtyard is surrounded by the Cacique Cafe and shops featuring work by Tigua artists.

Nearby, at 119 South Old Pueblo Road, is **Mission Corpus Christi.** Formerly known as Ysleta Mission, it was built in 1681 and is the oldest mission in Texas. Call (915) 859-9848.

Texas Indian Reservations

Texas has three Native American reservations:

- The **Alabama-Coushatta Reservation** near Woodville in east Texas. The Alabama-Coushattas have a restaurant, gift shop, and campsites; offer tours through the Big Thicket and the reservation, and present dances and other cultural attractions.

- The **Ysleta del Sur Pueblo,** south of El Paso in west Texas, serves as the Tigua Reservation. The Tiguas have a small gift shop and present dances. They also run a casino and excellent restaurant nearby. The Ysleta Mission was the first Spanish settlement in Texas.

- The **Kickapoo Reserve,** south of Eagle Pass in south Texas, is small and has no tourist facilities or attractions except for a casino. Before the reservation was established in the 1980s, the Kickapoo lived in a makeshift encampment under the international bridge at Eagle Pass. Most of the time, the Kickapoos live across the Rio Grande in Nacimiento, Coahuila.

Where to Eat

Casa Jurado. *226 Cincinnati, El Paso 79902 (915–532–6429) and 4772 Doniphan, El Paso 79922 (915–833–1151).* If you're hungry, try one of the six distinct styles of enchiladas for a real treat, the best in Texas. $–$$

Cracker Barrel. *7540 Remcon Circle, El Paso 79912 (915–581–9742).* Family-style southern cooking with a huge gift shop in the lobby. $–$$

Wyngs Restaurant. *122 South Old Pueblo Road, El Paso 79907 (915–858–1033).* Operated by the Tiguas; adjacent to their Speaking Rock Casino and Bingo Center. Has great portions of great food. Kids will love the hamburger served on Indian fry bread, so large it can be shared by two adults or several small children. The best burger in the state. $$

Where to Stay

Cowboys and Indians Board and Bunk. *40 Mountain Vista, SantaTeresa, New Mexico 88008 (505–589–2653; www.smart.net/~cowboysbb/home.html).* Huge adobe hacienda. Choose from four theme rooms furnished with many items handcrafted by the owners, have breakfast in the Kiva Room, and enjoy spectacular sunsets from the veranda. $$

Howard Johnson Inn. *8887 Gateway West, El Paso 79925 (915–591–9471 or 800–446–4656).* Trolley stops at the hotel. $$

La Quinta Inns. *7550 Remcon Circle, 11033 Gateway West and 6140 Gateway West, El Paso 79925 (800–531–5900).* Perfect for families: Children under twelve stay **Free**; pools and **Free** breakfast. $$

For More Information

El Paso Convention and Tourism Department. *One Civic Center Plaza, El Paso, TX 79901–1187; (915) 534–0696. Visit the Web site at www.visitelpaso.com.*

Fabens and Sierra Blanca

As you travel east along I-10 to Fabens and Sierra Blanca, you'll see just how desolate this area of Texas can be. Just make sure you have a full tank of gas, some snacks, and water before you leave El Paso. Sierra Blanca is historically important as the juncture of the nation's second transcontinental rail route when the Southern Pacific and the Texas & Pacific lines met up in 1881. You'll find a historical marker commemorating that event downtown on U.S. Highway 80.

CATTLEMAN'S STEAK HOUSE (ages 4 and up)

At Indian Cliffs Ranch, Fabens 79838; east on I–10 about thirty minutes to exit 49 in Fabens, then north 4 miles to the Indian Cliffs sign (915–544–3200; www.cattlemanssteakhouse.com). Zoo area **Free**.

If your kids have never gotten excited about a restaurant before, they will over the Cattleman's Steak House. Although the restaurant is justly famous for items like its two-pound T-bone and the Royale ground steak, it's the ranch itself that your children will love. Sprawled over several acres around the restaurant are a small zoo, buffalo and longhorn herds, a snake pit, a frontier fort replica, a kids' playground, and a complete Western town. Donkey rides and covered-wagon rides are available to other areas of the ranch. Prices are moderate to expensive, mostly moderate. *People* magazine said this was the best steak in the country.

RAILROAD DEPOT HUDSPETH COUNTY MUSEUM (ages 6 and up)

U.S. Highway 80, Sierra Blanca 79851. Open Wednesday 1:00 to 5:00 P.M. **Free**.

Near the post office is the Railroad Depot Hudspeth County Museum, where you'll find exhibits of railroad memorabilia, Native American artifacts, and county history housed in a Southern Pacific depot built in 1882.

Nearby, at Highway 80's intersection with Ranch Road 1111, is the **Hudspeth County Courthouse,** the only adobe structure currently in use by a government in the entire Southwest. The building is a favorite place for photos.

Fort Davis

Take Texas Highway 118 south at Kent for one of the finest scenic drives in Texas. The road travels through the rugged Davis Mountains with a number of twists and sharp turns. The land here is almost all working ranches, and you're likely to see pronghorn antelope roaming the range by the side of the road, so have the kids keep a sharp lookout. This *is* where the deer and the antelope play, and the skies are not cloudy (usually) all day.

MCDONALD OBSERVATORY (ages 6 and up)

On Spur 78 just off Texas Highway 118, Fort Davis 79734 (915–426–3640; www.as.utexas.edu/mcdonald/vc/). Open daily 9:00 A.M. to 5:00 P.M., except

Thanksgiving, Christmas, and New Year's Day. Solar viewing and self-guided tours **Free**; *tours: $4.00 adults, $3.00 children 6–12; $10.00 family; Star Party: $4.00 adults, $3.00 children 6–12, $10.00 family; both tour and Star Party: $7.00 adults, $5.00 children 6–12, $15.00 family.*

McDonald Observatory is perched atop 6,800-foot Mount Locke. The University of Texas operates this complex of deep-space telescopes, including a new one that has the largest telescope mirror in the nation. Kids love the visitors center, which has daily programs, films, guided tours, and solar viewing. Star Parties are held on smaller telescopes Tuesday, Friday, and Saturday evenings so even the smallest children can enjoy the stars and planets. Once a month the public can peer through the "Big Eyes" of the 107-inch telescope, but reservations must be made months in advance.

DAVIS MOUNTAINS STATE PARK (ages 4 and up)

On Park Road 3 off Texas Highway 118, Fort Davis 79734 (915–426–3337).

A few miles farther south is Davis Mountains State Park. This is one of the best state parks in Texas, with picturesque campsites, picnic areas, several hiking trails, and a scenic driving loop. One of the trails runs over a mountain 4 miles into Fort Davis National Historical Park. One of the best things about Davis Mountains Park is the Indian Lodge motel, built during the Depression by the Civilian Conservation Corps.

FORT DAVIS NATIONAL HISTORICAL PARK (ages 4 and up)

On Texas Highway 17, Fort Davis 79734 (915–426–3225). Open daily 8:00 A.M. to 5:00 P.M., except Christmas.

Just north of downtown is Fort Davis National Historical Park, one of the best restored Indian Wars forts in the country. Officers' Row and an enlisted men's barracks are just as they were back in the 1880s. During the summer, volunteers don period uniforms and roam the fort giving living-history talks and presentations. A museum in the visitors center offers a slide show, several displays, and a gift shop.

OVERLAND TRAIL MUSEUM (ages 6 and up)

Old Overland Trail, Fort Davis 79734 (915–426–3904). Open March through the second week in November, Monday through Saturday, except Wednesday, from 10:00 A.M. to 5:00 P.M. Adults $2.00, children $1.00.

The Overland Trail Museum commemorates the Overland Stage route that passed through here. The small museum is 2 blocks south of the fort, 2 blocks west of the highway.

NEILL MUSEUM (ages 6 and up)
On Seventh Street, Fort Davis 79734 (915–426–3838 or 915–426–3969). Open June through Labor Day, Tuesday through Saturday 10:00 A.M. to 5:00 P.M., Sunday 1:30 to 5:00 P.M. **Free***.*

The Neill Museum, in the 1898 Truehart Home, 7 blocks west of the courthouse, preserves antique toys made in Texas and antique dolls, bottles, and furniture. The museum also has a two-room bed-and-breakfast with antique furnishings.

 CHIHUAHUAN DESERT RESEARCH INSTITUTE (ages 6 and up)
4 miles south of Fort Davis on Texas Highway 118, Fort Davis 79734 (915–837–8740; www.cdri.org). Open April through August, weekdays 1:00 to 5:00 P.M. and weekends 9:00 A.M. to 6:00 P.M. **Free***.*

About 4 miles south of town is the Chihuahuan Desert Research Institute. An arboretum and desert garden display more than 500 species of plants you'll find in the area, and there is an interesting nature hike to some hidden springs.

Night of Lights One evening in April 1989, my wife and I were returning to Fort Davis after viewing the mysterious Marfa Lights. We had taken the long way around, through Alpine, and just as we were about to ascend into the Davis Mountains, we saw a bright light streaking to Earth in the eastern sky. The streak blossomed into a bright green flash. We had seen a meteor that had fallen somewhere in the field to the east.

When we arrived at the Indian Lodge in Davis Mountains State Park, we were treated to more mysterious lights. An entire portion of the sky was lit up in undulating orange and red lights. We, along with everyone else in the park, stood amazed at the light, wondering what the size of a fire would have to be to cause such a display. Having lived in both Alaska and Vermont, I thought the lights kind of looked like the aurora borealis, except for their color. The next day, while visiting McDonald Observatory, one of the astronomers asked if we had seen the spectacular Northern Lights. I had thought it impossible for the Northern Lights to be seen so far south, but the astronomer said this was a rare occurrence caused by high sunspot activity, and the difference in color was because the solar wind that causes the aurora had to penetrate a thicker layer of atmosphere in Big Bend than in Alaska.

Where to Eat

Black Bear Restaurant. *At Davis Mountains State Park, Fort Davis 79734 (915–426–3254).* Good food, great view, and a nearby hill to climb afterward to work off the calories. $

Fort Davis Drugstore. *On the town square, Fort Davis 79734 (915–426–3118).* Get a bona fide fountain Coca-Cola made from syrup and fizzy water. The marble-top counter and old-

fashioned glasses should bring back memories. One of the few places in town open for breakfast. $

Limpia Restaurant. *On the town square, Fort Davis 79734 (915–426–3237).* The best food in town. Lobby has many books about Big Bend; adjacent gift shop filled with unusual items. $–$$

Where to Stay

Hotel Limpia. *Main Street, Fort Davis 79734 (915–426–3237 or 800–662–5517; www.hotellimpia.com).* Across the street from the drugstore is the Hotel Limpia, a Texas Historic Landmark whose creaking hallway boards give testament to the fact that it has been serving travelers since 1912. In addition to pleasant, low-to moderate-priced rooms, the Limpia has an herb garden,

a gift shop, a comprehensive bookstore, and the best restaurant in town, with moderate prices. $$

Indian Lodge. *At Davis Mountains State Park, Fort Davis 79734 (915–426–3254).* Rooms have hand-hewn ceiling beams and are furnished with hand-crafted items. There's even a good-size pool to cool off in. $$

For More Information

Fort Davis Chamber of Commerce. *In the Union Trading Co. building near the Limpia Hotel, P.O. Box 378, Fort Davis, TX 79734; (800) 524–3015 or (915) 426–3015. Visit the Web site at www. fortdavis.com.*

Alpine and Marfa

If you're lucky enough to be in Alpine during early March, don't miss the annual **Cowboy Poetry Gathering** at the university. This is a real family-friendly celebration of western heritage and a wonderful time. Call (915) 837-2326 or (915) 837-8191.

In Marfa you can get information on the newly formed **Chinati Mountains State Natural Area** by calling (915) 229-3416, but as of this writing the park was open only via special tours.

MUSEUM OF THE BIG BEND (ages 6 and up)

At Sul Ross University, Alpine 79830 (915–837–8143). Open Tuesday through Saturday 9:00 A.M. to 5:00 P.M., Sunday 1:00 to 5:00 P.M. Donations welcomed.

Your family won't get a better introduction to the Big Bend area of Texas than in Alpine at Sul Ross University's Museum of the Big Bend, located on campus. The museum showcases area history with dioramas, paintings, photographs, and many artifacts, including a stagecoach full of bullet holes.

WOODWARD AGATE RANCH (ages 6 and up)

18 miles south of town on Texas Highway 118, Alpine 79830 (915–364–2271).

The kids are always picking up rocks anyway, so take them to the Woodward Agate Ranch, where they can search more than 3,000 acres for their own rainbow-hued agates. Quite a souvenir to take home. The ranch has its own lapidary shop that will cut or polish your stones or sell you more.

MARFA LIGHTS (ages 6 and up)

Off U.S. Highway 90, Marfa 79843, 9 miles east of Marfa. After dark.

If you head west of Alpine on U.S. Highway 90, you'll notice a road-side park about 9 miles before you get to Marfa. This is the prime viewing site for the famous, elusive Marfa Lights. No one knows what the lights are, but you're likely to see them on almost any night. Some of the lights are just refractions of vehicle headlights, but not all. Look across the plain toward the base of the mountains in front of you. Unless the lights are mighty active, though, younger kids might get bored waiting for a show.

In Marfa there is a nice view of the surrounding area from the public viewing spot at the top of the 1886 **Presidio County Courthouse.** Don't worry, you can't miss the courthouse; it's the biggest, most ornate building in town.

Texas Trivia The Big Bend gecko lizard *(Coleonyx reticulatus)* wasn't discovered until the mid-1950s, but it is now seen frequently in the Big Bend region, usually at night after a summer rain.

For More Information

Alpine Chamber of Commerce. *106 North Third Street, Alpine, TX 79830; (800) 561–3735. Visit the Web site at www.alpinetexas.com.*

Marfa Chamber of Commerce. *On U.S. Highway 90, Marfa, TX 79843; (800) 650–9696 code 1845 or (915) 729–4942. Visit the Web site at www. marfalights.com/marfa.html.*

Presidio

Presidio is one of the oldest continuously inhabited places in all of North America. For an interesting walk through a non-typical Mexican border town, cross into **Ojinaga.** The square is quite scenic, making for great photographs, and a few bargains are available in the shops. Call (915) 229-3199 for information on both towns.

FORT LEATON STATE HISTORICAL PARK (ages 6 and up)

4 miles east on Farm Road 170, Presidio 79845 (915–229–3613). Open daily 8:00 A.M. to 4:30 P.M., except Christmas.

Fort Leaton is a huge adobe fortress built by trader Ben Leaton in 1848. The private fort, now almost completely restored, was once the only civilized place for hundreds of miles. The visitors center includes a small museum and a slide show on the region. At various times, local high schoolers don costumes and present living-history programs inside the fort. Picnic areas outside overlook the Rio Grande and mountains in Mexico.

*S*cenic Drive Head south on U.S. Highway 67 for the best drive into the Big Bend. Mountains and desert surround you along the entire trip. The ghost town of Shafter, almost 40 miles from Marfa, presents an opportunity to stretch your legs and have a picnic lunch. Keep the kids away from the old silver mine because many of the shafts there are hidden and dangerous.

An alternate route—south on Farm Road 2810 from Marfa to Ruidoso—is even more scenic, passing through the stunning Pinto Canyon. However, the road is way off the beaten path, you'll find no services whatsoever along its entire 50-mile length, and the ranch owners are adamant that you don't even stop alongside the road.

Scenic Drive

Scenic Drive Farm Road 170 from Presidio to Lajitas is known as El Camino del Rio, the River Road, and it's one of the most scenic drives in Texas. The road runs alongside the Rio Grande for several miles, with mountains looming up on both sides. Just off the highway, 29 miles east of Presidio, is Closed Canyon, a nice, short walk into a unique canyon that offers plenty of shade as it closes in on you the farther you walk inside. Look carefully for the trailhead parking area on the south side of the road.

The scenic overlook at the top of Big Hill (don't worry, you can't miss Big Hill; it's really big) is not to be missed. Many stunning photos have been taken from this spot looking back upriver.

One of the interesting places along the drive is at Contrabando Creek on the south side of the road on the banks of the Rio Grande. It's easy to miss, so keep an eye peeled. This is the movie site, a complete border town of authentic looking, 1880s-era ruins, where several films—including the TV miniseries *Streets of Laredo*—were shot. This is an absolutely wonderful place for photos of children.

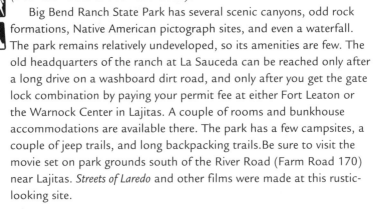

BIG BEND RANCH STATE PARK (ages 4 and up)

North of Farm Road 170, Presidio 79845 between Presidio and Lajitas (915–229–3613 or 915–424–3327).

Big Bend Ranch State Park has several scenic canyons, odd rock formations, Native American pictograph sites, and even a waterfall. The park remains relatively undeveloped, so its amenities are few. The old headquarters of the ranch at La Sauceda can be reached only after a long drive on a washboard dirt road, and only after you get the gate lock combination by paying your permit fee at either Fort Leaton or the Warnock Center in Lajitas. A couple of rooms and bunkhouse accommodations are available there. The park has a few campsites, a couple of jeep trails, and long backpacking trails. Be sure to visit the movie set on park grounds south of the River Road (Farm Road 170) near Lajitas. *Streets of Laredo* and other films were made at this rustic-looking site.

For More Information

Presidio Chamber of Commerce. *On U.S. Highway 67 Business Loop, P.O. Box 2497, Presidio, TX 79845; (915) 229–3199.*

Lajitas

After traveling along scenic Farm Road 170, you'll arrive at the tiny village of Lajitas (La-hee-tahs). No more than a couple of shacks and a tumbling-down trading post a few years ago, the town has been turned into an oasis in the Big Bend desert thanks to the Lajitas Resort. Paso Lajitas is its tiny Mexican counterpart across the river. You won't find any bridges here. To get across, stand on the American bank and hail a boatman from the opposite bank, who will come across and row you over to the Mexican side for a dollar or two.

 ### LAJITAS TRADING POST (ages 4 and up)

Overlooking the Rio Grande, Lajitas 79852 (915–424–3234).

No one is certain how long the Lajitas Trading Post has been around, but it's said that Pancho Villa shopped here. You can find supplies here as well. To get your family into the border mood, punch up a Mexican *corrido* on the jukebox and relax under the *ramada* with a cool drink. The adobe building is near the river and is home to Clay Henry III, a beer-drinking goat certain to delight your kids.

 ### BARTON WARNOCK ENVIRONMENTAL EDUCATION CENTER (ages 6 and up)

On Farm Road 170, Lajitas 79852, just a mile east of town (915–424–3327).

Barton Warnock Center, a part of Big Bend Ranch State Park, has a museum focusing on the pioneer history and natural history of the area, with several dinosaur bones, a library, and a desert garden featuring all the plants you're likely to see in the area.

Texas Trivia

The largest state park is Big Bend Ranch in west Texas, sprawling over 277,140 acres. This park is so large that when the area was designated a park in 1988, it effectively doubled the amount of land in the state park system.

Where to Eat and Stay

Lajitas Resort. HC 70, Box 400, Lajitas 79852 (915–424–3471 or 800–944–9907; www.lajitas.com). What looks like an Old West town is actually Lajitas Resort. Here you'll find the largest number of hotel rooms in the area, a laundry, a bakery, a good restaurant, a saloon with occasional live entertainment, a golf course, a swimming pool, tennis courts, and a boardwalk with a number of shops. Room rates are low in the summer, moderately priced otherwise. One portion of the hotel is built on the ruins of an original cavalry post where Gen. John Pershing's troops were headquartered during his chase of Villa over the desert south of here. The town is so rustic looking that it has been used in a number of movies. $$

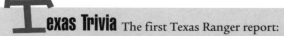

Texas Trivia The first Texas Ranger report:

Date: August 10, 1876

Name of Offender: Bill Jones

Offense: Stealing cattle

Disposition: Mean as hell. Had to kill him.

Terlingua and Study Butte

Known primarily for the chili cook-off championships held near here the first weekend of every November, Terlingua is an old mining ghost town that probably has more activity today than it ever did. The little town, just north of Farm Road 170 (look for the sign), offers many opportunities to take cute pictures of your children. The largest, and best, gift shop and bookstore in the region is here and is called **Terlingua Trading Co.,** (915) 371–2234.

The **Terlingua Cemetery** is an interesting place, certain to give you a very real idea of what life was and is like in the midst of a true desert. If you do visit, make sure the kids show proper respect for the graves; it's not a playground.

Study Butte (Stew-dee Bewt), another old mercury-mining town, is just down the road at the intersection of Farm Road 170 and Texas Highway 118. You'll find several shops, motel rooms, gas stations, RV accommodations, a wonderfully rustic grocery store, and a restaurant or two, depending on the time of year.

BIG BEND NATIONAL PARK (ages 4 and up)

Just east of Study Butte, Big Bend National Park 79834 (915–477–2374).
Entry fee: $10 per vehicle per week.

Big Bend National Park is remote, huge, and spectacular. The 800,000 acres encompass the Rio Grande, the Chihuahuan Desert, and the Chisos Mountains, offering three very different ecosystems and a multitude of plant and animal life for your family to marvel at. The park is as accessible as you want it to be, with paved roads to many scenic areas, dirt roads to others, four-wheel-drive routes to backcountry locations, and miles and miles of hiking trails ranging from easy walks to strenuous treks. Rangers present daily educational programs at amphitheaters at Rio Grande Village, Cottonwood Campground, and the Chisos Basin. You'll find weather forecasts and road accessibility posted at all ranger stations. The park has many campsites and picnic areas, two gas stations, three grocery stores, and motel rooms in the Basin area.

Pay your entry fee at the Maverick or Persimmon Gap entrances to the park. Then stop at the park headquarters at Panther Junction to get information, peruse the bookstore, and go outside to take the self-guided quarter-mile nature walk that will familiarize your family with the plants in the park. A post office is next to the park headquarters.

The **Lost Mine Trail** is a nice half-day hike into the high Chisos that will afford you one of the best vistas in the park, a breathtaking view looking down on other mountains. You're also likely to see a lot of wildlife along this trail, especially if you begin early in the morning. Don't miss a trip across the river to **Boquillas,** Mexico. And even if it's hot, your kids are going to want to soak in the **Hot Springs.**

Scenic Drive The very best introduction to Big Bend National Park—and the best thing to do if you have only a day or two here—is to make the **Old Maverick Road/Ross Maxwell Scenic Drive** loop. The Old Mavrick Road is a well-maintained dirt road across the desert that passes by a couple of old ruins and ends at the mouth of Santa Elena Canyon, where you can either enjoy the view or hike a mile or so upriver into the depths of the canyon.

Returning on the paved Ross Maxwell Scenic Drive, you'll pass many stunning landscapes—including Mule Ears Peak, Cerro Castellan, Tuff Canyon, Sotol Vista, Burro Mesa Pouroff—and the Castolon Store, where the kids can sit in the shade and have some ice cream.

Chili Cook-Offs

Since chili legends Frank X. Tolbert, Wick Fowler, H. Allen Smith, and Carroll Shelby started the whole chili cook-off craziness as a lark back in 1967, the Big Bend *despoblado* known as Terlingua has become the place to be on the first weekend of November. People gather from all over the country to test their chili against everyone else's in this town, whose population of just a few dusty souls inflates into the thousands for the weekend.

Why? No one is really certain why bragging rights to an eye-watering cowboy staple has such magnetism, but it does. Participants say it's the camaraderie, meeting all the other chili heads at all the other cook-offs, then gathering for the world championship in a place so desolate even the cactus seem lonely. Of course, the zany shows the various teams put on while waiting for their chili to simmer may be one big reason. It's never boring. The legendary BeBop Chili Team used to dress in dark glasses and white sport coats with pink carnations and sing dozens of 1950s and early '60s. songs with lyrics altered to impress chili judges, like, "It's My Chili and I'll Cry If I Want To", and "You Ain't Nothin' But a Chili Dog." Some folks will tell you that chili heads have lost their minds, but they don't seem to miss 'em none.

For more information on chili cook-offs, contact the Chili Appreciation Society International, 1307 Smiley, Amarillo, TX 79106; (806) 352-9783 or www.bigbend.com/casi/.

Where to Eat

Chisos Mountain Lodge Restaurant. *In the Chisos Basin, Big Bend National Park 79834 (915–477–2291).* Good food; a stunning view of sunsets through the Window, an impressive V-shaped formation in the mountain walls that form the basin. Large gift shop in lobby. $-$$

La Kiva Restaurant and Bar. *At Terlingua Creek on Farm Road 170, Terlingua 79852 (915–371–2250).* Funky restaurant built underground with a tree growing in the middle of it. Truly a unique experience. Kids are certain to love the rest rooms. $$

Starlight Theatre Restaurant. *In the Ghost Town, Terlingua 79852 (915–371–2326).* The best restaurant for hundreds of miles. Live entertainment fairly common. Kids will marvel at the huge cowboy campfire mural on the back wall, which is also a good place for taking photographs. $$

Where to Stay

Chisos Mountain Lodge. *In the Chisos Basin, Big Bend National Park 79834 (915–477–2291).* Many motel rooms in several buildings, from cabins built by the Civilian Conservation Corps to new units built in the past decade. The cool, beautiful Basin location is a prime one in Big Bend, so reservations should be made many months in advance, a year in advance for Easter, Thanksgiving, Christmas, and chili cook-off weekends. You'll also find a camping supply store and ranger station in the Basin. $$

For More Information

Superintendent, *Big Bend National Park, TX 79834; (915) 477–2251. Visit the Web site at www.nps.gov/bibe.*

Stillwell and Marathon

Just outside the park on Highway 385, south on Ranch Road 2627.

 HALLIE'S HALL OF FAME (ages 6 and up)
On Ranch Road 2627, Stillwell 79830 (915–376–2244).
This was the home of Hallie Stillwell, a legend in the Big Bend, who died just before her one hundredth birthday. Stillwell was a teacher, ranch manager, and longtime justice of the peace in Brewster County. The Stillwell Store offers an RV park, camping, jeep tours of Maravillas Canyon, rock hunting on her ranch, a gas station, and a grocery store. You'll find Hallie's Hall of Fame next door. Inside the adobe

The state dish is chili.

walls, Hallie's world is preserved with a reproduction of her one-room ranch home and displays of her guns, clothing, books, awards, citations, newspaper clippings, and other memorabilia.

Where to Eat and Stay

Gage Hotel. *On U.S. Highway 90, Marathon 79842 (800–884–4243; www. gagehotel.com).* Built in 1927, restored in 1987, now offering thirty-seven rooms decorated with artifacts and furnishings that represent the Native American, Mexican, and Anglo cultures of the Big Bend. The hotel has a newer area of rooms and a nearby bed-and-breakfast inn. Several of the rooms in the main house do not have private baths, so it would be good to ask when making reservations. The hotel's restaurant serves good food in a great atmosphere. The hotel can also arrange a variety of tours and activities for your family, including Rio Grande float trips, horseback riding, and guided tours of the national park. $$

Fort Stockton and Sheffield

You'll experience more of that Big Bend desolation as you drive north from Marathon on U.S. Highway 385 to I-10 East and Fort Stockton. Even though you're on a main highway, it's a long and lonely drive. The city was established as an army outpost at the crossroads of the Old San Antonio Road, the Butterfield Overland Mail Route, and the Comanche War Trail. Today the town is mostly a center for oil and natural gas production, ranching, and hunting. Farther east on I-10, at the Texas Highway 290 exit, is tiny Sheffield. Once off the interstate, the bleakness is palpable, broken only by an occasional oil pump jack creaking away in the desert silence.

The Big Bend

You go south from Fort Davis
Until you come to the place
Where rainbows wait for rain,
And the river is kept in a stone box
And water runs uphill.
And the mountains float in the air,
Except at night when they run away to play
With other mountains.

—*Anonymous Mexican Vaquero*

ANNIE RIGGS MUSEUM (ages 6 and up)

301 South Main Street, Fort Stockton 79735 (915–336–2167). Adults $2.00, children 6–12 $1.00, children under 6 Free.

The Annie Riggs Museum in Fort Stockton is housed in a 1900 adobe hotel, featuring displays of archaeology, geology, and pioneer history in fourteen rooms and two outside areas. Hours vary with the seasons.

HISTORIC FORT STOCKTON (ages 4 and up)

At Third and Rooney Streets, Fort Stockton 79735 (915–336–2400). Open Monday through Saturday, 10:00 A.M. to 1:00 P.M. and 2:00 to 5:00 P.M. Adults $2.00, children 6–12 $1.00, children under 6 Free.

Historic Fort Stockton is a reconstruction of part of the army fort that was here from 1858 to 1886, one of the main Comanche Trail Forts protecting Anglo settlers along the primary raiding trail of the Comanche Indians. The fort visitors center and museum is just east of downtown.

FORT LANCASTER STATE HISTORICAL PARK (ages 4 and up)

Highway 290, Sheffield 79781; take exit 343 off I–10 at Sheffield, follow the scenic loop on Highway 290 about 8 miles east of town (915–836–4391). Open daily Memorial Day through Labor Day from 9:00 A.M. to 6:00 P.M. Open the remainder of the year Thursday through Monday from 9:00 A.M. to 5:00 P.M.

You can walk over the old parade ground and view the cemetery. Looking at the ruins of the fort in the incredible stillness and blistering heat, your family will be amazed that people survived in this bleak frontier outpost. The park has picnic tables, a nature trail, and a museum.

Texas Trivia Although Judge Roy Bean believed the town of Langtry was named for the famous English actress and singer Lillie Langtry—a claim repeated in many stories, films, and in letters he wrote to Miss Langtry—Bean was mistaken. The whistle-stop village was named for George Langtry, a railroad construction foreman. Bean was so obsessed with Miss Langtry that he put a sign on his home, calling it an "Opera House," and wrote Langtry several letters in hopes she would drop in and perform there. She finally accepted but didn't arrive until 1904, several months after Bean died.

Langtry

If you want to get a good feel for what ranch life in west Texas is like, take Texas Highway 349 south from Sheffield to Dryden; just make sure you gas up the car before you tackle this arid landscape that hasn't changed in hundreds of years. The same is true of U.S. Highway 90 into Langtry. Except for the paved road, old Judge Roy Bean would still recognize the area.

JUDGE ROY BEAN VISITOR CENTER (ages 4 and up)

On Park Road 25, Langtry 78871 (915–291–3340). Open daily from 8:00 A.M. to 5:00 P.M., except Thanksgiving, Christmas Eve, Christmas Day, and New Year's Day. **Free**.

The visitors center presents the history of the area in a series of dioramas and displays a few of Bean's personal items. The center is also full of travel brochures from attractions around the state. The judge's original Jersey Lilly saloon, where he dispensed his Law West of the Pecos, still stands behind the visitors center. Next to it is an impressive cactus garden that children love to roam through. The adjacent **Opera House,** which used to be Bean's residence, has been renovated into a theater. The complex is operated by the Texas Department of Transportation.

Where to Eat and Stay

For restaurants and lodgings see the listings under Comstock and Del Rio.

South Plains

The South Plains area is a true melting pot, a unique blend of American and Mexican cultures you won't find in any other state. No matter where you go here, you can expect to find that nearly everyone has a good command of both Spanish and English, regardless of their native tongues; you'll also find fine Mexican restaurants and a history that dates back to before the first Spanish missions.

It was here that cowboying began hundreds of years ago with the Spanish vaqueros and where modern-day buckaroos continue the tradition on spreads like the famous King Ranch.

Tejano music, that upbeat conglomeration of polka, pop, country, and blues set to a distinctly Latin beat, could only have originated in the unique South Plains environment.

The South Plains region sprawls across vast distances between population centers here, from the thriving metropolis of San Antonio to the heavily agricultural, alluvial plain along the Rio Grande that Texans call "The Valley." The population swells here during the winter, when thousands of "Winter Texans," many from as far away as Canada, make The Valley their home during the coldest months of the year.

When you travel the South Plains, you'll discover just how big Texas really is because you won't have the scenic attractions of west Texas or the Hill Country to distract you from those miles and miles of miles and miles.

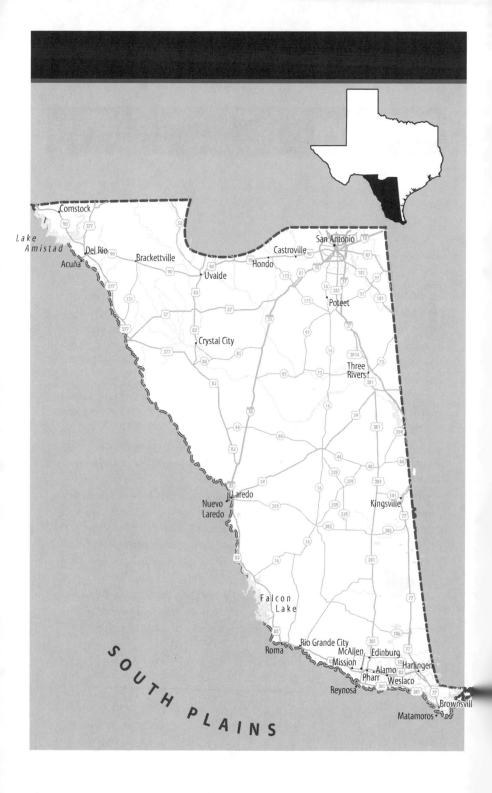

Allan's Top Annual Family Fun Events

- San Antonio Stock Show and Rodeo, San Antonio, February (210–225–5851)
- Washington's Birthday Celebration, Laredo, February (956–722–0589)
- Poteet Strawberry Festival, Poteet, April (830–742–8144)
- Cinco de Mayo Celebration, San Antonio, May (210–207–8600)
- Texas Folklife Festival, San Antonio, June (210–558–2300)
- St. Louis Day Festival, in August, Castroville (830–538–3142)
- Fiesta de Amistad, Del Rio/Acuña, October (830–775–3551)
- Holiday River Parade and Fiesta de las Luminarias, San Antonio, November and December (210–227–4262)

Comstock

SEMINOLE CANYON STATE HISTORICAL PARK
(ages 4 and up)

9 miles west of Comstock on U.S. Highway 90, Comstock 78837 (915–292–4464). Guided tours to Fate Bell Shelter within the canyon Wednesday through Sunday at 10:00 A.M. and 3:00 P.M.

Seminole Canyon State Historical Park is one of the few public areas in the state where you can get a close-up look at prehistoric Native American pictographs. It's a fairly strenuous return hike, especially during hot weather, and not recommended for smaller children, but it offers some spectacular pictographs that time is gradually fading away. The visitors center has exhibits on the inhabitants of the area. The park also has many camping and picnic areas and hiking and mountain-bike trails.

AMISTAD NATIONAL RECREATION AREA (ages 4 and up)

Between Comstock and Del Rio, adjacent to U.S. Highway 90, Del Rio 78840
(830–775–7491 or 800–889–8149).

Amistad National Recreation Area, just west of Del Rio on Highway 90, is a family recreation mecca with many swimming beaches, marinas, boat ramps, and campgrounds. The 64,900-acre Lake Amistad is jointly owned by the United States and Mexico. Its waters are usually so blue as to defy description. Even if you don't stop and play in the lake or by the shore, take the drive over the international bridge that runs across the top of the dam. At the center of the bridge is a small visitors center showing the history and construction of the dam; there's also an

Texas Trivia Among the pictographs you can see in the Fate Bell Shelter at Seminole Canyon State Park is one, more than 4,000 years old, that looks exactly like a 1950s television set complete with rabbit-ears antenna.

interesting double-eagle monument at the borderline dedicated to *amistad* (friendship). At the Mexican end of the bridge is an imposing statue of Tlaloc, the rain god, and a picnic area along the beach. Both the double-eagle monument and Tlaloc make very nice backdrops for photos of the kids.

Many families like to spend a few days on a houseboat on Lake Amistad. It's a relaxing combination of recreation and accommodation. You can explore the lake's many bays, fish, bask in the sun, or boat up to Panther Cave to view more pictographs, some dating back more than 10,000 years. Call the **Lake Amistad Resort and Marina** at (830) 774-4157 or (800) 255-5561 for more information.

For More Information

National Park Service Visitors Center. *On U.S. Highway 90 West, Del Rio, TX 78840; (830) 775–7491. Visit the Web site at www.nps.gov/amis.*

Del Rio

The Mexican city of Ciudad Acuña, across the Rio Grande over the bridge at Garfield Avenue in Del Rio, has a number of good Mexican crafts shops but focuses more on night life than family fare.

The cities of Del Rio and **Acuña** celebrate binational friendship with the **Fiesta de Amistad** in mid-October, a festival so big it's held on both sides of the border. The parade across the International Bridge is the only parade in the world that starts in one country and ends in another. Your family will be delighted by the entertainment, arts-and-crafts and food booths, and fun run. Call (830) 775-3551.

WHITEHEAD MEMORIAL MUSEUM (ages 6 and up)

1308 South Main Street, Del Rio 78840 (830–774–7568). Open Tuesday through Saturday 9:00 A.M. to 4:30 P.M. Open Sunday and some holidays 1:00 to 5:00 P.M. Adults $3.00, children 13 through 18 $2.00, children 12 and under $1.00.

The Whitehead Museum is dedicated to the life and legends of this frontier region. The famed Judge Roy Bean and his son, Sam, are buried on the museum grounds, made up of several historic buildings, an old train caboose, and a replica of Bean's Jersey Lilly saloon.

SAN FELIPE SPRINGS AND MOORE PARK (ages 4 and up)

About 2 miles east of Del Rio off U.S. Highway 90, Del Rio 78840 (830–775–3551).

San Felipe Springs and Moore Park may be just what your family is looking for if you visit here during the summer. This is a true oasis surrounded by the semiarid South Plains landscape. The springs pump ninety million gallons of pure water every day into a large swimming pool.

Where to Eat

Cripple Creek. *U.S. Highway 90 West, Del Rio 78840 (830–775–0153).* Steaks and chicken-fried steaks galore. $-$$

The Feed Store. *1001 Ogden Street, Del Rio 78840 (830–775–2998).* Heaping helpings of barbecued brisket, sausage, ribs, and all the fixings. Special smoked turkey breast on Sunday. $-$$

Luby's Cafeteria. *2205 Avenue F, Del Rio 78840 (830–768–1057).* A favorite among longtime Texans for good food and a good selection. $-$$

Where to Stay

Best Western Inn. *810 Avenue F, Del Rio 78840 (830–775–7511 or 800–528–1234).* Pool, **Free** continental breakfast. $$

La Quinta Inn. *2005 Avenue F, Del Rio 78840 (830–775–7591).* Pool, **Free** continental breakfast. $$

Lakeview Inn. *U.S. Highway 90 West, Del Rio 78840 (830–775–9521).* On Lake Amistad. $$

For More Information

Del Rio Chamber of Commerce. *1915 Avenue F, Del Rio, TX 78840; (830) 775–3551. Visit the Web site at www.chamber.delrio.com.*

Brackettville and Uvalde

At Brackettville, on U.S. Highway 90, your family will find the best place to stay in all of the South Plains and enjoy both real and reel western history.

In Uvalde, you can see the graves of famous westerners Pat Garrett, the man who killed Billy the Kid, and outlaw-turned-sheriff King Fisher at **Pioneer Park,** at the corner of Leona and Park Streets.

FORT CLARK SPRINGS (ages 4 and up)
At Fort Clark, Brackettville 78832 (830–563–2493).

Fort Clark Springs is a modern resort built on the grounds of historic Fort Clark, one of the largest of Texas's frontier forts. The fort was active from 1852 to 1946. Black pioneer history is strong here; the fort was home to the renowned Seminole Negro Indian Scouts and several troops of Buffalo Soldiers. The **Fort Clark Museum** and nearby **Sutler's Store** gift shop are open Saturday and Sunday 1:00 to 4:00 P.M.

SEMINOLE NEGRO INDIAN SCOUT CEMETERY (ages 6 and up)
Farm Road 3348, Brackettville 78832, 3 miles south of Brackettville (830–563–2466).

If your family is interested in history, don't miss visiting the Seminole Negro Indian Scout Cemetery. The scouts were runaway slaves who had assimilated into Seminole culture by the time some bands were forced out of Florida. Many of the black Native Americans settled in the Brackettville area and scouted for the army, fighting in virtually every major Indian War campaign. They lost not a man, and four of them won Medals of Honor. Their graves are here, along with those of other Seminole Negroes who fought in many other American wars. You can leave a donation at the Fort Clark Museum to help maintain the cemetery.

Texas Trivia The state mammal is the armadillo.

ALAMO VILLAGE (ages 4 and up)
7 miles north of Brackettville on Farm Road 674, Brackettville 78832 (830–563–2580). Open daily 9:00 A.M. to 5:00 P.M. except Christmas week. Adults $7.00, children $3.50.

Alamo Village, a family delight, is a movie set built for John Wayne's 1960 production of *The Alamo* and used for dozens of other films, television shows, and commercials since. The set, on the Shahan HV Ranch, is a complete town with jails, saloons, general stores, hotels, a blacksmith shop, a mission church, and, of course, a replica of the Alamo as it was in 1836. Several of the buildings house historic displays of either bona fide artifacts or movie memorabilia. A gift shop is also on the set. Between Memorial Day and Labor Day actors perform on the village streets with music and melodrama.

FORT INGE (ages 4 and up)
Located at the base of an extinct volcano on the Leona River, 2 miles south of Uvalde on Farm Road 140, Uvalde 78801 (800–588–2533).

At Fort Inge your family can picnic, camp, hike nature trails, or inspect the ruins of the old fort.

Where to Eat and Stay

Fort Clark Springs Resort. *P.O. Box 528, Brackettville 78832 (830–563–2493).* Has it all for family travelers. Las Moras Restaurant has the best food from Del Rio to Castroville. The motel is located in the center of town and has an RV park, a wilderness campground, a huge spring-fed swimming pool, tennis courts, two golf courses, a gun range, a health spa, and a museum displaying the history of the fort. Rooms are remarkably affordable. $–$$

For More Information

Kinney County Chamber of Commerce. *(830) 563–2466, or check with the gate guard at Fort Clark Springs on U.S. Highway 90 in Brackettville. Visit the Web site at www.brackettville.com.*

Uvalde Chamber of Commerce. *300 East Main Street, Uvalde, TX 78801; (800) 588–2533 or (830) 278–4115. Visit the Web site at www.uvalde.org.*

Allan's Top Family Fun Ideas

1. Sea World of Texas, San Antonio
2. Gladys Porter Zoo, Brownsville
3. Six Flags Fiesta Texas, San Antonio
4. Witte Museum, San Antonio
5. San Antonio Zoological Gardens, San Antonio
6. Alamo Village, Brackettville
7. San Antonio Missions Baseball, San Antonio
8. Houseboating on Lake Amistad, Comstock
9. Laredo Children's Museum, Laredo
10. Seminole Canyon State Historical Park, Comstock

Crystal City and Laredo

If you head south on Highway 83 from Uvalde, your kids will be able to visit **Popeye** in Crystal City, or at least they can have their picture taken in front of his statue. The town produces a prodigious amount of spinach, which is why it built the monument to the world's most famous spinach eater. It's located on The Square downtown.

Laredo, much farther south on Highway 83, has such a heavy Hispanic influence you might think you've crossed the border into Mexico.

Two bridges will now take you into **Nuevo Laredo** across the Rio Grande, but be warned that the area is so popular now because of the NAFTA agreement that traffic is usually backed up for miles. Best to leave your car at your hotel, take a shuttle, and walk across. Nuevo Laredo is one of the nicer border towns and offers some great bargains in its crafts shops. **El Mercado,** 2625 Guerrero, just a couple of blocks from the bridges, is a marvelous maze of shops featuring modern and traditional items and several snack bars.

In February your family will be amazed at the scale of the **George Washington's Birthday** celebration held in Laredo. It's said to be the largest anywhere, and it's been going on, on both sides of the border, every year since 1898. Two different parades feature entries from both the United States and Mexico, with one showcasing area schoolchildren. This is a birthday Washington never imagined: a jalapeño festival, a Mexican rodeo, and special Native American events. You'll have a great time. Call (956) 722-0589.

Texas Trivia More tourists enter Mexico via the Laredo/Nuevo Laredo international bridge than at any other border crossing in the United States.

 ### LAREDO CHILDREN'S MUSEUM (ages 4 and up)

1 West Washington Street, Laredo 78040 (956–725–2299). Open Thursday through Saturday 10:00 A.M. to 5:00 P.M., Sunday 1:00 to 5:00 P.M. Adults $1.00, children $2.00.

The Laredo Children's Museum guides kids through history, the arts, and science with hands-on exhibits that encourage creativity. The museum is located on the campus of Laredo Junior College.

 ### REPUBLIC OF THE RIO GRANDE MUSEUM (ages 8 and up)

1003 Zaragosa Street, Laredo 78040 (956–727–3480). Open Tuesday through Saturday 9:00 A.M. to 4:00 P.M., Sunday 1:00 to 4:00 P.M. **Free**.

The Republic of the Rio Grande Museum, across the plaza from historic San Agustin Church, is in a building that once served as the capitol for the Republic of the Rio Grande, an unsuccessful attempt in the mid-1800s to break away from Mexico. The museum has many pioneer displays.

 ### LAKE CASA BLANCA STATE PARK (ages 4 and up)

5201 Bob Bullock Loop, Laredo 78044 east of Laredo off U.S. Highway 59 (956–725–3826).

Lake Casa Blanca offers your family camping, screened shelters, picnic areas, a fishing pier, a boat ramp, a baseball diamond, and basketball, volleyball, and tennis courts. The lake is known for its black bass fishing.

Where to Eat

El Cafe. *1000 Zaragosa, Laredo 78040 (956–722–1701).* True Mexican food by folks who truly know how to do it. $-$$

Emperor Garden. *620 West Calton Street, Laredo 78041 (956–791–4848).* Laredo has a long tradition of offering great Chinese food, and you can find the best in town, some say the best in the state, here. Live music on weekends. $$

Golden Corral. *5930 San Bernardo, Laredo 78041 (956–791–3373).* Steaks and an all-you-can-eat buffet make for a dining bargain. $-$$

Where to Stay

Family Gardens Inn. *5830 San Bernardo, Laredo 78041 (956–723–5300 or 800–292–4053).* Targeted to families, with pool, Jacuzzis, and playground. Children stay **Free**. $$

La Posada Hotel. *1000 Zaragosa, Laredo 78040 (956–722–1701).* Beautifully landscaped, pool and courtyard areas, boasts a couple of fine restaurants, and is within walking distance of shopping areas in Laredo and both bridges across the Rio Grande. $$

For More Information

Laredo Chamber of Commerce. *501 San Augustine Street, Laredo, TX 78040; (800) 361–3360 or (956)* *795–2200. Visit the Web site at www. visitlaredo.com.*

Texas Campgrounds
If your family loves the outdoors, they'll love Texas. Its enormous size means there's still plenty of wide open spaces for you to explore on foot or horseback, by bicycle or canoe, and campgrounds abound.

For a complete list of Texas public campgrounds, write the Travel and Information Division of the Texas Department of Transportation, P.O. Box 5064, Austin, TX 78763.

For a list of commercial campgrounds, contact the Texas Association of Campground Owners, P.O. Box 14055, Austin, TX 78761; (800) 657-6555.

Roma and Rio Grande City

Taking U.S. Highway 83 south from Laredo will have you traveling along the Rio Grande and bring you into the area Texans call simply "The Valley," the heart of Texas agriculture. The route from Laredo to Falcon Lake isn't quite as desolate as some of the drives in west Texas and the Big Bend, but almost. Only a few small towns and very large farms break up the landscape.

FALCON STATE PARK (ages 4 and up)

Along the shores of the Falcon Reservoir, about 14 miles northwest of Roma via Highway 83, Farm Road 2098, and Park Road 46, Falcon Heights 78545 (956–848–5327).

The park has cabins, boat docks, camping, swimming, picnicking, fishing, and RV sites. There's also a grocery store and snack bar. The 87,210-acre Falcon Lake is jointly owned by the United States and Mexico, like Lake Amistad, and is known for its black bass and catfish fishing. You can also see the old town of Guerrero, now buried under the waters of the lake.

OUR LADY OF LOURDES GROTTO (ages 4 and up)

305 North Britton, Rio Grande City 78582.

This is a replica of the famed shrine in Lourdes, France.

Where to Stay

La Borde House. *601 East Main Street, Rio Grande City 78582 (956–487–5101).* This National Historic Landmark was a home and trading post from 1899 to the 1930s and is a mix of several architectural styles. The inn has been restored to its century-old splendor. $$

Mission, McAllen, and Pharr

Continuing to follow the Rio Grande along U.S. Highway 83, you'll soon be in the very bustling cities of Mission, McAllen, and Pharr. Heavily Hispanic in influence, the area's main business is agriculture, especially citrus farming around Mission, the home of the famous Texas Ruby Red grapefruit, a very sweet fruit. Just after Mission was founded in the early 1800s, Mexican priests planted an orange grove, the first experiment with citrus in The Valley. Pharr, too, is a citrus wonderland.

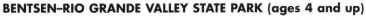

McAllen is so lush, you'll occasionally see palm trees. It's a favorite tourist location, especially with birders. Thousands of Canadians and Midwesterners spend the colder months of the year here, becoming what locals call "Winter Texans."

Across the McAllen-Hidalgo-Reynosa International Bridge on Route 336 is the Mexican city of Reynosa, which is widely known in Texas for fine restaurants. You'll also find many crafts shops and traditional Mexican markets downtown. The largest market is **Mercado Zaragosa**, at Hidalgo and Matamoros Streets.

BENTSEN–RIO GRANDE VALLEY STATE PARK (ages 4 and up)

6 miles west of Mission off Farm Road 2062, Mission 78573 (956–585–1107).
One of the few nature reserves in the South Plains, Bentsen–Rio Grande Valley State Park encompasses 600 acres on the Rio Grande, preserving subtropical plants and wildlife. More than 200 species of birds have been documented here. Your family can fish, camp, have a picnic, or walk along the nature trails.

ANZALDUAS PARK (ages 4 and up)

3 miles south of Mission on Farm Road 1016, Mission 78572 (956–581–2725). Open daily 8:30 A.M. to 4:30 P.M.
Tiny La Lomita Chapel was built in 1865 for itinerant priests and is still used today for private services like weddings. Surrounding Anzalduas Park has a bird-observation pier, boat docks, and picnic areas.

LOS EBANOS FERRY (ages 2 and up)

14 miles west of McAllen on Highway 83, then south on Farm Road 886, McAllen 78505 (956–485–2855). Ferry runs daily 8:00 A.M. to 4:00 P.M. $1.50 for car and driver, 25 cents per pedestrian.
Even if you're not crossing the border, your kids are sure to love seeing the Los Ebanos Ferry, the only existing hand-operated ferry on the United States–Mexico border. The platform holds only two cars, so if you do want to cross, it's better to do so on foot unless you're planning to drive somewhere else in Mexico from here.

MCALLEN INTERNATIONAL MUSEUM (ages 6 and up)

1900 Nolana, McAllen 78504 (956–682–1564). Open Tuesday through Saturday 9:00 A.M. to 5:00 P.M., Sunday 1:00 to 5:00 P.M. Adults $2.00, children $1.00.
The McAllen Museum has rotating exhibits of Mexican folk art, American fine art, and European paintings. The science wing features several hands-on exhibits for children.

SMITTY'S JUKE BOX (ages 6 and up)
116 West State Street, Pharr 78577 (956–787–0131). Open Monday through Friday 9:00 A.M. to 5:00 P.M. **Free**.

This museum displays a large variety of restored, nostalgic jukeboxes.

 THE OLD CLOCK MUSEUM
929 East Preston Street, Pharr 78577 (956–787–1923). Open daily 10:30 A.M. to noon and 2:30 to 4:00 P.M. **Free**.

This museum preserves scores of antique clocks, some dating back to 1690.

Where to Eat

El Patio. *3019 North Tenth Street, McAllen 78501, and other locations (956–682–1576).* Good Mexican food in a family setting at good prices. $–$$

Furr's Cafeteria. *Expressway 83 at Tenth Street, McAllen 78501, and other locations (956–687–9571).* A true family bargain with a wide selection of food and all-you-can eat prices. $

Tony Roma's. *2121 South Tenth Street, McAllen 78501 (956–631–2121).* One of the finest barbecue restaurants in Texas. $$

Where to Stay

La Quinta Motor Inn. *1100 South Tenth Street, McAllen 78501 (956–687–1101 or 800–531–5900).* Pool. **Free** continental breakfasts, and children under eighteen stay **Free**. $$

McAllen Inn. *1401 South Tenth Street, McAllen 78501 (956–686–8301 or 800–781–1005).* **Free** breakfast, and children under seventeen stay **Free**. $$

Thrifty Inn. *620 West Expressway 83, McAllen 78501 (956– 631–6700).* Pool, **Free** breakfast, and children under eighteen stay **Free**. $$

For More Information

McAllen Chamber of Commerce. *10 North Broadway Street, McAllen, TX 78505–0790; (956) 682–2871. Visit the Web site at www.McAllen.org.*

Mission Chamber of Commerce. *220 East Ninth Street, Mission, TX 78572; (956) 585–2727. Visit the Web site at www.mission.lib.tx.us/chamber.*

Pharr Chamber of Commerce. *308 West Park Street, P.O. Box 1341, Pharr, TX 78577; (956) 787–1481.*

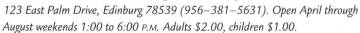

Edinburg, Alamo, and Weslaco

Edinburg is just north of McAllen on U.S. Highway 281, while Alamo and Weslaco are just east on U.S. Highway 83.

Now you're in the middle of an immense citrus-, vegetable-, and cotton-producing area with hundreds of food processing industries. Dozens of RV parks dot the landscape, home to all those Winter Texans in cooler months.

EDINBURG WATERPARK (ages 4 and up)

123 East Palm Drive, Edinburg 78539 (956–381–5631). Open April through August weekends 1:00 to 6:00 P.M. Adults $2.00, children $1.00.

Cool off in three swimming pools at the Edinburg Waterpark. The city park also features a water slide, water basketball, beach volleyball, barbecue grills, and picnic tables.

HIDALGO COUNTY HISTORICAL MUSEUM (ages 6 and up)

121 East McIntyre, Edinburg 78539 (956–383–6911). Open Tuesday through Friday 9:00 A.M. to 5:00 P.M., Saturday 10:00 A.M. to 5:00 P.M., and Sunday 1:00 to 5:00 P.M. Adults $2.00, students $1.00, children under twelve 50 cents.

The Hidalgo County Historical Museum, in the restored county jail in Edinburg, has a number of displays highlighting the area's history.

SANTA ANA NATIONAL WILDLIFE REFUGE (ages 4 and up)

7 miles south of Alamo on U.S. Highway 281, Alamo 78516 (956–787–3087). Visitors Center open weekdays 8:00 A.M. to 4:30 P.M. and weekends 9:00 A.M. to 4:30 P.M.

The Santa Ana Wildlife Refuge preserves what The Valley looked like before agricultural development, with many species of birds nesting here during winter months. An interpretive tour operates from November through April on a 7-mile loop; you drive your own car during the other months. Or you can walk along several nature trails.

BICULTURAL MUSEUM (ages 6 and up)

515 South Kansas Avenue, Weslaco 78596 (956–968–9142). Open Wednesday and Thursday 1:00 to 3:00 P.M., Friday 10:00 A.M. to noon and 1:00 to 3:00 P.M. **Free**.

Weslaco's Bicultural Museum has exhibits about the pioneer Hispanic and Anglo settlers of the area.

Brownsville and Harlingen

For a quaint, entertaining way to see all the highlights of the city, hop aboard a **Historic Brownsville Trolley Tour,** beginning at the Convention and Visitors Bureau Information Center at the corner of Farm Road 802 and Expressway 77/83. Cost is $7.00 for adults, $3.50 for children 12 and under. Call (956) 546-3721 for reservations.

Matamoros, Mexico, is just across the river, and its mission for decades has been catering to U.S. visitors, with more restaurants, nightclubs, and gift shops than you could count. Bargains are still available, especially in leather goods and pottery. Take the Gateway International Bridge at East Fourteenth Street. **Mercado Juarez,** at Matamoros and Nueve Streets, is a huge, well-known market.

 HISTORIC BROWNSVILLE MUSEUM (ages 6 and up)
641 East Madison Street, Brownsville 78520 (956–548–1313). Adults $2.00, children 50 cents.

    The Historic Brownsville Museum will familiarize you with the history of Brownsville, the founding of which touched off the Mexican War in 1846. The museum has photos and other displays housed in a restored railroad depot.

 CONFEDERATE AIR FORCE MUSEUM (ages 6 and up)
Brownsville Airport, Brownsville 78520 (956–541–8585). Open Tuesday through Saturday from 9:00 A.M. to 4:00 P.M. Adults $5.00, children $3.00, children under 8 accompanied by an adult ℱ𝓇ℯℯ.

    The Confederate Air Force, which used to be headquartered in nearby Harlingen before it moved to Midland, still maintains its Rio Grande Valley Wing at the Brownsville Airport. The wing shows off a number of restored World War II aircraft and memorabilia.

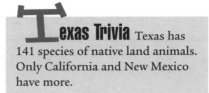

Texas Trivia Texas has 141 species of native land animals. Only California and New Mexico have more.

GLADYS PORTER ZOO (ages 2 and up)

500 Ringgold Street, near the intersections of U.S. Highways 281 and 77 Brownsville 78520 (956–546–2177; www.gpz.org). Open daily 9:00 A.M. to 5:00 P.M. Adults $6.50, children 2 to 13 $3.25. Train tour: $1.00 adults, 50 cents children.

Your children will revel in the Gladys Porter Zoo, which has one of the world's best collections of rare animals, including lowland gorillas. The animals are all in a natural setting without bars or cages. You can get close-up views looking through one-way glass in a series of caves adjacent to animal dens. The Zoofari Express train offers guided tours every Sunday.

Texas Trivia The longest highway in Texas is U.S. Highway 83, stretching 899 miles from the Mexican border at Brownsville in the South Plains to the Oklahoma border in the Panhandle.

IWO JIMA WAR MEMORIAL (ages 6 and up)

320 Iwo Jima Boulevard, Harlingen 78550 (956–423–6006 or 800–365–6006). Open Monday through Saturday 10:00 A.M. to 4:00 P.M., Sunday 1:00 to 4:00 P.M. **Free**.

The original working model of the famous Iwo Jima War Memorial is on display at the **Marine Military Academy,** a prep school next to the Harlingen airport. (The final bronze is at Arlington National Cemetery.) Various Texas and military souvenirs are available in an adjacent gift shop.

RIO GRANDE VALLEY MUSEUM (ages 6 and up)

On Loop 499, Harlingen 78550, 2 blocks from Valley International Airport, (956–430–8500). Open Wednesday through Saturday 10:00 A.M. to 4:00 P.M., Sunday 1:00 to 4:00 P.M. **Free**.

The Rio Grande Valley Museum complex in Harlingen includes a stagecoach inn from 1850, the original city hospital with vintage medical equipment on display, a pioneer home, and exhibits on the area's colorful history.

Where to Eat

Antonio's. *2921 Boca Chica Boulevard, Brownsville 78521 (956–542–6504).* $–$$

Bonanza Family Restaurant. *803 South Expressway 77, Harlingen 78550 (956–425–6517).* Mostly steaks. Wide selection, good food. $–$$

Golden Corral. *2912 Boca Chica Boulevard, Brownsville 78521 (956–982–0393).* Steaks and all-you-can-eat buffet are true bargains. Special kids' desserts. $-$$

Pepe's Mexican Restaurant. *117 South Expressway 77, Harlingen 78550 (956–423–3663).* Excellent Mexican food. $-$$

*S*cenic Drive

$\mathcal{S}$**cenic Drive** For a glimpse at the unspoiled, real tropical Texas, head out east from Brownsville on Farm Road 1419 to Texas Highway 4—from the **Sabal Palm Grove Sanctuary** to **Boca Chica State Park,** an undeveloped beach with no facilities. The route will take your family from a native palm forest to the shores of the Gulf of Mexico at the Rio Grande delta, one of the southernmost points in the United States. By the way, don't be tempted to drive on the beach, as some do, because the sand can be very unforgiving. Many plant and animal species found here are unique to the United States.

Where to Stay

Best Western Rose Garden Inn. *845 North Expressway 77/83, Brownsville 78520 (956–546–5501 or 800–528–1234).* Pool, **Free** continental breakfast. $$

Comfort Inn. *406 North Expressway 77, Harlingen 78520 (956–412–7771).* Pool, **Free** continental breakfast. $$

Holiday Inn Fort Brown. *1900 East Elizabeth Street, Brownsville 78520 (956–546–2201 or 800–465–4329).* Pool, convenient to the border. $$

La Quinta Inn. *1002 South Expressway 83, Harlingen 78550 (956–428–6888 or 800–531–5900).* Pool, **Free** continental breakfast. $$

For More Information

Brownsville Convention and Visitors Bureau. *650 Farm Road 802, Brownsville, TX 78520; (956) 546–3721. Visit the Web site at www.brownsville.org.*

Harlingen Chamber of Commerce. *311 East Tyler, Harlingen, TX 78550; (800) 531–7346 or (956) 423–5440. Visit the Web site at www.harlingen.com.*

Kingsville

KING RANCH (ages 6 and up)

405 North Sixth Street, Kingsville 78363 (361–595–1881; www.king-ranch. com). Museum open Monday through Saturday 10:00 A.M. to 4:00 P.M., Sunday 1:00 to 5:00 P.M. Admission: $4.00, or $2.00 with ranch tour. The Visitors Center is on Texas Highway 141 West and is open Monday through Saturday 9:00 A.M. to 4:00 P.M., Sunday noon to 4:00 P.M. Tour admission: $7.00 adults, $2.50 children. Tour times vary, so call (361) 592–8055 for more details.

The King Ranch is the largest ranch in the country: 825,000 acres across four counties. The ranch offers guided tours of an old cow camp, cattle pens, and the ranch headquarters.

The museum is in a restored ice plant in downtown Kingsville. It showcases photos of ranch life; antique coaches, cars, and saddles; and other historic ranching items.

The **King Ranch Saddle Shop,** 201 East Kleberg Street, was begun by the ranch to outfit its own cowboys with riding gear. Now they outfit everyone from visiting children to presidents. A most unusual shop, it's open Monday through Friday 10:00 A.M. to 6:00 P.M., Saturday 10:00 A.M. to 2:00 P.M. Call (512) 595-5761 or (800) 282-KING.

JOHN E. CONNER MUSEUM (ages 6 and up)

Located on the campus of Texas A&M University-Kingsville, at Santa Gertrudis at Armstrong Street, Kingsville 78363 (361–595–2819). Open Monday through Saturday 9:00 A.M. to 5:00 P.M., closed on university holidays. **Free**.

The John E. Conner Museum displays artifacts from Native American, Spanish, Mexican, and Texan cultures. It has exhibits focusing on natural history and a Discovery Area for kids to get their hands on displays. The Peeler Hall of Horns displays 264 trophy mounts of North American game.

Poteet and Three Rivers

Three Rivers is at Choke Canyon Lake on U.S. Highway 281 at I–37. Poteet is about 40 miles south of San Antonio on Texas Highway 16.

Poteet has the **World's Largest Strawberry,** a monument to the sweet fruit grown all around the area. You'll also discover a monument to Poteet Canyon, the Steve Canyon comic-strip character named after the city. Both are located at the chamber of commerce building on Farm Road 476.

In mid-April your family is certain to enjoy the **Poteet Strawberry Festival,** where they can overdose on all things strawberry: ice cream, cheesecake, shortcake, parfait, and plenty of plain old strawberries. In addition to the regular arts-and-crafts and food booths, the festival has six stages with continuous entertainment. Call (830) 276-3323 or visit the Web site at www.strawberryfestival.com.

CHOKE CANYON STATE PARK (ages 4 and up)

West of Three Rivers off Texas Highway 72, Three Rivers 78071 (Calliham 361–786–3868 or South Shore 361–786–3538).

You'll find very few places to swim in this region, and Choke Canyon is one of the best. Here your family can boat, swim, fish, have a picnic, or camp out on 26,000-acre Choke Canyon Lake. The relatively new park was designated within a wildlife management area, so spotting animals is relatively easy for kids. They might even spy an alligator in the marshes. The park is divided into two units: South Shore is 4 miles from Three Rivers while Calliham is 12 miles. The Calliham unit also has tennis and basketball courts, a baseball diamond, and a swimming pool.

For More Information

Three Rivers Chamber of Commerce. *(361) 786–4330. For information on Poteet call (830) 276–3323.*

Hondo and Castroville

On U.S. Highway 90, west of San Antonio.

All the Alsatians come out for Castroville's **St. Louis Day Festival** in late August, and your family is certain to enjoy it as well. The celebration features an auction, bingo, children's rides and games, barbecue and Alsatian sausage, an arts-and-crafts show, and Flemish and Alsatian dancers. Call (830) 538-3142, (800) 778-6775, or visit the Web site at www.castroville.net.

MEDINA COUNTY MUSEUM (ages 6 and up)

2202 Eighteenth Street, Hondo 78861 (830–426–8819). Open year-round Saturday 10:00 A.M. to 5:00 P.M. and Sunday 2:00 to 6:00 P.M.; also open Memorial Day through Labor Day Monday through Friday 10:00 A.M. to 5:00 P.M. Free.

The Medina County Museum features pioneer artifacts and exhibits in a restored 1897 railroad depot.

LANDMARK INN STATE HISTORICAL PARK (ages 4 and up)

At Florence and Fiorella Streets, Castroville 78009 (830–931–2133).

The Landmark Inn in Castroville used to serve stagecoach passengers and continues to serve travelers today. On the site is an old water-powered gristmill. You and the kids can also walk on a nature trail, fish, or picnic on the grounds. Park staff conducts several seminars on pioneer skills like soap making, so see what else is going on.

Texas Trivia In 1846, the Association for the Protection of Immigrants in Texas offered a package deal to Europeans wanting to settle in Texas. For 1,000 francs the immigrant would receive passage and meals from Bremen, Germany, to Castroville; transport of 300 pounds of luggage; a small log cabin; two oxen and yokes; two milk cows; twelve chickens and a rooster; a plow; and a "Mexican" wagon. In return the settler agreed to live on and work the land for at least three years.

CASTROVILLE REGIONAL PARK (ages 4 and up)

1209 Fiorella Street, Castroville 78009 (830–538–2224).

Castroville Park is a nice place to picnic under a covered shelter, swim in a pool, or play tennis or volleyball. You can fish or just relax by the Medina River. It has camping and RV sites.

Where to Eat

Alsatian Inn. *On U.S. Highway 90, Castroville 78009, at the south edge of town, (830–931–9451).* In a town known for its fine restaurants, this is one of the best, specializing in steaks and Alsatian cuisine. Many tables have a beautiful view of the Medina River Valley. $–$$

Haby's Bakery. *207 Highway 90 East, Castroville 78009 (830–931–2118).* If you're after some tasty pastries, go here. Bet you can't buy just one. $

Where to Stay

Landmark Inn. *At Florence and Fiorella Streets, Castroville 78009 (830–931–2133).* With only eight rooms to choose from, reservations should be made well ahead of time. The inn has been restored to the 1940s era with ceiling fans and rocking chairs but no televisions. Continental breakfasts served in the 1849 kitchen building adjacent to the inn. $$

For More Information

Castroville Chamber of Commerce. *802 London Street, Castroville, TX 78009; (800) 778–6775 or (830) 538–3142. Visit the Web site at www.castroville.net.*

San Antonio

Seems like people are always having a good time in San Antonio no matter where you go. It's a big, fun city with lots to do, from many historic locales to modern shopping centers to family amusement parks and one of the best minor-league baseball parks in the country.

One of the best rodeos in Texas is held here every February. The **San Antonio Stock Show and Rodeo** features professional riders, a huge livestock show, a carnival, and plenty of arts-and-crafts and food booths. Each evening and Sunday matinee features a top-name entertainer. Call (210) 225-5851.

San Antonio also celebrates **Cinco de Mayo** with great gusto. You'll find parades, pageants, dancing, singing, carnivals, and wonderful food in several places around the city. Call (210) 207-8600.

San Antonio Tours You can go on a **San Antonio City Tour,** (210) 228-9776, or a **Texas Trolley Tour,** (210) 225-8587, from the Alamo Visitor Center, between the Alamo and the Rivercenter Mall. Tours run daily 9:00 A.M. to 5:00 P.M. **Gray Line Lone Star Trolley Tours,** (210) 226-1706, also offers several tour options from their headquarters at 217 Alamo Plaza. If the family wants a guided boat tour of the river, go to the **Yanaguana Cruise** office below the Marriott Rivercenter Hotel. The company also offers special dining cruises along the river. Tour fares are $4.00 for adults, $3.00 for children. Call (210) 244-5700 or (800) 417-4139 for more information or dinner reservations.

You can get to the city's famous **San Antonio River Walk** across from Alamo Plaza. The walk lines both sides of the San Antonio River for a couple of miles, and along the way you'll discover some of the city's best restaurants, specialty stores, and hotels.

The River Walk is the jewel of San Antonio. It becomes a magical place during the month of December with the **Holiday River Parade** and **Fiesta de las Luminarias** celebrations. Lights are the key, hundreds of thousands of lights that will delight kids from ages one to 92. During the month, some sort of entertainment is featured almost every night. Don't miss out on the special performances on the bandstand by the River Center patio on the River Walk, or the **Las Posadas** procession through La Villita on December 8. Call (210) 270-8700 or (800) 447-3372.

ALAMO (ages 6 and up)

At Houston and Alamo Streets, San Antonio 78205 (210–225–1301). Open Monday through Saturday 9:00 A.M. to 5:30 P.M., Sunday 10:00 A.M. to 5:30 P.M. **Free**.

You can't talk about San Antonio without mentioning the Alamo, the mission turned into a fortress by Texans fighting for independence from Mexico in 1836. You might be surprised at its location: right in the middle of downtown next to the Rivercenter Mall. Texans treat the Alamo as a shrine, so speak softly inside. Only the old chapel is left of the original mission; the actual battleground stretches across Alamo Plaza and into the souvenir shops on the far side of Alamo Street.

The imposing monument you see across from the Alamo in Alamo Plaza is the **Alamo Cenotaph,** which is inscribed with the names of those who died defending the mission. Some of the defenders' remains are also buried here. Craft fairs and battle reenactments often occupy the plaza. If the kids want something cold, you can almost always find *raspa* (snow cone) vendors here.

THE TEXAS ADVENTURE (ages 4 and up)

307 Alamo Plaza, San Antonio 78205 (210–227–8224). Open daily 10:00 A.M. to 10:00 P.M. in summer, 10:00 A.M. to 6:00 P.M. in winter. Adults $7.50, children $4.50.

Across from the Alamo is The Texas Adventure, featuring a special-effects theater that re-creates the battle of the Alamo. The complex also has several displays, a souvenir shop, and a snack bar.

Texas Trivia While most Texans remember Gen. Antonio Lopez de Santa Anna as being the military dictator defeated in the fight for the state's independence, he made another lasting contribution to modern society: chewing gum. His troops used to chew chicle to relieve tension, and he introduced the idea to inventor Thomas Adams while on a visit to New York in 1837. Adams made some; it was a local hit, and the chewing gum industry was born. The Adams Gum Co. ruled the industry until Wrigleys entered the market in the 1900s. Adams's Chiclets are still popular; however, Santa Anna never got a dime of the fortune he made for Adams.

 IMAX THEATER (ages 4 and up)
Rivercenter Mall, San Antonio 78205 (210–225–4629; www.imax-sa.com). Adults $7.50, children 3 through 11 $4.75 . Double-feature prices: adults $13.00, children $7.50.

More Alamo history is available at the IMAX Theater. The IMAX shows a filmed account of the battle, *Alamo . . . The Price of Freedom,* on its huge, six-story screen. The sound system here is so good the explosions rattle your teeth. The theater also shows other special IMAX films and, in the evening, presents regular movies or classic films on that giant screen. For example: *Batman, Jurassic Park,* and *2001: A Space Odyssey* were real trips here.

 RIPLEY'S BELIEVE IT OR NOT! AND PLAZA THEATRE OF WAX (ages 6 and up)
 301 Alamo Plaza, San Antonio 78205 (210–224–9299). Open daily except Christmas from 10:00 A.M. to 7:00 P.M., extended hours in the summer. Adults $14.95, children $7.95.

Ripley's and the Theatre of Wax are quite popular with kids. Here they get to explore Ripley's famous collection of oddities and the eerie presentations in wax of heroes of the battle of the Alamo and of more modern celebrities.

 COWBOY MUSEUM AND GALLERY (ages 6 and up)
209 Alamo Plaza, San Antonio 78205 (210–229–1257). Open daily 10:00 A.M. to 7:00 p.m . Adults $3.00, children $2.00.

The Cowboy Museum is a replica of an 1870s rail town, along with exhibits from the heyday of the Texas cowboy and a western art gallery.

In warmer months, costumed staff members have a fake pony out front where you can take pictures of your kids for a small fee.

LA VILLITA (ages 6 and up)
Alamo at Villita Street, San Antonio 78205 (210–299–8610). Open daily 10:00 A.M. to 6:00 P.M.; individual shop hours vary widely.

Bordering on the River Walk is La Villita, San Antonio's original village. The historic homes have now become a diverse selection of arts-and-crafts shops that shouldn't be missed.

INSTITUTE OF TEXAN CULTURES (ages 4 and up)
801 South Bowie Street, San Antonio 78205 (210–458–2300 or 210–458–2330; www.cultures.utsa.edu). Open Tuesday through Sunday 9:00 A.M. to 5:00 P.M., closed Thanksgiving and Christmas. Hours are extended during the Texas Folklife Festival in June. Adults $4.00, children 3 through 12 $2.00. No charge for special exhibits.

The Institute of Texan Cultures, at Hemisfair Park downtown, is a unique museum that highlights the wide variety of cultures that have contributed to the history of Texas. The main exhibit floor allows children to touch and examine artifacts and other displays of twenty-seven ethnic groups. The gift shop has a number of ethnic products.

The **Texas Folklife Festival** is one of the premier celebrations in the state. Vendor booths and performance stages surround the Institute of Texan Cultures for several days in early June. Your family will be overloaded with food, dancing, singing, and crafts from the state's many cultures. Many of the performers are children's groups, and there is a special Storytelling Stage for kids. You shouldn't miss this one. Call (210) 458–2300.

Texas Trivia
When Spaniards first visited the area that is now San Antonio it was a Payaya Indian camp on the banks of a gently flowing river. The Indians called it *Yanaguana*, "the clear water." The Spanish called it San Antonio because they first stopped here on the feast day of Saint Anthony.

MARKET SQUARE (ages 6 and up)

On Commerce Street at I–35, San Antonio 78205 (210–207–8600). Open June through August 10:00 A.M. to 8:00 P.M. daily, September through May 10:00 A.M. to 6:00 P.M. daily.

Visit Market Square, and your family will feel like they're walking through Mexico. Three distinct shopping areas with hundreds of shops, cafes, and vendors will delight your senses with handicrafts, imports, and food.

Texas Trivia Near historic San Fernando Cathedral in downtown San Antonio is the intersection of Dolorosa and Soledad Streets. That means you can stand on the corner of Sad and Lonely Streets. There is no Heartbreak Hotel at the location, however.

HERTZBERG CIRCUS MUSEUM (ages 4 and up)

210 Market Street, San Antonio 78205 (210–207–7810). Open Monday through Saturday 10:00 A.M. to 5:00 P.M., and from June through Labor Day on Sunday and holidays 1:00 to 5:00 P.M. Adults $2.50, children $1.00.

Every child loves the circus, and historic circus items are preserved at the Hertzberg Circus Museum. Paintings, a mechanical clown, and various other artifacts are on display.

SAN ANTONIO MUSEUM OF ART (ages 6 and up)

220 West Jones, San Antonio 78215 (210–978–8100). Open Monday through Saturday 10:00 A.M. to 5:00 P.M. (to 9:00 P.M. on Tuesday) and Sunday noon to 6:00 P.M. Adults $5.00, students $4.00, children 4–11 $1.75.

The San Antonio Museum of Art is a six-building complex, formerly a renovated historic brewery, that houses excellent collections of pre-Columbian, Native American, Spanish colonial, and American paintings; photography; sculpture; and furnishings.

SAN ANTONIO MISSIONS NATIONAL HISTORICAL PARK (ages 6 and up)

On the Mission Trail, beginning on Alamo Street, San Antonio 78205 (210–534–8833). Open daily 8:00 A.M. to 5:00 P.M. **Free**.

Give your family a sense of area history by touring San Antonio's famous missions. The driving tour to the four old churches that make up the park begins on Alamo Street. Just follow the signs south. **Mission**

Concepción, Mission San José, Mission Espada, and Mission San Juan were built by the Spanish in the 1700s, and all are still active parish churches. Photographic possibilities at any of the missions are endless. A visitors

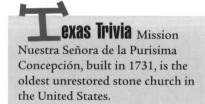

Texas Trivia Mission Nuestra Señora de la Purisima Concepción, built in 1731, is the oldest unrestored stone church in the United States.

center is located at Mission Concepción. Mission San José is justly famous for its Sunday noon mariachi mass.

 BUCKHORN HALL OF HORNS (ages 6 and up)

Houston and Presa Streets, San Antonio 78205 (210–247–4000). Open daily 10:00 a.m. to 6:00 p.m. Adults $9.95, children $7.95.

The entire family will enjoy this authentic Western experience that has been around for more than one hundred years. Recently relocated from an old brewery, the new two-level downtown museum offers thirteen rotating exhibits of more than 520 preserved animals and 3,300 artifacts, including horn and antler furniture, rattlesnake art, and a church made from 50,000 matchsticks. The museum features a saloon and restaurant with cowboy entertainment, an arcade and shooting gallery, a curio shop, and the Texas History Wax Museum.

 WITTE MUSEUM (ages 6 and up)

3801 Broadway, San Antonio 78209 (210–357–1900; www.wittemuseum. org). Open Monday through Saturday 10:00 A.M. to 5:00 P.M. (to 9:00 P.M. Tuesday) and Sunday noon to 5:00 P.M. Adults $5.95, children $3.95. Admission is Free on Tuesday from 3:00 P.M. to 9:00 P.M.

The Witte has extensive exhibits covering the natural history and science of Texas, including a Texas Rangers wing. Special exhibits, such as one with animated dinosaurs, are featured regularly. The Science Treehouse is a wonder of interactive fun and technology with four levels of hands-on exhibits and activities just for children, an absolute must-see.

 SPLASHTOWN USA (ages 4 and up)

3600 North Pan Am Highway, San Antonio 78219 (210–227–1100; www. splashtown.com). Open daily in the summer until mid-August, 11:00 A.M. to 9:00 P.M.; from mid-August to mid-September, 11:00 A.M. to 9:00 P.M. Saturday and 11:00 A.M. to 7:00 P.M. Sunday. Adults $17.99, children under 48 inches $12.99, children under 2 and seniors Free. Nonparticipant admission is $4.99. After 5:00 P.M., all admission is $9.99.

Splashtown USA is a sure way to cool the kids off in the Texas heat. The park has a number of water slides and other water-based attractions.

SAN ANTONIO ZOOLOGICAL GARDEN (ages 2 and up)

3903 North Saint Mary's Street, San Antonio 78212 (210–734–7183). Open daily 9:00 A.M. to 5:00 P.M., to 6:30 P.M. April through November. Adults $7.00, children 3–11 $5.00.

The San Antonio Zoological Garden is a family delight, fun for kids and parents alike. More than 3,000 animals, most in natural settings, are displayed here. More than 700 different species, including rare white rhinos, snow leopards, and whooping cranes, make the zoo the third largest collection in the United States. A special children's area features a tropical boat tour of animal and plant exhibits. Elephant and camel rides are available during most of the summer.

The Mission Trail

When the Spanish occupied Texas, they established about forty missions in the region in an attempt to convert Native peoples and protect the frontier, establishing colonies and forts at each mission. Although the missions ultimately did little of either, they did pave the way for later settlers. The oldest mission was established at El Paso. Today, ten missions or their ruins are open to the public in Texas.

San Antonio is the only city in the United States with five Spanish colonial missions within its city limits, all dating back to the early 1700s. All of them are along the San Antonio River. Missions Concepción, San José, Espada, and San Juan form the San Antonio Missions National Historic Park. The aqueduct at Mission Espada has been in continuous use since the 1730s. A series of markers showing the way along the Mission Trail begin on Alamo Street. Although the Alamo is one of the city's original missions, it is not managed by the National Park System, but by the Daughters of the Republic of Texas as a state historic site. The Daughters consider the Alamo a shrine, so you should maintain hushed tones and control small children while inside, or you may be chastised. Also, show respect inside the other churches along the Mission Trail as they are all active Roman Catholic congregations.

BRACKENRIDGE PARK (ages 4 and up)

3910 North St. Mary's Street, San Antonio 78209; adjacent to San Antonio Zoo (210–736–9534). Gardens open daily 8:00 A.M. until dark.

Next to the zoo, Brackenridge Park and the **Japanese Tea Garden** provide a beautiful, tranquil setting of rustic stone bridges and winding walks by pools and flowers. This is a great place for the children and you to decompress.

 ### SEA WORLD OF TEXAS (ages 2 and up)

10500 Sea World Drive, San Antonio 78251 (210–523–3611; www.seaworld.com). Hours vary widely with the seasons. Adults $32.95, children under 12 $22.95.

You might not find a better way to entertain your kids in all of the state than Sea World of Texas, the world's largest marine-life park. The park offers water slides, tube rides, beaches, surf, waterskiers, and a number of other shows featuring dolphins, killer whales, and birds. Aquariums and other exhibits teach children about marine life.

 ### SIX FLAGS FIESTA TEXAS (ages 4 and up)

At I–10 and Loop 1604, San Antonio 78230 (210–697–5050 or 800–473–4378). Adults $33.99, children under 48 inches $16.99.

Six Flags Fiesta Texas is a 200-acre theme park with more than enough rides and shows to keep any kid entertained, from roller coasters to water slides to trains. Not only does the park put on its own themed music shows, but concerts by top-name performers are scheduled throughout the summer months. The park also brags that it is one of the most accessible theme parks in the nation for people with disabilities or hearing impairments.

 ### MALIBU CASTLE (ages 6 and up)

3330 Castle Ridge Drive, San Antonio 78230 (210–341–6664). Golf is $5.95 for adults, $4.95 for children; boats are $4.50; batting cages are $1.25 for twenty-five balls; go-carts are $4.50. Gran Prix cars, next door (210–341–2500), are $13.95 for five laps for adults, $12.95 for children 4 feet 6 inches or taller.

Your family can spend an entire day at Malibu Castle and never get bored. Choose from a challenging miniature golf course, bumper boats, batting cages, and race cars. There also are a snack bar, video arcade, and game room.

MONARCH COLLECTIBLES (ages 4 and up)

 2012 NW Military Highway, San Antonio 78213, near the airport (210–341–3655 or 800–648–3655). Open Monday through Saturday 10:00 A.M. to 5:00 P.M.

If you or your children like dolls, Monarch Collectibles is the place for you. Monarch is home to more than 2,500 dolls on display and hundreds of limited-edition collectors' plates. The shop also sells dolls, dollhouses, and accessories.

 SAN ANTONIO MISSIONS BASEBALL (ages 4 and up)

5757 U.S. Highway 90 West, San Antonio 78227 (210–675–7275). Tickets: $4.50 to $8.50.

The San Antonio Missions baseball team (a farm club of the Seattle Mariners) plays in the Class AA Texas League, in a new ballpark, one of the best minor-fields in the United States, that will take you back to the golden age of baseball. The team caters to families, with a large picnic area and a special section that prohibits beer sales. Sure, you can get peanuts and Cracker Jack, but you can also get nachos.

 SAN ANTONIO SPURS BASKETBALL (ages 6 and up)

100 Montana Street, San Antonio 78203 (210–554–7787; www.spurs.com). Tickets: $5.50 to $52.50.

The San Antonio Spurs are a class act in the National Basketball Association; they won the championship in 1999. They play at the Alamodome on the frontage road of I-37 east of downtown. The Alamodome not only has regular concessions but features several fast-food franchise restaurants as well.

SAN ANTONIO IGUANAS (ages 6 and up)

8546 Broadway, San Antonio 78217 (210–227–4449 for game dates and times). Tickets: $8.50 to $15.50.

If hockey's your game, the Central Hockey League San Antonio Iguanas are your team. The Iguanas have tons of fun blazing around the ice at Freeman Coliseum off I-35.

Where to Eat

Casa Rio. *430 East Commerce Street, San Antonio 78205 (210–225–6718).* Oldest and largest Mexican restaurant on the River Walk. $-$$

Michelino's. *237 Losoya Street, San Antonio 78205 on the River Walk* *(210–223–2939).* The best Italian food in town. $$

Schilo's (Shee-lows). *424 East Commerce Street, San Antonio 78205 (210–223–6692).* This German-style delicatessen is a city tradition. $

Where to Stay

Bullis House Inn. *621 Pierce Street, San Antonio (210–223–9426).* Nice, quiet place to stay, just 2 miles from downtown. It's a historic landmark, and several of the rooms will accommodate you and your children. There's no charge for kids under three; cribs provided with advance notice. $$

Comfort Inn Fiesta. *6755 North Loop 1604 West, San Antonio 78230 (210–696–4766).* Pool, continental breakfast, convenient location to Six Flags Fiesta Texas. $$

Family Gardens Inn. *2383 Northeast Loop 410, San Antonio 78230 (800–314–3424).* Pool, playground, large suites. $$

La Quinta Inn Market Square. *900 Dolorosa, San Antonio 78205 (210–228–0663 or 800–687–6667).* Pool; convenient to Market Square and much of downtown. $$-$$$

For More Information

San Antonio Convention and Visitors Bureau. *317 Alamo Plaza, San Antonio, TX 78205; (800) 447–3372 or* *(210) 270–8700. Visit the Web site at www.SanAntonioCVB.com.*

The Hill Country

The Hill Country is the heart of Texas. It's centrally located, the capital city of Austin is here, and it's an area so universally loved that most Texans wish they lived here. Although its rugged hills and hardscrabble land don't allow many folks to make a living, the Hill Country stills draws visitors from every corner of the state to bask in its quiet and its beauty over and over and over again.

Formed by the Balcones Escarpment, the limestone ledges and steep, green hills of the Edwards Plateau are crisscrossed by spring-fed rivers and creeks, dotted with farms, scattered with arts-and-crafts communities, and underlain with several spectacular caverns. For centuries the Hill Country was an Apache stronghold; it was later cultivated by German immigrants, whose influence remains substantial, and finally invaded by tourists. Except for I-35, which follows the Balcones Fault Line separating the eastern edge of the Hill Country from the Coastal Plains, and I-10 that bisects the plateau, most roads through the area are twisty, narrow, and hilly, their scenic routes unchanged for a hundred years. And except for the ever-growing metropolis of Austin, the cities in the Hill Country remain small and rustic, windows to Texas's past.

New Braunfels

New Braunfels is one of the key Hill Country cities founded by German immigrants in the mid-1800s, and it still shows through the town's architecture, its street and family names, and most of the restaurants. In the summertime, Texans flock to the town for refuge in the cooling waters of the Comal and Guadalupe Rivers and the state's best water park, and in the shade of the giant oak and cypress trees.

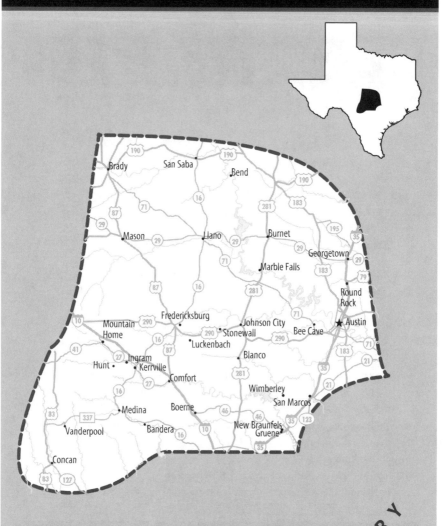

THE HILL COUNTRY

Allan's Top Annual Family Fun Events

- Travis County Livestock Show and Rodeo, Austin, March (512–477–6060)

- Eeyore's Birthday Party, Austin, April (512–448–5160)

- Texas State Arts and Crafts Fair, Kerrville, May (830–896–5711)

- Cowboy Capital Rodeo, Bandera, May (830–796–3045 or 800–364–3833)

- Peach JAMboree, Stonewall, June (830–644–2735)

- Texas International Apple Festival, Medina, July (830–589–7224)

- Chilympiad, San Marcos, September (888–200–5620 or 512–393–5900)

- Wimberley Gospel Music Festival, Wimberley, October (512–847–9916)

- The Great Turkey Escape, Johnson City, November (830–868–7684)

- Trail of Lights, around the Hill Country, December (830–868–7684 or 830–997–6523)

 NATURAL BRIDGE CAVERNS (ages 4 and up)

26495 Natural Bridge Caverns Road, Natural Bridge Caverns 78266; take exit 175 from I–35 and follow the signs (210–651–6101; www.naturalbridgecaverns. com). Opens at 9:00 A.M.; last tour leaves at 6:00 P.M. June through August, 4:00 P.M. during the remainder of the year. Adults $12.00, children 4–12 $7.00.

Natural Bridge Caverns is a great family adventure: You'll descend hundreds of feet into the earth to encounter the largest underground formations in Texas. All but one of the seven show caves in the state can be found in the Hill Country. Named for the 60-foot natural limestone bridge that spans its entrance, Natural Bridge is a living cave, and the sound of water dripping through the limestone to create the subterranean formations can be heard everywhere along the tour. Some formations here are huge, like the 50-foot Watchtower. Aboveground you'll find an interpretive center, snack bar, gift shop, and picnic area.

NATURAL BRIDGE WILDLIFE RANCH (ages 2 and up)

Adjacent to Natural Bridge Caverns, Natural Bridge Caverns 78266 (830–438–7400; www.nbwildliferanchtx.com). Open daily 9:00 A.M. to 5:00 P.M., to 6:30 P.M. June through August. Closed Thanksgiving, Christmas, and New Year's Day. Adults $9.50, children $6.00.

Next door to the cavern is Natural Bridge Wildlife Ranch, a way for the kids to get up close and personal with more than sixty-five exotic species of animals, such as rhinoceros, giraffe, wildebeest, gazelle, zebus, Cape buffalo, aoudad, and baboon. The main tour is through 200 acres of ranchland in your own vehicle; there's also a visitors center, where you can watch newborns being cared for and ostriches hatching; a children's petting zoo; a snack bar; and shaded picnic tables.

SNAKE FARM (ages 4 and up)

5640 I–35 South, New Braunfels 78132; at the Engle Road exit (830–608–9270). Open daily 10:00 A.M. to 7:00 P.M. Memorial Day through Labor Day, to 6:00 P.M. daily the remainder of the year. Closed Tuesday. Adults $4.95, children 3–12 $3.95, children under 3 **Free**.

Your kids will get an educational and slithering good time at the Snake Farm, home to around 800 reptiles of all types, including a 275-pound constrictor. Owners John and Susan Mellyn give frequent hands-on demonstrations. The farm is also home to a variety of alligators, turtles, and longhorn cattle.

THE HUMMEL MUSEUM (ages 6 and up)

199 Main Plaza, New Braunfels 78130 (830–625–5636 or 800–456–4866). Open Monday through Saturday 10:00 A.M. to 5:00 P.M., Sunday noon to 5:00 P.M. Adults $5.00, students $3.00.

The Hummel Museum has the largest collection of original works by German artist Maria Innocentia Hummel in the world. Her drawings of cute children were the inspiration for the popular Hummel figurines, which you can buy in the museum's gift shop.

THE CHILDREN'S MUSEUM (ages 2 and up)

In the New Braunfels Marketplace, exit 188 off I–35, New Braunfels 78130 (830–620–0939). Open Tuesday through Friday 9:00 A.M. to 5:00 P.M., Saturday 10:00 A.M. to 5:00 P.M., Sunday noon to 5:00 P.M. Admission: $3.00.

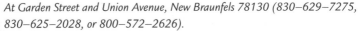

The Children's Museum allows kids the chance to explore and discover on their own with many hands-on exhibits, including a television studio and puppet palace.

LANDA PARK (ages 4 and up)

At Garden Street and Union Avenue, New Braunfels 78130 (830–629–7275, 830–625–2028, or 800–572–2626).

Landa Park is at the headwaters of the Comal River, a stream that begins and ends within the New Braunfels city limits. The towering shade trees, spring-fed swimming pools, hike and bike trails, golf course, miniature train tours, and picnic areas make this one of the most popular parks around. Adjacent, on Liberty Street, is **Prince Solms Park,** where you can slide down a chute from the pool in Landa Park into the Comal River.

SCHLITTERBAHN (ages 4 and up)

305 West Austin Street, New Braunfels 78130 (830–625–2351; www. schlitterbahn.com). Hours vary widely, so call for exact details. Closed from mid-September through mid-April. All-day pass is $25.19 adults, $21.99 children.

Schlitterbahn means "slippery road" in German, and you'll find more than enough ways to slip and slide at the state's largest water park and resort. The park has everything from radically fast and steep chutes to leisurely floats to surf. The resort area offers more than 130 riverside rooms, cottages, and private Jacuzzi suites. Four shops stock water fashions and accessories.

THE GUADALUPE RIVER (ages 6 and up)

Along River Road, north of New Braunfels.

One of the most popular recreational activities in this part of Texas is running the Guadalupe River in an inner tube, raft, canoe, or kayak. The scenery can be spectacular, and the river has enough small rapids to keep your interest. A large number of outfitters are scattered along the river from New Braunfels almost to Sattler. One of the oldest, and most reliable, is **Whitewater Sports,** (830) 964-3800.

Gruene

On Gruene Road off Loop 337, or on Hunter Road off Route 306.

The historic community of Gruene (pronounced "Green") is now a part of New Braunfels, but it maintains its century-old character in its restored old homes that are now country inns, restaurants, or boutiques. The Guadalupe River flows through, providing the most popular summer attraction in all the Hill Country: rafting, canoeing, kayaking, or tubing downstream. Two river outfitters call Gruene home: **Gruene River Raft Co.** (830-625-2800) and **Rockin' R River Rides** (830-629-9999 or 800-55-FLOAT). Both companies' offices are just across the river from the town. If you've never been here before, taking a guided raft ride with your family is a good way to get acquainted with the area and have some safe fun at the same time.

Shopping is abundant in Gruene, where you can buy anything from T-shirts to antiques, pottery to western gifts. Kids love the shop where they can get their picture taken in an Old West costume. You can also shop at **Gruene Market Days,** one of the best outdoor markets in the Hill Country, on the third weekend of each month from April through December.

CANYON LAKE (ages 2 and up)

14 miles north of Gruene on Texas Highway 306 (830–964–2223 or 800–528–2104).

North of Gruene is Canyon Lake, 80 miles of protected shoreline with several parks around it providing ample opportunities for boating, fishing, camping, picnicking, swimming, sunning, or just relaxing. The lake is one of the most popular in the state for scuba diving.

Where to Eat

The Grist Mill Restaurant. *1287 Gruene Road, Gruene 78130 (830–625–0684).* Laid-back atmosphere (shorts and sandals are OK) in a barely restored hundred-year-old mill on the banks of the Guadalupe River. The best food in Texas and incredible strawberry shortcake. $$

Guadalupe Smoked Meat Co. *1299 Gruene Road, Gruene 78130 (830–629–6121).* Great barbecue and burgers. $

Oma's Haus Restaurant. *541 Highway 46 South, New Braunfels 78130 (830–625–3280).* Delicious, authentic German food. Special children's selections, gift shop, homemade fudge and strudel. $-$$

Where to Stay

Gruene Mansion Inn. *1275 Gruene Road, Gruene 78130 (830–629–2641).* Luxurious lodging in the Victorian home of H. D. Gruene, the town's founder, within walking distance of everything in Gruene. $$

Holiday Inn. *1051 I–35 East, New Braunfels 78130 (830–625–8017 or*

800–465–4329). Convenient to everything in New Braunfels or Gruene, exercise room and hot tub. $$

Maricopa Ranch Resort. *Texas Highway 306, Canyon Lake 78130 (830–964–3731; www.texhillcntry.com/stagestop).* Centrally located. Pool, kitchenettes, washers and dryers. $$

San Marcos

AQUARENA SPRINGS (ages 4 and up)

1 Aquarena Springs Drive, San Marcos 78666; west of I–35 at exit 206 (512–245–7575).

For decades San Marcos was known as the home of Ralph the Swimming Pig, who performed along with mermaids at Aquarena Springs. Ralph and the mermaids were retired, however, when Southwest Texas State University bought the amusement park and resort. Developing new programs with the Texas Parks and Wildlife Department, it's open without charge but with few of its former attractions operating. The park now specializes in education, and the always-interesting glass-bottom boat tours continue to fascinate families. A new feature is the **Natural Aquarium of Texas,** showcasing several of the endangered species found only at Aquarena Springs.

WONDER WORLD (ages 2 and up)

1000 Prospect Drive, San Marcos 78667; off I–35 at the Wonder World Drive exit, south of downtown (512–392–3760 or 800–782–7653, ext. 2283; www.wonderworldpark.com). Open June through August 8:00 A.M. to 8:00 P.M.; September and October 9:00 A.M. to 5:00 P.M.; November through February 10:00 A.M. to 3:00 P.M. weekdays, 9:00 A.M. to 5:00 P.M. weekends. Adults $13.95, children $9.95.

Wonder World is a fun place to take younger children. It includes a wildlife park, an observation tower, an antigravity house, and a train tour. The central attraction for adults and older children here is Wonder Cave, unique because it was formed by an earthquake, so it lacks the usual cavern formations. The tour into the cave allows you to see the actual Balcones Fault Line that separates the Hill Country from the Coastal Plains.

THE SAN MARCOS RIVER (ages 6 and up)

At City Park, 170 Bobcat Drive, San Marcos 78666 (512–396–LION). Tube rentals open 11:00 A.M. to 6:00 P.M. weekdays, 10:00 A.M. to 6:00 P.M. weekends. Regular tube rental: $3.00 weekdays, $4.00 weekends.

When the weather is warm, the most popular family activity in San Marcos is tubin' down the San Marcos River. You bring your own inner tube or rent one from the Lions Club facility at City Park and go on a leisurely float down the most beautiful river in the state. Most tubers take out after shooting the chute at Rio Vista Dam. The Lions Club provides a **River Taxi** (512–392–8255) to shuttle you from that location back to City Park. You can keep doing it until you're shriveled up. For the more experienced river runners, canoes and shuttles are available from **Spencer's Canoes** in Martindale (512–357–6113).

Allan's Top
Family Fun Ideas

1. Schlitterbahn Water Park, New Braunfels
2. Enchanted Rock State Natural Area, Fredericksburg
3. Natural Bridge Caverns, New Braunfels
4. Austin Children's Museum, Austin
5. Guadalupe River, New Braunfels
6. Zilker Park, Austin
7. San Marcos River, San Marcos
8. Longhorn Cavern/Inks Lake State Park, Burnet
9. Natural Bridge Wildlife Ranch, New Braunfels
10. Wonder World, San Marcos

Wimberley

About 15 miles north of San Marcos on scenic Ranch Road 12.

Wimberley is a growing arts-and-crafts community at the confluence of the Blanco River and Cypress Creek. The village is known around Texas for its monthly **Wimberley Market Day,** held the first Saturday of each month from April through December on Ranch Road 2325 just north of downtown. This is the second largest outdoor flea market in the state, after Canton's, with more than 450 booths selling everything from junk to art to jams and jellies, from antiques to cactus to handcrafted furniture. Barbecue and live entertainment are served up at lunchtime. Call the chamber of commerce at (512) 847-2201 for more information.

A large number of artists call Wimberley home, and their work can be seen all over town. Downtown around **The Square,** you'll find a number of arts-and-crafts galleries, an old-fashioned ice cream parlor, and a few restaurants where you can get everything from chicken-fried steaks to barbecue to Navajo tacos.

 ### THE CORRAL THEATER (ages 6 and up)

Flite Acres Road at Ranch Road 3237, Wimberley 78676 (512–847–2513). Films begin at dusk, Memorial Day through Labor Day. Admission: $2.50.

Kids love watching first-run movies under the stars at the Corral, an outdoor theater where you can either bring your own chairs, use one of the theater's, or sit in the bleachers. The films are always limited to family fare, and the popcorn has been rated the best in the state.

 ### WIMBERLEY GLASS WORKS (ages 4 and up)

111 West Spoke Hill Drive, Wimberley 78676; turn at the sign 1.6 miles south of Wimberley off Ranch Road 12 (512–847–9348; www.wgw.com). Open Friday through Monday noon to 5:00 P.M., 10:00 A.M. to 5:00 P.M. Memorial Day to Labor Day. **Free**.

You and the kids will be mesmerized at the Wimberley Glass Works. Glassblower Tim de Jong and his staff put on public demonstrations at their modern studio, maneuvering liquid fire on long poles to create impressive art. Visitors sit on bleachers while the artists work from several white-hot vats and furnaces. Finished work is available next door in the showroom.

PIONEER TOWN (ages 6 and up)
333 Wayside Drive, Wimberley 78676 (512–847–2517).

Pioneer Town at 7A Ranch Resort can be a fun place for kids to roam around. An Old West village is re-created on the grounds, including an old fort, chapel, and popular glass-bottle house, as well as an ice cream parlor, gift shop, and video arcade. The resort offers twenty-six rustic cottages, a half mile of Blanco River frontage for swimming and fishing, a pool, and tennis courts, at low-to-moderate prices.

Where to Eat

Casa Olé. *1617 Aquarena Springs Drive, San Marcos 78666 (512–353–5788).* Best Mexican food in town. $–$$

The Salt Lick. *18300 Ranch Road 1826, Driftwood 78619 (512–858–4959).* Long rated the top barbecue in the Hill Country—some say all of Texas—and worth the drive. $

Texas Reds Steakhouse. *120 Grove Street, San Marcos 78666 (512–754–8808).* Great food in a restored mill, and the kids get to toss peanut shells on the floor. $$

Where to Stay

Amerihost Inn. *4210 I–35 South, San Marcos 78667 (512–392–6800 or 800–434–5800).* Indoor pool, exercise room, close to outlet malls and Wonder World. **Free** continental breakfast. $$

Mountain View Motel. *On Ranch Road 12, Wimberly 78676, 3 miles south of downtown (512–847–2992).* Best view around, pool, nature trail, **Free** breakfast. Secluded yet convenient. $$

For More Information

San Marcos Convention and Visitors Bureau. *202 North C. M. Allen Parkway, P.O. Box 2310, San Marcos, TX 78667; (888) 200–5620 or (512) 393–5900.*

Austin

Texas's capital city is famous for its live music scene, the number of festivals it stages throughout the year, and the hundreds of thousands of bats that live under a downtown bridge.

JOURDAN-BACHMAN PIONEER FARM (ages 4 and up)
11418 Sprinkle Cut-Off Road, Austin 78754 (512–837–1215). Open Sunday 1:00 to 5:00 P.M. year-round, September to May Monday through Wednesday 9:30 A.M. to 1:00 P.M., June through August Monday through Thursday 9:30 A.M. to 1:00 P.M.

Aimed at teaching children what life was like for pioneer Texans a hundred years ago, this working farm has several hands-on exhibits, costumed interpreters, and regular programs where children can milk cows, make old fashioned toys or candy, or harvest crops.

STATE CAPITOL (ages 6 and up)
Congress Avenue at Fifteenth Street, Austin 78701 (512–463–0063). **Free** *tours Monday through Friday 8:30 A.M. to 4:30 P.M., Saturday 9:30 A.M. to 4:30 P.M., Sunday 12:30 to 4:30 P.M.* **Free**.

This pink-granite building is a replica of the U.S. Capitol, but just a little bit taller (of course). Portraits of the state's governors line the rotunda walls, and statues of Texas heroes crowd the foyer. The building was recently restored, and the House and Senate chambers are an impressive sight. The adjacent **Capitol Complex Visitors Center** at 112 East Eleventh (512–305–8400) is housed in the historic Old General Land Office Building and is filled with information about local tours and attractions.

AUSTIN CHILDREN'S MUSEUM (ages 2 and up)
201 Colorado Street, Austin 78701 (512–472–2494; www.austinkids. org/museum.html). Open Tuesday through Saturday 10:00 A.M. to 5:00 P.M., Sunday noon to 5:00 P.M. Adults and children 2 and older $4.50.

The Austin Children's Museum recently moved into an expanded facility, showcasing a fascinating collection of hands-on exhibits where kids can climb, touch, and play to their heart's content. The focus is on cultural diversity and science. Unique features include model cities and weather galleries.

MEXIC-ARTE MUSEUM (ages 6 and up)

419 Congress Avenue, Austin 78701(512–480–9373). Open Monday through Saturday 10:00 A.M. to 6:00 P.M. **Free.**

Exhibits include masks and photographs and other artworks highlighting Hispanic culture. Special exhibits throughout the year feature works by Latin American artists.

O. HENRY HOME AND MUSEUM (ages 6 and up)

409 East Fifth Street, Austin 78701 (512–472–1903; www.artcom.com/museums). Open Wednesday through Sunday noon to 5:00 P.M. **Free.**

The O. Henry Museum is where renowned short-story writer William Sydney Porter lived in 1888. A relatively small place, it houses many of the writer's personal items. The museum hosts the annual O. Henry Pun-Off in early May, an event that will delight every member of the family as hundreds of people get on stage vying to tell the punniest stories.

ZILKER PARK (ages 2 and up)

2220 Barton Springs Road, Austin 78746 (park, 512–499–6710; pool, 512–867–3080). Open Monday through Friday 5:00 A.M. to 10:00 P.M.; Saturday, Sunday, and holidays 10:00 A.M. to 6:00 P.M. Gardens open 7:00 A.M. to dusk.

Pool hours vary considerably with seasons and other factors and can be closed even in the summer; call (512) 476–9044 for details. Pool admission: $2.75 adults, $2.50 ages 18–21, $1.00 children 12–17, 50 cents children under 12.

Zilker Park is where Austinites take their kids, and for good reason. The park has an impressive botanical garden, an outdoor theater, picnic areas, a playscape,

Texas Trivia The capital of Texas has been located in more cities than capitals in any other state. The towns that have served are San Felipe, Washington-on-the-Brazos, Harrisburg, Velasco, Columbia, Houston, and Austin.

and famous Barton Springs Pool. The Austin Nature Center in the park gives children the chance to learn with hands-on exhibits. A miniature train tours the park.

UNIVERSITY OF TEXAS (ages 8 and up)

Visitors Center at Martin Luther King Boulevard and I–35, Austin 78705
(512–475–7348). **Free** *campus tours Monday through Saturday.*

The University of Texas campus is home to four museums:

- The **Texas Memorial Museum,** 2400 Trinity Street, has historical, archaeological, and geological collections. Open Monday through Friday 9:00 A.M. to 5:00 P.M., Sunday 1:00 to 5:00 P.M., closed holidays. Call (512) 471-1604.

- The **Harry Ransom Center,** Twenty-first and Guadalupe Streets, showcases UT's permanent collection, which features a 1455 Gutenberg Bible, Western art, and Latin American art. Open Monday through Saturday 9:00 A.M. to 5:00 P.M., Sunday 1:00 to 5:00 P.M. Call (512) 471-8944.

- The **Archer M. Huntington Art Gallery,** Twenty-third and San Jacinto Streets, features rotating and traveling art exhibits. Call (512) 471-7324.

- The **Lyndon B. Johnson Presidential Library and Museum,** 2313 Red River. The LBJ Library houses the papers and personal effects of our thirty-sixth president. On display are a replica of Johnson's Oval Office, a Vietnam War exhibit, and gifts the president received from other heads of state. Also has a nice gift shop. Open 9:00 A.M. to 5:00 P.M. daily. Call (512) 482-5136.

GEORGE WASHINGTON CARVER MUSEUM (ages 6 and up)

1165 East Angelina Street, Austin 78702 (512–472–4809). Open Tuesday through Thursday 10:00 A.M. to 6:00 P.M., Friday and Saturday noon to 5:00 P.M. **Free**.

Black history and culture are showcased here with changing exhibits displaying photographs, artifacts, and folk art.

Texas Trivia The capitol was completed in 1888, covering two and a quarter acres. It's built of 4,000 carloads of Texas pink granite and 11,000 carloads of limestone, both quarried in Marble Falls and shipped to the site on a specially built railroad and by ox teams. The dome is made of iron with copper, covering 85,000 square feet.

BAT EMERGENCE (ages 4 and up)

Congress Avenue Bridge at Riverside Street, Austin 78701 (512–416–5700, ext. 3636 or 512–327–9721).

Don't leave downtown Austin without showing your children all the bats. The world's largest colony of Mexican free-tailed bats hangs out under the Congress Avenue Bridge from April to October. At dusk you can watch about 1.5 million of them take off in search of supper, one of the most unique wildlife spectacles in the United States. Best viewing areas are from the pedestrian walkway on the bridge itself, the adjacent hike and bike trail, observation decks at nearby restaurants and hotels, or the **Bat Observation Center** on the southeast shore of Town Lake at the bridge. A great photo opportunity for the kids is in front of the new 20-foot, free-swinging purple bat sculpture in the small park at Barton Creek Road and Congress Avenue.

Texas Trivia More bats and more species of bats—thirty-two—make their home in Texas than in any other state. The largest urban bat colony in the world—about 1.5 million Mexican free-tailed bats—lives under the Congress Avenue Bridge in Austin.

ICE BATS HOCKEY (ages 6 and up)

7311 Decker Lane, Austin 78724 (512–927–7825; www.icebats.com). Tickets: $10 to $18.

Austin has another sort of bat, the kind on ice skates. The minor-league Ice Bats take to the ice at the Travis County Exposition Center every winter and have become one of the most popular attractions in town.

KIDDIES ACRES (ages 4 and up)

4800 West Howard Lane, Austin 78728 (512–255–4131). Open Tuesday and Friday noon to 7:00 P.M.; Wednesday and Saturday 10:00 A.M. to 9:00 P.M.; Sunday noon to 7:00 P.M. Ride tickets are $1.50 each (it takes ten tickets to take a spin on all rides).

Amusement park rides, miniature golf, pony rides, and train rides at the Austin institution for little folk.

Texas Trivia

The Texas Department of Transportation plants 60,000 pounds of wildflower seeds along Texas highways every year.

MCKINNEY FALLS STATE PARK (ages 4 and up)

7102 Scenic Loop Road, Austin 78744 (512–243–1643; 512–389–8900 for camping reservations).

South of Austin, at the confluence of Onion and Williamson Creeks, is McKinney Falls State Park, a quiet retreat from the nearby big city. Trails throughout the park lead to two waterfalls, a Native American rock shelter, and ruins of an old homestead and a gristmill. The park has picnic, camping, and swimming areas.

 ### LADY BIRD JOHNSON WILDFLOWER CENTER (ages 4 and up)

4801 La Crosse Avenue, Austin 78739 (512–292–4200). Open Tuesday through Sunday 9:00 A.M. to 5:30 P.M. Adults $4.50, students $2.50, children 4 and under Free.

Wildflowers abound at the Wildflower Research Center, founded by former First Lady Lady Bird Johnson and recently renamed in her honor. The huge facility in South Austin has several gardens, a nature trail, a visitors gallery, indoor exhibits, picnic areas, a gift shop, and a beautiful observation tower. The center also offers many classes and workshops specifically for children.

AUSTIN ZOO (ages 2 and up)

10807 Rawhide Trail, Austin 78736; off Highway 290 southwest of town (512–288–1490; www.austinzoo.org). Open 10:00 A.M. to 6:00 P.M. Adults $6.00, children $4.00.

The Austin Zoo isn't like typical large city zoos. This one was designed for children, giving them a chance to have a hands-on encounter with a variety of animals native to Texas. It has pony rides and a picnic area.

Where to Eat

Mexico Tipico. *1707 East Sixth Street, Austin 78702 (512–472–3222).* Not the fanciest Mexican restaurant in town, just one of the best. $

The Texas Chili Parlor. *1409 Lavaca Avenue, Austin 78701 (512–472–2828).* Legendary for serving up the state's official dish in the shadow of the capi-tol. Go for the chili pie. The cook gives you the option of three degrees of heat in your chili, and if you're not sure, start low. $

Threadgills. *6416 North Lamar, Austin 78752 (512–451–5440).* An Austin institution with good, family-style food. $$

Where to Stay

Days Inn. *820 Anderson Lane, Austin 78752 (512–835–4311 or 800–DAYS–INN).* Pool, 𝐅𝐫𝐞𝐞 breakfast. $$

La Quinta. *5812 North I–35, Austin 78701 (512–452–9401 or 800–531–5900).* Conveniently located. 𝐅𝐫𝐞𝐞 breakfast, pool. $$–$$$

For More Information

Austin Visitors Center. *201 East Second Street, Austin, TX 78701; (800)* *926–2282 or (512) 478–0098. Visit the Web site at www.austintexas.org.*

Round Rock and Georgetown

History buffs will want to visit the Round Rock Cemetery, on Sam Bass Road west of I-35. The bandit Sam Bass was buried here after being shot to death by Texas Rangers during an attempted bank holdup in Round Rock.

INNER SPACE CAVERN (ages 6 and up)

At exit 259 off I–35, Georgetown 78626 (512–863–5545). Open daily 9:00 A.M. to 6:00 P.M. Memorial Day through Labor Day and 10:00 A.M. to 5:00 P.M. Labor Day through Memorial Day. Adults $9.00, children $6.00.

A few more miles north, just south of Georgetown, is Inner Space Cavern. The cave, Texas's newest, was discovered when construction crews were building the interstate. Visitors travel down on a cable car, then proceed on a walking tour around many impressive natural formations and by mastodon, dire wolf, and other Ice Age animal remains. The tour is enhanced with a light and sound show.

ROUND ROCK EXPRESS (ages 4 and up)

3400 East Palm Valley Boulevard, Round Rock 78664 (512–255–2255; www.roundrockexpress.com). Tickets range from $5.00 to $8.00.

Texas League baseball returned to the capital area in a big way in 2000 when the Round Rock Express, owned by Hall of Famer Nolan Ryan, began play at the Dell Diamond, a small state-of-the-art ballpark. The Express is affiliated with the Houston Astros.

For More Information

Georgetown Convention and Visitors Bureau. *103 West Seventh Street, Georgetown, TX 78627–0409; (800) 436–8696 or (512) 930–3545. Visit the Web site at www.georgetown.org.*

Round Rock Chamber of Commerce. *212 East Main Street, Round Rock, TX 78664; (800) 747–3479 or (512) 255–5805.*

Burnet

If you mispronounce the name of this city, you'll be corrected by a resident very quickly: It's Burn-it, durn it! The city proclaims itself the Bluebonnet Capital of Texas, and rightly so. The best blooms of the state flower can be found on the rural roads all around Burnet every April, especially near Lake Buchanan.

Want to take the kids fishing? **Lake Buchanan,** 10 miles west of Burnet on Route 29, has some of the best fishing in the Hill Country, in addition to great swimming and picnic areas. For more information or a list of fishing charter companies, contact the Lake Buchanan Chamber of Commerce at (512) 793-2803.

Historic buildings, some dating back to 1854, surround The Square in the center of town. Most house antiques and arts-and-crafts shops now. If you walk over to the train depot on Jackson Street around noon, you can welcome the Hill Country Flyer steam train, and the kids can watch a staged gunfight.

HILL COUNTRY FLYER (ages 2 and up)

Burnet Depot on East Jackson Street, Burnett 78611, 2 blocks east of the downtown square (512–477–8468; www.main.org/flyer). Departs 10:00 A.M. weekends. Tickets range from $24 to $38.

Everyone loves to ride an authentic steam train. The Hill Country Flyer runs between Cedar Park near Highway 183 and Ranch Road 1431 to the city of Burnet. It's a four-hour scenic tour of the Hill Country, over creeks and through canyons, with a layover in Burnet for shopping and lunch. It's a special trip when spring wildflowers are blooming.

 ### FORT CROGHAN MUSEUM (ages 6 and up)

703 Buchanan Drive, Burnet 78611, on Texas Highway 29 (512–756–8281). Open from April through the second weekend of October, Monday and Thursday through Saturday 8:00 A.M. to 5:00 P.M., Sunday 1:00 to 5:00 P.M. **Free***.*

This restored fort depicts frontier days in Texas with several buildings and more than 1,200 items of pioneer history, from musical instruments to dental instruments.

 CONFEDERATE AIR FORCE MUSEUM (ages 6 and up)
At Municipal Airport on U.S. Highway 281, Burnet 78611 (512–756–2226). Open Saturday 9:00 A.M. to 5:00 P.M., Sunday 1:00 to 5:00 P.M. Donations requested.

The Hill Country Squadron of the Confederate Air Force is stationed at the airport, just south of town. The museum features World War II planes, firearms, photographs, and other memorabilia.

 LONGHORN CAVERN STATE PARK (ages 6 and up)
 On Park Road 4, Burnet 78611, 9 miles west of Burnet off Texas Highway 29 (512–756–6976). Open daily except Christmas Eve and Christmas. Adults $6.50, children $4.00.

 Most of the work on this Registered Natural Landmark was done by the Civilian Conservation Corps during the Depression, and an exhibit honoring the CCC is on display near the Visitors Center. The cave is unique for the way rushing water, in addition to the usual dissolving water, carved the cavern. Some of the walls are as smooth as glass. The park also has picnic areas, two nature trails, a snack bar, and a gift shop.

 INKS LAKE STATE PARK (ages 2 and up)
On Park Road 4, Burnet 78611, adjacent to Longhorn Cavern (512–793–2223; for camping reservations call 512–389–8900).

This is one of the most popular parks in the state, a 1,200-acre panorama of cedar and oak woodlands, wildflowers, and pink granite. The park borders Inks Lake and offers 7 miles of beautiful hiking trails, camping, picnicking, swimming, canoeing, waterskiing, scuba diving, sailing, and fishing. There also are a nine-hole golf course, a playground, and a store for groceries and camping supplies. Deer, turkey, quail, and songbirds are abundant in the park. At dusk, it's common to see small children feeding deer from their hands.

 VANISHING TEXAS RIVER CRUISE (ages 4 and up)
At Canyon of the Eagles Nature Park, Ranch Road 2341, Burnet 78011, 20 miles north of Texas Highway 29 (512–756–6986). Tour at 11:00 A.M. daily except Tuesday. Sunset dinner cruises are also available. Fare: $15 adults, $13 children.

The Vanishing Texas River Cruise is a true delight. The two-and-a-half-hour tour will take your family through unspoiled wilderness, focusing on bald eagle nesting areas November through March, on wildflowers April through June, and on majestic scenery and wildlife July through October. By the way, Ranch Road 2341 has some of the best wildflower viewing in Texas in spring.

Marble Falls, San Saba, and Bend

On Ranch Road 1431 you'll drive by Lake LBJ and Lake Marble Falls, two more of the Highland Lakes chain formed by several dams on the Colorado River in this area of the Hill Country. Fishing is excellent in both, especially bass fishing. Waterskiing and sailing are also popular. Both lakes have several boat docks, marinas, and picnic areas. The land surrounding the lakes is said to be the oldest dry land on Earth.

The Lower Colorado River Authority maintains several lakeside and riverside parks with swimming and picnic areas. Call (512) 473–4083 for more information.

The pink granite used for the state capitol was quarried from Granite Mountain in Marble Falls. You can see the huge stone dome from a roadside picnic area on Ranch Road 1431 just north of the city. They've been cutting and carrying out granite from this mountain for more than one hundred years, but it hasn't seemed to have made a dent in it.

In San Saba your family can relax at two cooling places. **Reisen Park** is on the banks of the San Saba River east of town on Highway 190 and has a playground, picnic areas, and volleyball courts all beneath large, shady pecan trees. (The city is known for its pecan crop.) **Mill Pond Park** has a spring-fed lake, waterfalls, a swimming pool, picnic areas, baseball fields, tennis courts, and a playground. It's 5 blocks east of the courthouse.

COLORADO BEND STATE PARK (ages 4 and up)

6 miles south of Bend; go to Bend on Ranch Road 501 or 580, follow the signs, and take the gravel road out of town south 6 miles to the entrance (mailing address: P.O. Box 118, Bend 76824; 915–628–3240; 512–389–8900 for camping reservations).

Near Bend you'll find the most beautiful waterfall in Texas at Colorado Bend State Park. The park, the most isolated in

Texas Trivia So far 153 caves have been discovered at Colorado Bend State Park.

the Hill Country, includes 6 miles of the Colorado River before it empties into Lake Buchanan, lots of wildlife, and scenery and solitude. You
can camp, hike, fish, mountain bike, or watch the teeming bird life,
including bald eagles. Rangers conduct guided tours to Gorman Falls
and several caves, areas accessible only by tour.

For More Information

**Marble Falls/Lake LBJ Chamber of
Commerce.** *801 Highway 281, Marble
Falls, TX 78654; (800) 759–8178.*

*Visit the Web site at www.lone-star.net/
marblefalls.*

Llano, Brady, and Mason

Brady Lake, with 29 miles of shoreline, offers waterskiing, swimming, camping, and fishing. You'll also find screened shelters and picnic areas. Call (915)
597-1823.

The little town of Mason prides itself on the amount of topaz that has
been found in the surrounding hills. If
your kids love beautiful rocks, they'll
love trudging around the brush looking
for raw gems. Several area ranches
allow rock hounds to search for the
state gem on their lands, except during
deer season. For a list of participating
ranches, call (915) 347-5758.

Texas Trivia The
geographic center of Texas is
15 miles northeast of Brady in
northern McCulloch County.

 HEART OF TEXAS HISTORICAL MUSEUM (ages 8 and up)
*High and Main Street, Brady 76825 (915–597–3491). Open Saturday through
Monday 1:00 to 5:00 P.M. and by appointment.* **Free**.

The imposing old county jail in Brady, in the geographical center of
Texas, has been converted into a museum. It displays the typical area
historical exhibits as well as jail cells and a gallows.

 LLANO COUNTY MUSEUM (ages 8 and up)
*On Texas Highway 16, Llano 78643, north of Llano River Bridge (915–247–
3026). Open June through August Tuesday through Saturday 10:00 A.M. to noon
and 1:30 to 5:30 P.M., Sunday 1:30 to 5:30 P.M.; September through May same
hours except closed Tuesday.* **Free**.

The museum is housed in an old drugstore just north of the Llano River Bridge on Route 16 in Llano and gives visitors a glimpse of what the area was like when it was an iron-ore boomtown.

Fredericksburg and Luckenbach

Fredericksburg is another of those Hill Country cities founded by German immigrants and is well known for its German restaurants and bakeries. The town is so steeped in its heritage that many natives still speak German. You'll notice that Main Street is exceptionally wide. It was built that way by founding families so they could turn wagons around in the middle of the street. More than a hundred quality antiques and arts-and-crafts shops and galleries line the street.

Near Fredericksburg is what may be the most famous small town in Texas: Luckenbach. You go 5 miles east on Highway 290 to Ranch Road 1376 and drive another 5 miles south. I'd tell you to follow the signs, but the Luckenbach signs are often stolen, so remember that if you get to the Grape Creek bridge, you've gone too far. What's left of the town is a general store and dance hall. On Sunday, singers and strummers from the famous to the obscure can often be found performing in the shade by the store near the bust of the late Hondo Crouch, a renowned storyteller who first popularized Luckenbach. Call (830) 997-3224 or visit the Web site www.luckenbachtexas.com.

WILDSEED FARMS (ages 4 and up)

7 miles east of Fredericksburg on U.S. Highway 290, Fredericksburg 78624 (830–990–1393 or 800–848–0078; www.wildseedfarms.com). Open daily 9:30 A.M. to 6:00 P.M. **Free**.

This place is really something to see in the spring when brilliant red poppies and bluebonnets blanket acres and acres just north of the highway. Hike around at any time of year, and something is always blooming here. The owners have set aside special areas where you may take pictures of the family sitting among the flowers. You can shop for seeds, potted flowers, plant tools and accessories, and Texas wines

Texas Trivia Notice the street names as you pass through Fredericksburg. The first ten streets east of the courthouse—Adams, Llano, Lincoln, Washington, Elk, Lee, Columbus, Olive, Mesquite, and Eagle—spell "All Welcome." And the streets west of the courthouse—Crockett, Orange, Milam, Edison, Bowie, Acorn, Cherry, and Kay—invite you to "Come Back."

and foods at the impressive Market Center. Grab a bite to eat and a cool drink at the adjacent Blubonnet Biergarten. A very impressive place.

OLD TUNNEL WILDLIFE MANAGEMENT AREA (ages 4 and up)

8 miles south of U.S. Highway 290 at the sign, 1 mile east of Fredericksburg (mailing address: P.O. Box 1167, Comfort 78013; 830–644–2478). **Free** *tours given June through October Thursday and Saturday.*

If you have kids who like bats, they'll like the bat tour at the Old Tunnel Wildlife Management Area. There's an observation deck near the parking lot where you can see hundreds of thousands of bats emerging from the Old Tunnel area around dusk. Directions to the area are complicated, so call for details and tour reservations.

FORT MARTIN SCOTT (ages 6 and up)

2 miles east of Fredericksburg on U.S. Highway 290, Fredericksburg 78624 (830–997–9895). Open Friday through Sunday 9:00 A.M. to 5:00 P.M. **Free**.

Texas Wildflowers Texas has more than 5,000 wildflower species. Visitors flock from all over in the spring to see blooming bluebonnets, Indian paintbrush, and Indian blankets coloring the fields blue, red, white, and yellow. But yucca, ocotillos, and cactus also burst forth with colors.

Each region of Texas has its own special places to see the wildflowers, and they are all connected by the state's highway system. In the 1930s, Texas became the first state to develop a plan for beautification of roadsides with flowers and plants. Along the roads are more than 700,000 acres of right-of-way that the Texas Department of Transportation carefully grooms and maintains so that each spring highway medians and roadsides burst into color all around the state. The department plants about 60,000 wildflower seeds a year along the roadways. In addition, cultivated varieties are planted along highways, like the miles of crape myrtles on U.S. Highway 271 north of Paris.

You can get a **Free**, full-color wildflower booklet from the Travel and Information Division, Texas Department of Transportation, P.O. Box 5064, Austin, TX 78763.

This fort was the first U.S. Army post in Texas. You can tour the grounds and several buildings now being reconstructed, including the guardhouse, a log cabin, and officers' quarters. The visitors center displays documents and artifacts recovered from the site. Costumed volunteers are often at the fort giving living-history demonstrations.

BAUER TOY MUSEUM (ages 4 and up)

223 East Main Street, Fredericksburg 78624 (830–997–6523). Open Wednesday through Monday 10:00 A.M. to 5:00 P.M. **Free**.

The Bauer Toy Museum features more than 3,000 antique toys from 1875 through the 1950s. Items include toy guns, dolls, and toy cars; a diorama of Charles Dickens's *A Christmas Carol;* and a miniature replica of a small Texas town accented with antique iron toys.

ADMIRAL NIMITZ MUSEUM AND HISTORICAL CENTER (ages 6 and up)

 304 East Main Street, Fredericksburg 78624 (830–997–4379; www.nimitzmuseum.org). Open daily 8:00 A.M. to 5:00 P.M. except Christmas. Adults $3.00, students $1.50.

That steamboat-looking building you see on Main Street is the Admiral Nimitz Museum. The nine-acre center is a state park honoring Chester Nimitz, a World War II hero who was born here. The park features the restored Nimitz Steamboat Hotel, the Museum of the Pacific War, the Garden of Peace (a gift from Japan), and a History Walk. A gallery dedicated to former president George Bush's war service recently opened.

PIONEER MUSEUM AND VEREINS KIRCHE MUSEUM (ages 6 and up)

 309 West Main Street, Fredericksburg 78624 (830–997–2835). Pioneer Museum open March through mid-December 10:00 A.M. to 5:00 P.M. Monday through Saturday, 1:00 to 5:00 P.M. Sunday, closed on Tuesday. Open mid-December through February 10:00 A.M. to 5:00 P.M. Saturday and 1:00 to 5:00 P.M. Sunday. Adults $3.00, children $1.00. Vereins Kirche open Monday through Saturday 10:00 A.M. to 4:00 P.M., Sunday 1:00 to 4:00 P.M. Admission: $1.50 for ages 12 and up.

Texas Trivia Six different species of bluebonnets can be found in Texas. They are all the state flower.

Up the street is the Pioneer Museum complex, preserving several old buildings with pioneer artifacts. The Volunteer Fire Department Museum has items from the earliest days of organized fire fighting. Across the street is the Vereins Kirche, a uniquely shaped old church that's now a museum detailing the history of the area.

ENCHANTED ROCK STATE NATURAL AREA (ages 4 and up)
18 miles north of Fredericksburg on Ranch Road 965, Fredericksburg 78624 (915–247–3903; 512–389–8900 for camping reservations).

Straddling Llano and Gillespie Counties is massive Enchanted Rock. The landscape here is dominated by an immense, smooth pink granite dome more than one billion years old, the oldest exposed rock in North America. The rock, sacred to Native Americans, is surrounded with legends and was the site of a battle between Texas Rangers and Native Americans. Visitors love walking to the top of the rock, or trying to, but other trails in the park also offer sight-seeing and photo opportunities of unusual rock formations. Enchanted Rock has a couple of fissure caves children love to scramble around. The park also has picnic and camping facilities. Be advised to arrive early on weekends between May and October, because rangers close the park once capacity is reached.

Where to Eat

Altdorf Biergarten and Restaurant. *505 West Main Street, Fredericksburg 78624 (830–997–7865).* Famous German dinners, homemade desserts make this the most popular cafe in town. $$

Auslander Biergarten and Restaurant. *323 East Main Street, Fredericksburg 78624 (830–997–7714).* International menu, children's specials. $-$$

Friedhelm's Bavarian Restaurant. *905 West Main Street, Fredericksburg 78624 (830–997–6300).* As authentically German as it gets outside of Europe. $$

Wheelers Restaurant. *204 East Main, Fredericksburg 78624 (830–990–8180).* Hearty and delicious specials. $-$$

Where to Stay

Bed-and-breakfast inns are plentiful in the Fredericksburg area, either in town or out in the countryside. **Gasthaus Schmidt Reservation Service** will help you connect with one that suits your family. Call (830) 997-5612. $$-$$$

Best Western Sunday House. *501 East Main, Fredericksburg 78624 (830–997–4484 or 800–274–3762).* Large rooms, pool. $$

Fredericksburg Inn and Suites. *201 South Washington, Fredericksburg 78624 (830–997–5740 or 800–446–0202).* Comfortable, convenient; pool. $$

Scenic Drive

*S*cenic Drive In springtime when the bluebonnets, coreopsis, Indian blankets and paintbrushes, and wine cups are in bloom, the Willow City Loop is ablaze in blues, yellows, and reds against the most rustic and scenic backgrounds you will find anywhere.

Begin the drive by taking Ranch Road 965 northeast from Enchanted Rock, then turning south onto Texas Highway 16. Go about 5 miles to the Willow City Loop sign and turn east, following the county road to the small village of Willow City, where you turn west onto Ranch Road 1323 and return to Highway 16. If you don't want to make the drive a complete loop, turn east onto Ranch Road 1323 at Willow City, traveling through more scenic hills, past the village of Sandy, until you reach U.S. Highway 281 about 5 miles north of Johnson City.

The narrow, winding back road is extremely popular, so drive carefully and respect private property. Be aware that on weekends during peak blooms, sheriff's deputies patrol the road and ticket every car illegally parked or trespassing flower peepers.

For More Information

Fredericksburg Convention and Visitors Bureau. *106 North Adams Street, Fredericksburg, TX 78624;* *(830) 997–6523. Visit the Web site at www.fredericksburg-texas.com.*

Mountain Home

Y.O. RANCH (ages 4 and up)

15 miles west of Mountain Home on Texas Highway 41, Mountain Home 78058 (830–640–3222 or 800–967–2624). Tours leave at 10:00 A.M., and reservations are required. Cost is $27.70.

The Y.O. Ranch in Mountain Home was founded more than a hundred years ago and is still going strong. In addition to longhorn cattle, the ranch is home to thirty-five exotic species of animals. A tour of the ranch includes visiting a pioneer cabin, an old schoolhouse, and a Wells Fargo office. In addition to the regular tour, the ranch offers overnight guest packages, photo safaris, hiking, mountain biking, and horseback and hayrides.

Hunt

On Texas Highway 39.

Just south of Hunt is a roadside picnic area at a low-water crossing over the Guadalupe River where families always seem to gather. The area has several shaded picnic tables, great fishing, and a beautiful series of waterfalls just upriver from the bridge.

Two miles west of Hunt on Farm Road 1340 you'll discover Stonehenge. Well, it's **Stonehenge II,** an exact three-quarter-scale replica of the famous stone circle plopped down in an open field. There are even several Easter Island statue replicas.

Kerrville and Ingram

The **Kerrville Folk Festival** is held at Quiet Valley Ranch, 9 miles south of Kerrville on Route 16. The event features more than twenty straight days of the best music from singer-songwriters and folklife activities at the end of May and the first week of June. There's a special children's area with music just for kids. Most visitors camp out on the grounds since impromptu performances occur regularly around almost every campfire. Call (830) 257-3600 or (800) 221-7958.

The city also hosts the official **Texas State Arts and Crafts Fair** at the end of May, the largest and best such event in the state. Call (830) 896-5711.

 COWBOY ARTISTS OF AMERICA MUSEUM (ages 6 and up)
1550 Bandera Highway, Kerrville 78028 (830–896–2553; www.caamuseum. com). Open Tuesday through Saturday 9:00 A.M. to 5:00 P.M. and Sunday 1:00 to 5:00 P.M. Adults $5.00, children $1.00.

The Cowboy Artists of America Museum has an international reputation for collecting the best in contemporary and classic western paintings and sculpture. The museum features special shows, traveling exhibits, and workshops. The grounds and building are as beautiful as the art, and the museum store is first-rate.

 HILL COUNTRY MUSEUM (ages 8 and up)
226 Earl Garrett Street, Kerrville 78028 (830–896–8633). Open Monday through Thursday 1:00 to 4:30 P.M., Friday and Saturday 10:00 A.M. to noon and 1:00 to 4:30 P.M. **Free.**

Hill Country antiques, artifacts, and memorabilia are on display at the Hill Country Museum, in the former home of Capt. Charles Schreiner, a Texas Ranger and founder of the city.

RIVERSIDE NATURE CENTER (ages 4 and up)

150 Francisco Lemos Street, Kerrville 78028 (830–257–4837). Open Tuesday through Saturday 10:00 A.M. to 2:00 P.M. **Free**.

The Riverside Nature Center has special programs for children, blending cultural history with the area's natural history. The center includes a wildflower meadow, walking paths, and butterfly gardens.

KERRVILLE-SCHREINER STATE PARK (ages 4 and up)

2385 Bandera Highway, Kerrville 78028 (830–257–5392). Call (512) 389–8900 for camping reservations.

Kerrville-Schreiner State Park is nestled on the cypress-shaded, sloping banks of the Guadalupe River. The 517-acre park has ample opportunities to view wildlife up close, and offers campsites, or shelters, picnic tables, and hiking trails.

HILL COUNTRY ARTS FOUNDATION (ages 6 and up)

507 West Texas Highway 39, Ingram 78025 (830–367–5121). Gallery admission is **Free**. *Performance tickets vary with event.*

The Hill Country Arts Foundation is a combination of things: the **Alice Naylor Art Library,** full of information on art instruction and history; the **Duncan-McAshan Visual Arts Center,** with exhibition space for fine arts and a regular schedule of workshops; and the **Smith-Ritch Point Theatre,** which has two venues for the performing arts. Summer plays are geared for children, such as *Peter Pan.* And it's all tucked away on the banks of the scenic Guadalupe River.

Where to Stay

Inn of the Hills. *1001 Junction Highway, Kerrville 78028 (830–895–5000 or 800–292–5690).* Play tennis, putt some golf balls, swim in one of two indoor or three outdoor pools, work out in the gym, play racquetball or basketball, or take a hike. Rooms overlook the Guadalupe River. $$–$$$

Y.O. Ranch Holiday Inn. *2033 Sidney Baker Boulevard, Kerrville 78028 (830–257–4440 or 800–531–2800).* Kid-friendly hotel with bunk beds, Nintendo games, pool. $$

For More Information

Kerrville Chamber of Commerce. 1700 Sidney Baker Street, Suite 200, Kerrville, TX 78028; (800) 221–7958 or

(830) 792–3535. Visit the Web site at www.ktc.net/kerrvillecvb.

Medina, Vanderpool, and Concan

Take Route 16 south.

Medina is the apple capital of Texas. Yes, Texas does manage to raise apples, despite the lack of really cold weather. There's even an apple festival here in July. Several shops in town sell a huge variety of apple-based food items, and even apple trees. A large apple sculpture, billed as the World's Largest Apple, is on display downtown. For information on the **Texas International Apple Festival,** call (830) 589-7224.

Texas Trivia The top ten state parks for overnight visits are Garner, Inks Lake, Galveston Island, Cedar Hill, Tyler, Lake Texana, Goose Island, Lake Ray Roberts, Lake Livingston, and Bastrop.

LOVE CREEK ORCHARDS AND STORE (ages 6 and up)

112 Broadway (Ranch Road 337), Medina 78055, west of Medina (800–449–0882 or 830–589–2588; www.lovecreekorchards.com).

Love Creek Orchards gives guided tours on Saturday mornings May through October. Tours leave at 10:00 A.M. from the Cider Mill Store—filled with all sorts of apple goodies and gifts—on Broadway.

LOST MAPLES STATE NATURAL AREA (ages 4 and up)

5 miles north of Vanderpool on Ranch Road 187, Vanderpool 78885 (830–966–3413; 512–389–8900 for camping reservations).

Just north of Vanderpool, hidden in a remote canyon, lies a fall color display that rivals any found in New England. If the weather has been kind, bigtooth maples at Lost Maples blaze red, yellow, and orange and attract thousands of Texans in the know in late October and early November. It's still a fairly obscure park, however. Lost Maples is great even at other times of the year, too. Its 10 miles of hiking trails are mostly shaded, and you can cool off in a nice small lake. The park has camping and picnic facilities, an interpretive center, a gift shop, and rewarding bird-watching in the spring.

GARNER STATE PARK (ages 4 and up)

On Park Road 29, Concan 78838, 7 miles north of Concan off U.S. Highway 83 (830–232–6132; 512–389–8900 for camping reservations).

Garner State Park is so popular among Texans that someone wrote a popular rock song about it in the sixties. Generation after generation return so often, the park is a family tradition among many. Your family can admire the scenic Hill Country; splash in the sparkling cool Frio River; canoe; hike; mountain bike; camp; picnic; relax in the shade of cypress, elm, oak, or pecan trees; or stay in rustic cabins built by the Civilian Conservation Corps in the 1930s. There also are an eighteen-hole miniature golf course and a park store.

Scenic Drive Ranch Road 337 is an attraction in itself. This stretch of road between Medina and Vanderpool is one of the most scenic highways in the state, rolling over spectacular, pristine Hill Country and through secluded valleys. The hills are higher and steeper than in the rest of the area, the towns smaller, the traffic very light.

For a lovely scenic loop, start in Bandera going west on Texas Highway 16 to Medina, then west on Ranch Road 337 to Vanderpool, south on Ranch Road 187 to the junction with Ranch Road 470 just north of Utopia. Turn east and return to Bandera. This is also a convenient route if you wish to visit either Lost Maples State Natural Area or Hill Country State Natural Area.

Bandera

Bandera calls itself the Cowboy Capital of the World with good reason: It was the staging area for the great cattle drives of the late 1800s, many champion rodeo cowboys call the city home, and dozens of dude ranches surround the city. For a list of which ranches are operating guest facilities, call the **Bandera Visitors Center** at (830) 796-3045 or (800) 364-3833. Rates run moderate to high and usually include some, if not all, meals, horseback riding, hayrides, hiking trails, and, sometimes, pools.

FRONTIER TIMES MUSEUM (ages 6 and up)

506 Thirteenth Street, Bandera 78003 (830–796–3864). Open daily 10:00 A.M. to noon and 1:00 to 4:30 P.M. **Free**.

This rustic building, once the editorial offices of *Frontier Times* magazine, now houses hundreds of western artifacts, art and antiques, Native American items, and Wild West Show posters.

The Camel Experiment

The Camel Experiment Camels used to be seen all over Texas in the mid-1800s, thanks to then Secretary of War Jefferson Davis. Davis talked Congress out of $30,000 so the Army could determine if camels would be better than mules as beasts of burden in the desolate areas of the western states. The camel training headquarters was at Camp Verde, Texas, and before the Civil War camel caravans went west from there through the Big Bend of Texas all the way to California.

Although the camels proved to be a success, the experiment was never reactivated after the Civil War, probably because the idea had been the brainchild of Davis, who served as president of the Confederacy. The camels were subsequently abandoned by soldiers, and many were sighted roaming the Texas hills and deserts until well into the 1920s.

Camp Verde was destroyed by a fire in 1919, but the foundation of the post remains near the current **Camp Verde General Store**, about 16 miles north of Bandera on Texas Highway 173.

HILL COUNTRY STATE NATURAL AREA (ages 4 and up)

10 miles west of Bandera on Farm Road 1077, Bandera 78003 (830–796–4413). Closed Tuesday and Wednesday.

Hill Country State Natural Area is a 5,369-acre park maintained in its primitive state. You'll find a number of equestrian, hiking, and mountain-bike trails over rugged Hill Country. Through a local ranch, the park also occasionally offers guided horseback tours.

Boerne

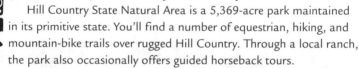

Located at the junction of Texas Highway 46 and I–10.

Another village settled by German pioneers, Boerne (pronounced Bur-nee) has a downtown area full of quaint shops, restaurants, and historic buildings and offers more than enough outdoor activities for anyone.

AGRICULTURAL HERITAGE CENTER AND CIBOLO WILDERNESS TRAIL (ages 4 and up)

In City Park on Texas Highway 46, Boerne 78006 (830–249–8000). The Heritage Center is open Wednesday and Sunday 1:30 to 4:30 P.M. **Free**.

The Agricultural Heritage Center and Cibolo Wilderness Trail combine education and recreation. The Heritage Center includes indoor and outdoor exhibits of antique farm machinery and implements and an operating blacksmith shop. The trail covers a sixty-five-acre inner-city greenbelt that crosses three distinct ecosystems.

CASCADE CAVERNS (ages 6 and up)

226 Cascade Caverns Road, Boerne 78006; take exit 543 off I–10, then follow the signs (830–755–8080). Open daily 9:00 A.M. to 6:00 P.M. except Tuesday. Tours leave every thirty minutes. Adults $6.95, children $4.95.

Cascade Caverns is the most distinctive cave in Texas and should not be missed. At the end of the one-hour tour, your family will see the 90-foot underground waterfall that gives the cavern its name. The cave has many large rooms, crystal pools, and growing formations. Above ground are a swimming pool, camping facilities, a store, and a dance hall.

CAVE WITHOUT A NAME (ages 6 and up)

On Kruetzberg Road, Boerne 78006 (830–537–4212). Open daily 9:45 A.M. to 4:30 P.M. except Tuesday. Adults $5.00, children $2.00.

Cave Without a Name can be difficult to find, but it's worth it. Travel northeast on Farm Road 474, go right on Kreutzberg Road for about 4.5 miles, then follow the signs. The huge cave system has some beautiful formations and is said to be 98 percent active—meaning the formations are still growing.

GUADALUPE RIVER STATE PARK AND HONEY CREEK STATE NATURAL AREA (ages 4 and up)

3350 Park Road 31, Spring Branch 78070 (830–438–2656; for camping reservations call 512–389–8900).

Bisected by the river from which it takes its name, the park is noted for its rugged beauty. You can enjoy hiking, swimming, canoeing, tubing, fishing, picnicking, camping, or watching wildlife. Adjacent is **Honey Creek State Natural Area,** a park kept so primitive that the public is allowed in only once a week, on Saturday, on guided tours. The 9:00 A.M. tour passes through wonderful Honey Creek Canyon, a true wilderness.

Comfort

West of Boerne at the junction of I–10 and Texas Highway 27.

Comfort is in many ways a mirror of Boerne, although smaller. It also was founded by German immigrants and has many historic buildings. Its downtown area is full of antiques and arts-and-crafts shops. For more information call the Comfort Chamber of Commerce, (830) 995-3131.

Blanco

On U.S. Highway 281, south of Johnson City.

Blanco has restored its old courthouse and will turn it into a museum of the Hill Country. On the third Saturday of each month from April through November, hundreds of vendors set up around the Courthouse Square for the city's **Market Day.** On streets surrounding the square you'll discover many antiques and arts-and-crafts shops and restaurants. By the way, the city and the river are pronounced "Blank-oh" by locals, despite the correct Spanish pronunciation.

BLANCO STATE PARK (ages 4 and up)

U.S. Highway 281, Blanco 78606, at the Blanco River (830–833–4333; 512–389–8900 for camping reservations).

Blanco State Park is an unpretentious little park offering great fishing (rainbow trout, perch, catfish, and bass), swimming, hiking trails, camping, and picnic facilities.

Where to Eat

Blanco Bowling Club. *Farm Road 1623 at Pecan Street, Blanco 78606 (830–833–4416).* You can bowl here, but the BBC is best known for its good eats. There's nothing like roast beef and mashed potatoes with the clink of falling bowling pins in the background. Home-cooked food in huge portions and the best pies in the Hill Country. $–$$

Peach Tree Country Kitchen. *448 South Main Street, Boerne 78606 (830–249–8583).* Great home cooking, with the best cheese rolls and peach cobbler around. $–$$

Po Po Family Restaurant. *At exit 533 off I–10, Welfare 78006 (830–537–4194).* Housed in an old stone building, this is one of the nicest kid-friendly restaurants in the region. Admire the huge commemorative plate collection covering the walls. Often has all-you-can-eat dinner specials. $–$$

Where to Stay

Best Western Texas Country Inn. *35150 I-10, Boerne 78006 (830–249–9791).* Conveniently located, pool, **Free** deluxe breakfast. $-$$

Gast Haus Lodge. *944 High Street, Comfort 78013 (830–995–2304).* Has nine units, most dating back to the late 1800s when this was a stagecoach stop. Some units are large enough to house a large family; two have kitch-enettes. Swim in the pool or fish in Cypress Creek, just a stone's throw from the lodge. $-$$

Guadalupe River Ranch. *605 Farm Road 474, Boerne 78006 (830–537–4837; www.guadalupe-river-ranch.com).* More than lodging: horseback rides, mountain bikes, nature trails, canoeing and tubing the river, sports court, game room, and more. $$-$$$

Johnson City and Stonewall

Johnson City was home to President Lyndon B. Johnson, and several parks in the area honor the former president. The downtown area has also been recently rejuvenated with several boutiques, antiques shops, and restaurants.

LYNDON B. JOHNSON NATIONAL HISTORICAL PARK (ages 6 and up)

100 Lady Bird Lane Johnson City 78636, 2 blocks south of Highway 290 (830–868–7128; www.nps.gov/lyjo/index.html). Open daily 9:00 A.M. to 5:00 P.M. except Christmas and New Year's. Admission: $2.00, children under 6 **Free**.

The park has an impressive visitors center, complete with an audiovisual program and a full book and gift shop. Across the street is LBJ's boyhood home, furnished with Johnson family household items and period furniture. Connected by a footpath is the nearby Old Johnson Settlement, a ranch complex owned by LBJ's grandfather and great uncle. Many of the old buildings have been restored.

LYNDON B. JOHNSON STATE AND NATIONAL HISTORICAL PARK (ages 4 and up)

On Park Road 52, Stonewall 78671 (830–644–2252; www.tpwd.state.tx.us/park/lbj/lbj.htm). Visitors center open 8:00 A.M. to 5:00 P.M.

This park has several distinct areas, all along or near U.S. Highway 290 between Johnson City and Stonewall. Tours of the LBJ Ranch, just across the Pedernales (LBJ pronounced it Purrr-din-alice) River from the state park area, depart from the visitors center 10:00 A.M. to 4:00 P.M. daily. The center features exhibits on Lyndon Johnson and on the history and wildlife of the Hill Country. A nature trail winds past wildlife enclosures with buffalo, deer, turkey, and long-horn cattle, and through beautiful wildflower fields. LBJ's gravesite is also located here.

In addition, the state park facility caters to families by providing tennis courts, a swimming pool, picnic areas, a baseball field, and fishing opportunities along the Pedernales.

Texas Snacks The most popular snack foods in Texas:

- Frito pie
- Peanuts in Dr Pepper
- Beef jerky
- Jalapeños (fresh or pickled)
- Corn dogs

Frito pies are simple to make. You tear open a regular-size bag of corn chips, pour in some chili, sprinkle chopped onions and shredded cheese on top, and eat it straight from the bag. Some restaurants will now serve this concoction in a bowl, but in-the-bag is the only true Texan way.

Also part of the park is the Sauer-Beckmann Living History Farm, a place children love. Costumed interpreters carry out the day-to-day activities of a typical turn-of-the-twentieth-century Hill Country farm. Kids can see the hogs get slopped, the livestock fed, eggs collected, butter churned, and cheese made. They might see a farmer plowing the garden with a team of horses or catch a meal being made from scratch.

PEDERNALES FALLS STATE PARK (ages 4 and up)
6 miles north of U.S. Highway 290 off Farm Road 3232, Johnson City 78636 (830–868–7304; 512–389–8900 for camping reservations).

More than 20 miles of meandering trails and a wide, gently rolling waterfall make Pedernales Falls State Park a nice getaway place. Your family can have a picnic or camp out; fish, swim, or canoe the river; and hike or bike along challenging or easy trails. During wet springs, the falls are truly impressive. During drier months kids scramble around the rocks separating the pools. Get to the park off Farm Road 2766 about 9 miles south of Highway 281 in Johnson City or from Farm Road 3232 about 6 miles north of Highway 290 between Johnson City and Dripping Springs

Bee Cave

On U.S. Highway 71, west of Austin.

Two beautiful examples of collapsed grottoes can be found about 18 miles west of the small community of Bee Cave. Your kids can enjoy themselves swimming and hiking at one and go on a scenic informative walk at the other.

HAMILTON POOL PRESERVE (ages 4 and up)

On Farm Road 3238, 13 miles south of Texas Highway 71 (512–264–2740). Open 9:00 A.M. to 6:00 P.M. daily. Admission: $5.00 per vehicle, $2.00 per pedestrian.

 Gorgeous Hamilton Pool Preserve has been a popular swimming hole with Hill Country residents for many decades. Its 60-foot travertine waterfall spills into a deep jade-green pool. The park has picnic areas and a nice nature trail that follows Hamilton Creek through a heavily wooded canyon to the Pedernales River. Rangers close the park when the parking lot is full, so plan on arriving early on weekends during hot weather.

WEST CAVE PRESERVE (ages 4 and up)

On Farm Road 3238, 1 mile from Hamilton Pool, first gate on the right after crossing Pedernales River (512–825–3442). Tours at 10:00 A.M., noon, 2:00 and 4:00 P.M. weekends only. Donations requested.

If you think Hamilton Pool is lovely, and it is, wait until you see the exquisite West Cave Preserve. This private thirty-acre natural preserve is home to many rare and endangered plants and birds, so access is by guided tour only. The tour crosses a grassland savanna with wildflower meadows and stands of ashe juniper, then descends sharply into a narrow, riverine canyon to the collapsed grotto and cave at the end of the tour. The travertine waterfall into the crystal-clear pool surrounded by ferns is one of the most spectacular, yet rarely seen, sights in Texas. Tour groups are limited to thirty people, and no reservations are taken.

Where to Eat and Stay

For restaurants and lodgings see listings under Austin.

Coastal Plains

his may be the coast, but it ain't the French Riviera. Texans pride themselves on their friendliness and informality, but coastal Texans crank those
traits up a few notches instead of worrying about a new coat of paint for
the house or boat. If you want laid-back times, the Texas coast is where to
find them. Pirates used to love this place, especially the famous Jean Lafitte,
who, legends say, buried much treasure around Galveston. Today, most of the
gold found along the coast comes from fishing or tourism.

U.S. Highways 77 and 59 and I-37 are the main thoroughfares in this
region. Highway 77 is the only way to get from the South Padre Island area to
North Padre Island by car, but it doesn't come very close to the coast. You
should also be warned that the stretch of Highway 77 through Kenedy County
is very long with no facilities of any kind, so fill up both your car and your kids
before you set out. The road that most closely connects with the coast itself is
Texas Highway 35, a worthy scenic attraction in its own right, especially if you
wander off on the many farm roads that snake out to coastal towns. This is a
route that demands that you take your time. Highway 35 is also the only road
that will take you all the way from the Corpus Christi area directly to the
Galveston area.

Port Isabel

About 25 miles east of Brownsville on Texas Highway 48.

Port Isabel, a small, picturesque village on the Laguna Madre, the body of
water between the Texas mainland and South Padre Island, is a distinctly sea-
side community where marinas abound and the sport fishing is spectacular.

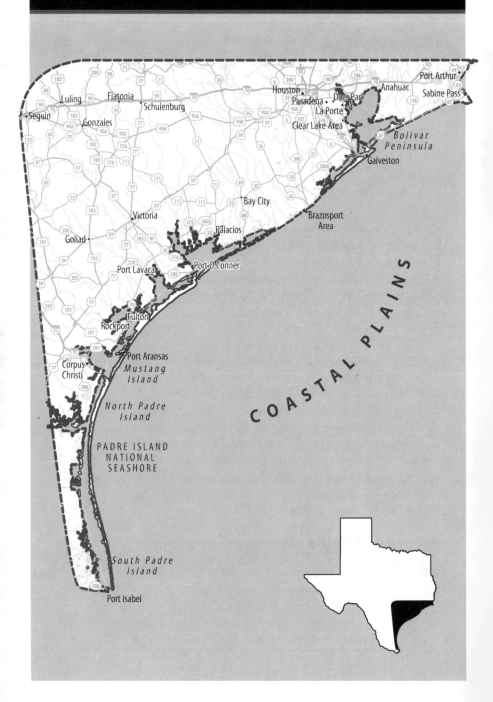

Allan's Top
Annual Family
Fun Events

- Houston Livestock Show and Rodeo, Houston, February (713–791–9000)
- Houston International Festival, Houston, April (713–654–8808)
- Texas Crab Festival, Crystal Beach, April (409–684–5940)
- Luling Watermelon Thump, Luling, June (830–875–3214)
- Rockport Art Festival, Rockport, July (361–729–6445 or 800–826–6441)
- Celebration of American Cultures, Goliad, July (361–645–3405)
- Pasadena Livestock Show and Rodeo, Pasadena, September (281–487–0240)
- Bayfest, Corpus Christi, September (361–887–0868)
- Czhilispeil, Flatonia, October (979–865–3920)
- Dickens on the Strand, Galveston, December (409–765–7834)

PORT ISABEL LIGHTHOUSE STATE HISTORIC SITE (ages 4 and up)

Alongside Texas Highway 100, Port Isabel 78578, at the causeway (956–943–1172). Open daily 10:00 to 11:30 A.M. and 1:00 to 5:00 P.M. Adults $1.00, children 50 cents.

Port Isabel, just east of Brownsville, is at the southernmost end of the Texas coast. You can see one of the few remaining lighthouses in the state here. Built in 1853, the lighthouse was used until 1905. You can climb the stairs inside for a panoramic view of the coastal plain. It's also a great place for photos of the kids.

LAGUNA ATASCOSA NATIONAL WILDLIFE REFUGE

At the intersection of Farm Roads 106 and 1847, Port Isabel (956–748–3607). Open daylight hours.

North of Port Isabel, on the shores of the Laguna Madre, is the Laguna Atascosa National Wildlife Refuge. The refuge includes 46,000 acres of habitat for wintering waterfowl and many area birds and mammals. You can walk or drive over several routes. The visitors center has exhibits, lists, and picnic areas.

Within the boundaries of Laguna Atascosa is **Adolph Thomas Jr. County Park,** which offers fishing piers, a boat ramp, picnic areas, a playground, a nature trail, and RV sites. Call (956) 748-2044 for information and reservations.

The Texas Coast From Port Isabel to Sabine Pass, the coast curves gently for 367 miles (624 if you count the bay areas), its many cities hiding behind barrier islands.

With such a large coast, Texas is frequently hit by hurricanes, a fact you should be aware of if you travel between June and November. One of the largest hurricanes ever to hit the state in recorded history was the Great Storm of 1900 that killed 6,000 people and nearly destroyed all of Galveston. Houston took advantage of its neighbor's misfortune and built itself a giant ship channel and more oil refineries than you can count to turn itself into the nation's fourth largest city, a metropolitan area with more than two million people.

South Padre Island

Connecting the mainland to South Padre Island is the Queen Isabella Causeway. At 2.6 miles long, this is Texas's longest bridge, and it offers a breathtaking view.

South Padre Island is a mecca for tourists year-round, although it hits its peak in late spring and summer. Your family can do it all here: bask in the sun, dive, swim, boat, sail, parasail, fish, ride horses, or frolic with dolphins.

The island is at the tropical tip of Texas, with the tranquil waters of Laguna Madre Bay on the west side and the vast beauty of the Gulf of Mexico on the east side. South Padre has 34 miles of white sand beaches, windswept dunes, and balmy weather. And it's close to both Brownsville and Mexico.

An exciting event, certain to delight children, is the **South Padre Island Windsurfing Blowout,** held in early May. The waters are filled with colorful windsurfers ripping across waves and flying in the wind. Call (800) 343-2368 for details and schedule information.

One time you might want to avoid South Padre is during spring break in March, when thousands upon thousands of college students descend on the area, turning the beaches into one giant party. If you do go then, the condos I've recommended do not accept spring breakers, so they're more quiet than most.

Texas Trivia More than one third of Texas's population lives on the coast.

ISLAND EQUESTRIAN CENTER (ages 8 and up)

On South Padre Boulevard, South Padre Island, 1 mile north of the Convention Center (800–761–HOSS).

One way your children are certain to enjoy the beaches of South Padre Island is trotting over them on horseback. The Island Equestrian Center has horses available for all levels and ages of riders, including pony rides for kids under six. The company offers guides and instruction at no extra cost. You can also enjoy carriage rides and hayrides.

JEREMIAH'S LANDING (ages 4 and up)

100 South Padre Boulevard, South Padre Island 78597 (956–761–2131). Open weekends April and May, then daily between Memorial Day and Labor Day. Adults $11.95, children $9.25.

For more conventional kid-style fun, visit Jeremiah's Landing, a water park featuring seven water slides, a video arcade, and a snack bar.

Where to Eat

Cross-Eyed Pelican. *823 Garcia Street, Port Isabel 78578 (956–943–8923).* One of the best seafood restaurants in the area, all-you-can-eat buffet lunches weekdays. $$

Mexquito. *802 Garcia, Port Isabel 78578 (956–943–6106).* More all-you-can-eat specials, featuring unique Mexican-style seafood. $$

Paulino's. *4600 Padre Boulevard, South Padre Island 78597 (956–761–4000).* Wonderful Italian food in a family-owned restaurant loved by locals. $–$$$

Where to Stay

Accommodations are plentiful around Padre Island. Smart families opt for a condo, giving them plenty of living space and the option of cooking many or all of their own meals. Prices range from very affordable to very expensive.

On the Gulf side of the island, check out:

La Playa. *2308 Gulf Boulevard, South Padre Island 78597 (956–761–4689).*

Sandpiper. *3708 Gulf Boulevard, South Padre Island 78597 (800–426–6530).*

Tiki. *6608 Padre Boulevard, South Padre Island 78597 (800–551–8454).*

On the Laguna Madre side, check out:

Las Brisas. *227 West Morningside Boulevard, South Padre Island 78597 (800–241–5111).*

Sunset on the Bay. *5101 Laguna Boulevard, South Padre Island 78597 (956–761–1399).*

For More Information

South Padre Island Convention and Visitors Bureau. *600 Padre Boulevard, South Padre Island, TX 78597; (800)*

SO–PADRE. Visit the Web sites at www. sopadre.com or www.south-padre-island.com.

Corpus Christi and North Padre Island

At the intersections of U.S. Highway 77 and I–37.

Almost in the center of the Texas Gulf Coast, Corpus Christi is a major deep-water port and one of the state's most popular coastal playgrounds. The bracing salt air blankets the city, begging for travelers to slow down and relax and enjoy themselves. Texans usually refer to the town by its first name, and Corpus has a lot to offer visitors, from first-rate museums to some great recreational areas.

  LAKE CORPUS CHRISTI STATE PARK (ages 4 and up)
35 miles north of Corpus Christi on Farm Road 1068, Mathis 78368 (361–547–2635; 512–389–8900 for camping reservations).

Lake Corpus Christi is a 365-acre site overlooking the impoundment of the Nueces River. The park has many campsites and two dozen screened shelters and offers your family swimming, fishing, boating, picnicking, and the opportunity to see and photograph a large nesting area for white doves.

CORPUS CHRISTI ZOO (ages 2 and up)

On County Road 33, off Weber Street, Corpus Christi 78411 (512–814–8000). Open Wednesday through Sunday 9:00 A.M. to 6:00 P.M. Adults $5.00, children $3.00.

In addition to a collection of exotic birds, primates, and other animals in this 145-acre park, the facility features **Kidz Zoo,** the largest petting area in the United States, with two acres of barnyard buddies.

BAYFRONT ARTS AND SCIENCE PARK (ages 4 and up)

1900 Shoreline Drive, Corpus Christi 78401 (361–882–5603 or 800–678–6232).

The heart of the city of Corpus Christi can be found in and around the Bayfront Arts and Science Park complex. The **Water Garden** here is a cooling, soothing circle of more than one hundred fountains that are lighted at night. In late June the Water Garden hosts **Fiesta de Corpus Christi,** a celebration of the city's Hispanic heritage, with music, historical exhibits, and other events. Call (361) 857-6222. An even bigger family event happens here in September. Called **Bayfest,** the festival includes an expansive arts-and-crafts show, fireworks, parades on city streets and on the water, a sailboat regatta, and other boat races. Call (361) 887-0868 for more information.

Included in the Bayfront complex are the following attractions:

- The **Art Museum of South Texas,** (361) 825-3500, features the work of many area artists and has rotating exhibits. Admission: $3.00 adults, $2.00 students. Open Tuesday through Saturday 10:00 A.M. to 5:00 P.M., Sunday 1:00 to 5:00 P.M.

- The **Bayfront Plaza Auditorium,** (361) 882-2717, is home to concerts, musicals, and other shows. Times and prices of shows vary.

- The **Corpus Christi Museum of Science and History,** (361) 883-2862, houses the natural history of the area, including artifacts from sixteenth-century shipwrecks, a live reptile exhibit, and interactive hurricane displays. Admission: $5.00 adults, $3.00 children. Open Monday through Saturday 10:00 A.M. to 5:00 P.M., Sunday 1:00 to 5:00 P.M.

- **Harbor Playhouse,** (361) 888-7469, has children's shows, summer melodramas, and other theater works throughout the year. Tickets range from $10 to $12.

- **Heritage Park,** (361) 883-0639, features eight restored century-old homes and a multicultural center with changing exhibits focusing on the city's heritage. Free.

Texas Trivia In 1845, Gen. Zachary Taylor and his troops camped at Corpus Christi before marching off to fight in the Mexican War. Among the troops were future Civil War generals Robert E. Lee and Albert Sydney Johnston, future president of the Confederacy Jefferson Davis, and future U.S. president Ulysses S. Grant. The troops put on a performance of *Othello*. Grant, wearing a skirt and carrying a fan, played Desdemona.

  ### TEXAS STATE AQUARIUM (ages 2 and up)
2710 North Shoreline Drive, Corpus Christi 78402 (361–881–1200 or 800–477–GULF; www.txstateaq.com/visitor.htm). Open Monday through Saturday 9:00 A.M. to 6:00 P.M., Sunday noon to 6:00 P.M. Adults $8.75, children 12–17 $6.75, children 4–11 $5.00.

The Texas State Aquarium is one way to explore the depths of the Gulf of Mexico without getting your feet wet. Kids and adults will learn about more than 250 species of marine life and the beauty of a coral reef at this facility. Also featured are a rare river otter family and a shark "touch tank" where children can get a feel for this fascinating creature. The aquarium is located on Corpus Christi Beach, across the channel from the Bayfront Arts and Science Park and next to the U.S.S. *Lexington*.

  ### U.S.S. *LEXINGTON* MUSEUM (ages 6 and up)
2914 North Shoreline Drive, Corpus Christi 78402 (800–LADY–LEX; www. usslexington.com). Open daily 9:00 A.M. to 8:00 P.M. Memorial Day through Labor Day, open daily 9:00 A.M. to 5:00 P.M. the rest of the year. Adults $9.00, children $4.00.

The U.S.S. *Lexington* Museum is a fascinating tour for any family. This old aircraft carrier is steeped in history; it served longer than any other U.S. Navy carrier. Tours run all around the ship, including the bridge, the engine room, and the flight deck full of vintage planes. Several maritime exhibits and multimedia programs are also on display.

 ### COLUMBUS FLEET (ages 6 and up)
Cargo Dock One, Port of Corpus Christi 78402 (361–882–1232 or 512–886–4492). Open Monday through Saturday 10:00 A.M. to 5:00 P.M., Sunday noon to 5:00 P.M. Adults $8.00, children $4.00.

History will come alive for your children at the Columbus Fleet, re-creations of the three famous ships of Christopher Columbus. The ships were built in Spain to be precise, authentic duplicates of the *Niña, Pinta,* and *Santa María.* Located under the Harbor Bridge. The fleet's shore facilities include an exhibit center with historical displays on Spain, a gift shop, and a snack bar.

DOLPHIN CONNECTION (ages 4 and up)

5151 East Causeway Boulevard, Corpus Christi 78402 (361–882–4126). Adults $17, children $12.

Take a trip into the bay on the *Dolphin Connection* to watch dolphins in their natural habitat. The company makes two trips each morning from March through October. The boat ride even allows children to feed the cavorting cetaceans. Call well in advance for required reservations.

FLAGSHIP PADDLE WHEELER (ages 4 and up)

Peoples Street Pier, Slip 49, Corpus Christi 78402 (361–884–8306). Adults $7.50 to $9.00, children $4.50 to $5.00.

Another enjoyable boat ride is on the paddle wheeler *Flagship.* The boat takes you on hour-long, narrated cruises of the bay and harbor. Evening trips last an hour and a half.

PLAYLAND AT THE BEACH (ages 6 and up)

3001 Seagull Boulevard, Corpus Christi 78402 (361–884–7251). Open as weather permits, March through November. $4.00 per ride.

Playland at the Beach is an outdoor family park featuring go-carts, bumper boats, bumper cars, a playground, and a game room.

PIRATES OF THE GULF MINIATURE GOLF (ages 6 and up)

2901 West Surfside Drive, Corpus Christi 78402 (361–884–4774). Open daily April through August from 11:00 A.M. to 11:00 P.M.; September through March from 4:00 to 10:00 P.M. Friday, from 11:00 A.M. to 10:00 P.M. Saturday, and from noon to 9:00 P.M. Sunday. Adults $13.00, children $4.00.

INTERNATIONAL KITE MUSEUM (ages 6 and up)

3200 Surfside Drive, Corpus Christi 78402 (361–883–7456). Open daily 10:00 A.M. to 6:00 P.M. Free.

Every kid likes kites, and you'll find the International Kite Museum, in the Sandy Shores Beach Hotel, has a history of kites from as long as 2,000 years ago told in exhibits and videos.

PADRE ISLAND NATIONAL SEASHORE (ages 4 and up)

South of Corpus Christi at the end of Park Road 22, Corpus Christi 78412 (361–949–8068). Visitors center open 9:00 A.M. to 6:00 P.M. daily. Weekly entry fee: $10.00 per vehicle, $1.00 per hiker or bus rider. Camping: $8.00 per night.

This 110-mile-long island is one of the last natural seashores in the United States. The tip of the island is developed, but the remainder is a preserve accessible only by four-wheel-drive vehicles or very long hikes. Several beach condos rent four-wheelers. North Padré is a beachcomber's paradise, and the National Park Service will allow your kids to collect seashells, driftwood, and glass floats (from as far away as Portugal or Asia), but not artifacts like flint points or antique coins. The visitors center has information, exhibits, gifts, concessions, a bathhouse, and a picnic area. Although North Padre and South Padre Islands are separated only by a narrow channel of water, the two are unconnected by bridge or ferry service, and visitors cannot get to one from the other.

Scenic Drive Don't miss the drive along Texas Highway 35 from Port Aransas to Port Lavaca. It's a sunny, refreshing drive braced with salt breezes and quaint beachfront communities that begins with a ferry ride across Aransas Pass. Depending on the time of year and time of day, you're likely to see dolphins playing in the water or rare whooping cranes overhead. Perhaps most startling are the huge, twisted oaks leaning over almost backwards that line the road in the Rockport and Fulton area. In some cases the trees have grown so close together they look like a giant hedge towering above your car.

Where to Eat

Frank's Spaghetti House. *2724 Leopard Drive, Corpus Christi 78408 (351–882–0075).* Favorite local restaurant in same little red brick house since 1947. $–$$

Golden Corral. *5274 South Padre Island Drive, Corpus Christi 78411 (361–992–8667).* It's difficult to beat all-you-can-eat good food. Special kids' desserts. $–$$

Landry's. *600 North Shoreline Drive, Corpus Christi 78401 (361–882–6666).* Well known throughout Texas as the place to go for seafood. Many entrees give you the choice of having them either baked, blackened, fried, or grilled. Children's plates available. $$

Where to Stay

Best Western Sandy Shores. *3200 Surfside Boulevard, Corpus Christi 78402 (800–528–1234).* Pool, sauna, whirlpool, self-service laundry, gift shop, snack shops, and several restaurants. Children under twelve stay **Free**. Within walking distance of several attractions and has its own beach. $$–$$$

La Quinta South. *6225 South Padre Island Drive, Corpus Christi 78411*

(361–991–5730 or 800–531–5900). Pool, **Free** breakfast, and children under 18 stay **Free**. $$

Sea Shell Inn. *202 Kleberg Place, Corpus Christi 78402 (361–888–5391).* On the beach and has an outdoor grill, kitchenettes, a self-service laundry, and a pool. Within walking distance of both the Texas State Aquarium and the U.S.S. *Lexington* Museum. $$˙

For More Information

Corpus Christi Information Center. *1201 North Shoreline Boulevard, P.O. Box 2664, Corpus Christi, TX 78403; (800)*

678–6232 or (361) 881–1888. Visit the Web site at www.cctexas.org/cvb.

Port Aransas

If your kids can't catch fish in Port Aransas, they just aren't trying. The Aransas Pass area advertises itself as the place "where they bite every day," and that's no exaggeration. You can fish **Free** from the beaches, the jetties, and the Station Street pier, or you can hire a boat for bay fishing or hop on a group charter boat for deep-sea fishing. The town is also full of curio shops, boutiques, and restaurants. Call (800) 633–3028 for information on the area and boat charters, or visit the Web site at www.portaransas.org.

ROBERTS POINT PARK (ages 4 and up)

At the ferry landing on Port Street off Texas Highway 361, Port Aransas 78373 (800–45–COAST).

   Big boats and dolphins are usually fascinating to children, so stop by Roberts Point Park. It's the perfect place to watch cargo ships pass by heading to and from the Port of Corpus Christi and to watch dolphins chase smaller craft across the bay. The park also has picnic areas, a fishing pier, and a children's playground.

MUSTANG ISLAND STATE PARK (ages 4 and up)

On Park Road 53, Port Aransas 78373 14 miles west of Port Aransas, just north of North Padre Island off Texas Highway 361 (361–749–5246; 512–389–8900 for camping reservations).

The 3,700-acre Mustang Island State Park is very popular with Texans. In addition to its pristine beaches, it has campsites, shower facilities, and hiking trails.

MUSTANG RIDING STABLES (ages 8 and up)

On Texas Highway 361, Port Aransas 78373 (361–991–RIDE or 361–749–5055). Open daily 9:00 A.M. to 6:00 P.M. Adults $20, children $15.

Enjoy horseback riding on the Mustang Island beach at Mustang Riding Stables. The company provides horseback riding, hayrides, and beach parties. Beginners are welcome, and instruction is provided.

Allan's Top Family Fun Ideas

1. Six Flags AstroWorld/WaterWorld, Houston
2. Moody Gardens, Galveston
3. Sun and surf along the Gulf Coast beaches
4. Space Center Houston, Clear Lake City
5. Houston Astros baseball, Houston
6. Houston Museum of Science, Houston
7. Texas State Aquarium, Corpus Christi
8. Houston Zoological Gardens, Houston
9. Port Lavaca State Fishing Pier, Port Lavaca
10. Center for Transportation and Commerce, Galveston

For More Information

Port Aransas Tourist and Convention Bureau. *421 West Cotter Street, Port Aransas, TX 78373; (800) 45–COAST or* *(361) 749–5919. Visit the Web site at www.portaransas.org*

Rockport and Fulton

Rockport, on Texas Highway 35, is more than just a great place to watch birds, go fishing, or swim in the surf. The town is full of crafts shops and art galleries, and each Fourth of July weekend it holds the **Rockport Art Festival,** one of the largest in the state. The festival includes art, food, fireworks, and a special children's art tent. Call (361) 729-6445 or (800) 826-6441 for more information.

Texas Trivia The top ten state parks for day visits are the San Jacinto Battleground, Cedar Hill, Garner, Caddo Lake, Lyndon B. Johnson, Lake Texana, Bastrop, Mustang Island, Lake Corpus Christi, and Eisenhower.

 ### TEXAS MARITIME MUSEUM (ages 6 and up)
On Texas Highway 35, Rockport 78382 at the Rockport Harbor (361–729–1271). Open Tuesday through Saturday 10:00 A.M. to 4:00 P.M., Sunday 1:00 to 4:00 P.M. Adults $4.00, children $2.00.

Learn about everything from Spanish explorers to pirates to Gulf oil-drilling rigs at the Texas Maritime Museum. The museum also has a number of changing displays and hands-on exhibits for kids.

 ### ROCKPORT BEACH PARK (ages 4 and up)
 Just north of the museum at 210 Navigation, Rockport 78382 (361–729–9392).
Your family can relax on the white sand beach, have a picnic in the shade, fish from the pier, swim in the saltwater pool, or have fun at the playground.

 ### GOOSE ISLAND STATE PARK (ages 4 and up)
 On Park Road 12, Rockport 78382, 10 miles north of Rockport off Texas Highway 35 (361–729–2858; for camping reservations call 512–389–8900).
More outdoor fun can be had at Goose Island State Park. Located at the conjunction of Aransas, Copano, and St. Charles Bays, the park is noted for its lovely campsites, good fishing, and opportunities to see whooping cranes and other waterfowl. Here you'll also find the Big Tree, the state-champion coastal live oak, a gnarled 1,000-year-old wonder of nature.

Bird Festivals Several local communities sponsor festivals celebrating their most popular local birds.

- Eagle Fest, Emory, January (903–473–3913)
- CraneFest, Big Spring, February (915–263–7641)
- Attwater's Prairie Chicken Festival, Eagle Lake, March (409–234–2780)
- Migration Celebration, Clute, April (800–938–4853)
- Bluebird Festival, Willis Point, April (903–873–3111)
- Hummerbird Celebration, Rockport, September (800–242–0071)
- Rio Grande Valley Birding Festival, Harlingen, November (800–531–7346)

FULTON MANSION STATE HISTORICAL PARK (ages 6 and up)
317 Fulton Beach Road, Fulton 78358 (361–729–0386).

Fulton Mansion is special for families at certain times of the year when staff members go all out. They conduct regular historical tours Wednesday through Sunday, but around Halloween they host a two-day event highlighting the mansion's history of hauntings, and every December they celebrate with a traditional Victorian Christmas. The house, built in the 1870s, was an architectural wonder at the time and a tribute to gracious living during the area's cattle-boom days.

COPANO BAY STATE FISHING PIER (ages 4 and up)
On Route 35, Fulton 78358, 5 miles from Rockport (800–792–1112).

Copano Bay State Fishing Pier is the longest lighted fishing pier in the world, more than 1.5 miles long. There are bait and tackle shops, snack bars, and rest rooms at each side of the pier, with boat ramps on the south side.

ARANSAS NATIONAL WILDLIFE REFUGE (ages 4 and up)
Off Texas Highway 35, Austwell 77950 (361–286–3559). Interpretive Center open daily 8:00 A.M. to 5:00 P.M. **Free**.

Aransas National Wildlife Refuge is famous as the winter home for the nearly extinct whooping cranes who fly 2,500 miles from their summer refuge in northern Alberta's Wood Buffalo National Park. More than 300 other species of birds also make Aransas their usual vacation spot, along with native deer, javelinas, and raccoons. Best time to see the rare whooping cranes is between November and March. The **Wildlife Interpretive Center** has mounted specimens and a slide show on the whoopers. Finding the refuge can be difficult if you miss one of the signs, so call ahead for directions.

The best way for your family to see whooping cranes is from the sea, since you can't walk very far out into the marshlands that make up much of the wildlife refuge. Prices are usually in the $20 to $30 per person range. **Fisherman's Wharf, Inc.,** out of Port Aransas conducts five-hour narrated trips to see the whoopers. Call (361) 749-5760. Other firms with varying itineraries operate out of Rockport. The most famous of these is **Captain Ted's,** docked at the Sandollar Pavilion in Rockport, (361) 729-9589 or (800) 338-4551, or visit his Web site at www. apluswebs.com/Capt.TedsWhoopingCraneTours.

Where to Eat

Crazy Cajun. *303 Beach Street, Port Aransas 78336 (361–749–5069).* Cajun-style seafood served up family style on butcher paper. $$

Hu Dat Restaurant. *61 Broadway, Fulton 78358 (361–790–7621).* Unique blend of Cajun and Vietnamese foods. $

Kline's Cafe. *106 South Austin Street, Rockport 78382 (361–729–8538).* Something for just about any taste here; steaks, seafood, Mexican food, and generous portions. $-$$

Seafood and Spaghetti Works. *710 South Alister Street, Port Aransas 78336 (361–749–5666).* Seafood, steaks, pasta and pizza; Sunday brunch buffet. $$

Silver Anchor. *115 South Fulton Beach Road, Fulton 78358 (361–790–7033).* All sorts of fresh seafood, special children's menu. $$

Where to Stay

Anthony's by the Sea. *732 Pearl Street, Rockport 78358 (361–729–6100 or 800–460–2557).* Gorgeous patio, secluded pool, sumptuous breakfasts, separate cabin perfect for families. $$$

Casa del Mar. *104 Dune Drive, Port Aransas 78336 (361–749–7116 or 800–799–CASA).* Walk down to the beach, swim in the pool, or cook outside on the barbecue grills. $$–$$$

Hummingbird Lodge and Educational Center. *5652 Farm Road 1781,* *Fulton 78358 (361–729–7555 or 888–827–7555).* Away from all the bustle of the beaches in a tropical setting, with educational programs on area wildlife, especially hummingbirds. $$

Laguna Reef Hotel. *1021 Water Street, Rockport 78382 (361–729–1742 or 800–248–1057).* Has its own fishing pier and a swimming pool; just 2 blocks from the shops and galleries in downtown Rockport. $$–$$$

For More Information

Rockport-Fulton Chamber of Commerce. *404 Broadway, Rockport, TX*   *78382; (800) 826–6441 from outside Texas or (800) 242–0071.*

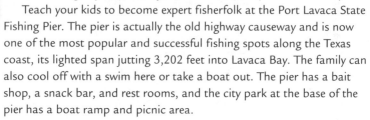

Port Lavaca, Port O'Conner, and Bay City

PORT LAVACA STATE FISHING PIER (ages 4 and up)

At the Texas Highway 35 Causeway, Port Lavaca 77972 (800–792–1112).

Teach your kids to become expert fisherfolk at the Port Lavaca State Fishing Pier. The pier is actually the old highway causeway and is now one of the most popular and successful fishing spots along the Texas coast, its lighted span jutting 3,202 feet into Lavaca Bay. The family can also cool off with a swim here or take a boat out. The pier has a bait shop, a snack bar, and rest rooms, and the city park at the base of the pier has a boat ramp and picnic area.

MATAGORDA ISLAND STATE PARK (ages 4 and up)

South Sixteenth at Maple Street, Port O'Conner 77982 (361–983–2215). Round-trip ferry fare is $10.00 for adults, $5.00 for children under 12. On weekends a shuttle makes trips from the docks to the Gulf beaches on the island for $2.00 for adults and $1.00 for children.

Located on a 38-mile-long barrier island, Matagorda Island State Park is one place you're certain to find uncrowded beaches. The fragile island, as narrow as .75 mile wide in some places, is both a state park and a national wildlife refuge. The island remains relatively secluded because the only access is by boat; either your own, a rental boat, or the ferry on weekends and holidays. Surfboards and bicycles are allowed on the ferry. Once on the island you can fish, hunt, hike, bicycle, comb the beach, swim, get some sun, or camp out.

Texas Trivia The first Texas tourist was Alonzo Alvarez de Piñeda, who visited the Matagorda area in 1514. He claimed the land for Spain and named it *Amichel.* The name didn't stick.

MATAGORDA COUNTY MUSEUM (ages 4 and up)

2100 Avenue F, Bay City 77404 (409–245–7502). Open Tuesday through Friday 10:00 A.M. to 4:00 P.M., Saturday and Sunday 1:00 P.M. to 4:00 P.M. Children's Museum hours are Friday 10:00 A.M. to 1:00 P.M., Saturday and Sunday 1:00 to 4:00 P.M. **Free**.

All the history of this unique area is here, along with a special Children's Museum section featuring "please touch" exhibits and programs.

Victoria

TEXAS ZOO (ages 4 and up)

110 Memorial Drive, Victoria 77901 (361–573–7681; www.viptx.net/texaszoo). Open daily 10:00 A.M. to 5:00 P.M. except Thanksgiving, Christmas, and New Year's. Adults $2.50, children $1.50.

Your family can get a close-up look at most of the animals of the Lone Star State at the Texas Zoo. Texas has wildly diverse natural habitats from one end of the state to the other, being home to more than 700 species of animals. The Texas Zoo exhibits a wide variety of these native animals: armadillo, bald eagle, black bear, coati, jaguarundi, margay, ocelot, otter, pelican, porcupine, prairie dog, rattlesnake, tortoise, and red wolf are just a few. Nestled in a curve of the Guadalupe River, the zoo also features native plants, a wildflower garden, an observation beehive, and special family programs and events.

Texas Trivia Matagorda Island State Park has recorded 317 species of birds, one of the largest numbers in the nation. Bird-watchers have spotted 110 different species in a single day there.

MCNAMARA HISTORICAL MUSEUM (ages 6 and up)

502 Liberty Street, Victoria 77901 (361–575–8227). Open Thursday and Friday noon to 5:00 P.M., Saturday and Sunday 1:00 to 5:00 P.M. **Free**.

This old Victorian homestead has a good collection of Texana, including documents and artifacts from the Spanish, Mexican, and Texan eras. The O'Conner gallery has changing exhibits of local artists and craftspeople.

VICTORIA RIVERSIDE PARK AND ROSE GARDEN (ages 4 and up)

502 McCright Drive, Victoria 77901 (361–572–2763).

If your family likes outdoor fun, they'll find a lot in and around Victoria. Riverside Park and Rose Garden is 562 acres of woodlands bordered by 4.5 miles of the Guadalupe River. The park has an exercise trail, a duck pond, baseball and softball diamonds, a playground, and 200 picnic spots. The garden features 1,500 rose bushes representing 105 varieties, an ornamental water fountain, a gazebo, and walkways.

SAXET LAKES PARK (ages 4 and up)

On Timberline Drive, Victoria 77905, 2 miles south of Victoria off U.S. Highway 59 (361–573–5277). Open daily from 6:00 A.M. to sunset.

More outdoor opportunities exist at Saxet Lakes Park, including fishing, swimming, picnic areas, and boat ramps.

COLETO CREEK RESERVOIR AND PARK (ages 4 and up)

15 miles west of Victoria on U.S. Highway 59, Victoria 77905 (mailing address: P.O. Box 68, Fannin 77960; 361–575–6366).

Coleto Creek features a 3,100-acre lake, and your family can fish, boat, swim, picnic, camp out, hike along nature trails, or have fun at the volleyball court or playground.

LAKE TEXANA STATE PARK (ages 4 and up)

On Farm Road 111, Edna 77957, off U.S. Highway 59, 35 miles east of Victoria (361–782–5718; 512–389–8900 for camping reservations).

Lake Texana State Park has 125 miles of shoreline around the reservoir. Fishing is excellent, as are opportunities to see some of the more than 225 bird species that have been spotted here along with animals like deer, rabbits, and raccoons. The park has three fishing piers (two of them lighted), one fishing jetty, a fish-cleaning station, nature trails, campsites, and shaded picnic areas.

Where to Eat

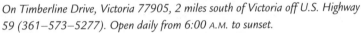

Golden Corral. *5102 North Navarro, Victoria 77904 (361–578–8176).* All-you-can-eat buffet and special children's desserts. $–$$

Pelican's Wharf. *2912 Houston Highway, Victoria 77901 (361–578–5253).* Variety of fare, including seafood and steaks. $$

Where to Stay

Comfort Inn. *1906 Houston Highway, Victoria 77901 (361–574–9393). Pool,* **Free** *continental breakfast.* $$

La Quinta. *7603 North Navarro, Victoria 77904 (361–572–3585). Pool,* **Free** *breakfast, many handicap-accessible rooms.* $$

For More Information

Victoria Convention and Visitors Bureau. *700 Main Center, Victoria, TX* *77901; (800) 926–5774 or (361) 573–5277.*

Goliad

Goliad means a lot to Texans. Not only was it a prime Spanish colonial city, but Col. James Fannin and 342 men were massacred here after surrendering to Mexican forces just after the fall of the Alamo. Also, Gen. Ignacio Zaragosa was born here. He led the Mexicans in their defeat of the French at the city of Puebla on May 5, 1862. That victory continues to be celebrated in Mexico and Texas as Cinco de Mayo, perhaps the premier holiday for Hispanic Texans.

GOLIAD STATE PARK (ages 4 and up)

On U.S. Highway 183, Goliad 77963, 1 mile south of Goliad (361–645–3405; 512–389–8900 for camping reservations).

Goliad State Park is a 2,208-acre park preserving the Mission Nuestra Señora del Espíritu Santo de Zuniga, established in 1749. In addition to interpretive displays, the park has camping and picnic areas. If the kids need a dunking, there is a city-operated swimming pool across the street that is open from noon to 8:00 P.M. during the summer.

PRESIDIO LA BAHIA (ages 6 and up)

On U.S. Highway 183, Goliad 77963, 2 miles south of Goliad (361–645–3752). Open daily 9:00 A.M. to 4:45 P.M. except Good Friday and Christmas. Adults $2.00, children 50 cents.

Presidio La Bahia, south of town just past the San Antonio River, is the Spanish fort built here to protect the mission and the colonists. The fortress has been excavated and restored, and the museum houses many items uncovered during that excavation. Included are artifacts

depicting nine levels of civilization at the site. The mass grave of Fannin
and his men are a couple hundred yards south of the Presidio.

 GENERAL ZARAGOSA STATE HISTORIC SITE (ages 6 and up)
*At Presidio La Bahia, Goliad 77963 (361–645–2282). Open Friday 1:00 to
5:00 P.M., Saturday and Sunday 8:00 A.M. to 5:00 P.M.*
This is the reconstructed birthplace of Ignacio Zaragosa.

For More Information

Goliad Chamber of Commerce. *205
South Market Street, P.O. Box 606, Goliad,
TX 77963; (361) 645–3563.*

Texas Weather You'll hear Texans often saying that if you
don't like the current weather, wait a few minutes and it'll change.
Don't believe them. In general, Texas weather is remarkably consistent,
even though it varies considerably from north to south because of the
size of the state. Temperatures range from a summer mean of seventy-
eight degrees and a winter mean of forty degrees in the Panhandle to
eighty-four degrees and sixty-one degrees, respectively, in the Lower Rio
Grande Valley. Average annual rainfall varies widely across the state,
from 59 inches in east Texas to less than 8 inches in west Texas. Only in
deep winter can you expect drastic, sudden changes of weather, when
what Texans call a "blue norther" blows in on an Arctic front and can
drop temperatures forty degrees in a few minutes.

Texas weather can be very violent, though. An average of 126 tornadoes strike Texas every year (the most of any state), usually from March
to May and usually along the Red River Valley. Also, hurricanes spawn
many tornadoes (like the record number of 115 tornadoes that swirled
into life by Hurricane Beulah in 1967). Hurricane season is June to
November, when you should pay close attention to weather reports if
you're traveling along the coast.

Gonzales, Luling, and Seguin

You'll discover more Texas history in Gonzales, home to the **Come and Take It! Celebration** in early October. The festival celebrates the first battle flag of Texas, created when Texians stitched the words COME AND TAKE IT along with a small cannon on a banner as they protected the village cannon against advancing Mexican troops. The Mexicans retreated after a brief skirmish. The celebration includes a parade, battle reenactment, arts-and-crafts fair, and canoe races. For information on the festival, call (830) 672-6532.

The city of Luling is known for two things. First are the numerous oil-rig pump jacks around town that are painted with a variety of designs or as cartoon characters. Some, like the woodpecker, are fascinating to little kids. Second is the annual Luling Watermelon Thump in late June. The Thump, like many such Texas festivals, has a parade, many arts-and-crafts booths, a carnival, musical entertainment, food, dances, and a rodeo, but it also features such contests as watermelon eating and the World Championship Watermelon Seed Spitting Contest. Call (830) 875-3214.

GONZALES MEMORIAL MUSEUM (ages 6 and up)

414 Smith Street, Gonzales 78629 (830–672–6350). Open Tuesday through Saturday 10:00 A.M. to noon and 1:00 to 5:00 P.M., Sunday 1:00 to 5:00 P.M. **Free**.

The Gonzales battle is commemorated at the Gonzales Memorial Museum. The star of the museum is the cannon the Texians were taunting the Mexicans with, the cannon that fired the first shot of the Texas Revolution.

GONZALES PIONEER VILLAGE (ages 6 and up)

On U.S. Highway 183, Gonzales 78629, just north of Gonzales (830–672–2157). Open Saturday 10:00 A.M. to 5:00 P.M., Sunday 1:00 to 5:00 P.M. Adults $2.50, children $1.00.

The Gonzales Pioneer Village will help your kids understand the hardships of pioneers on the Texas frontier in the 1800s. The site has several restored buildings, including a log cabin, blacksmith shop, and church. Costumed volunteers make the history come to life, demonstrating pioneer skills. Located on Highway 183, about .25 mile north of the city.

PALMETTO STATE PARK (ages 4 and up)

On Park Road 11, Gonzales 78629, off U.S. Highway 183 between Gonzales and Luling (830–389–8900; for camping reservations call 512–389–8900).

Palmetto State Park has a wide diversity of plant life in an area known as Ottine Swamp, where many eastern and western plant species merge. Also, more than 240 species of birds have been identified within the park's 178 acres. The park has picnic areas, campsites, hiking trails, swimming, and fishing. Facilities here were among those built at several Texas state parks by the Civilian Conservation Corps during the Depression.

MAX STARCKE PARK (ages 4 and up)

Texas Highway 123, Luling 78648, at the Guadalupe River, Luling (830–379–4853).

Max Starcke Park is a beautiful place to cool off or have a picnic during the summer. Nestled beneath towering oak and pecan trees, the park has a swimming pool and eighteen-hole golf course.

LAKE MCQUEENEY (ages 4 and up)

On Farm Road 725, Sequin 78156, about 4 miles northwest of Seguin (830–557–9900).

Lake McQueeney is a popular spot for swimming, fishing, and especially waterskiing.

For More Information

Gonzales Chamber of Commerce. *414 Saint Lawrence Street, Gonzales, TX 78629; (830) 672–6532.*

Luling Chamber of Commerce. *421 East Davis Street, Luling, TX 78648; (830)* *875–3214. Visit the Web site at www. bcsnet.net/lulingcc/chamber.htm.*

Seguin Chamber of Commerce. *427 North Austin Street, P.O. Box 710, Seguin, TX 78156; (830) 379–6382. Visit the Web site at www.seguin.net.*

Flatonia and Schulenburg

This area is well known for its Czech heritage, and you can find spicy sausage and kolaches (small dough-wrapped sausages) just about everywhere. Flatonia celebrates this tradition every October with **Czhilispeil,** an elaborate chili cook-off festival with a parade, arts-and-crafts booths, a carnival, and live entertainment. Call (979) 865-3920.

Where to Eat

Frank's. *I–10 feeder at the Schulenberg exit, Schulenberg 78956 (979–743–3555).* Eating here on Sunday after church is a long-standing ritual for most locals. Very generous portions; many German and Czech specialties. Lobby is filled with country gift items for sale. $–$$

Texians, Texans, and Texicans

It seems that from the beginning of Anglo settlement in Texas there has always been some confusion about what to call its residents. Those of Sam Houston's time, during the Republic of Texas, commonly referred to themselves as "Texians," and you will usually see that term in historical documents for the period. However, after Texas became a state, the term "Texan" was used more often, usually by outsiders. Slowly, "Texan" overtook "Texian," and after the Civil War the older term was seldom heard. John Wayne confused the issue by referring to Lone Star State inhabitants as "Texicans" in several of his movies. That term has become fairly popular, though it's not commonly used. A group of Old West shooters in the Hill Country, for example, are the "Texican Rangers," and several Texans who feel strong connections with Texans of old refer to themselves as "Texicans."

Palacios and Brazosport

About midway along the Gulf Coast between Corpus Christi and Galveston is Palacios (Puh-lash-ush), with several marinas, RV parks, fishing piers, and three bayshore parks. The town is located on the Central Flyway, so you're certain to see hundreds of waterfowl, and several sailing regattas are held here each year.

Brazosport is the area around where the Brazos River empties into the Gulf of Mexico and includes the cities of Freeport, Quintana Beach, Surfside Beach, Lake Jackson, Clute, and Angleton. The towns are closely united, and all feature an almost endless variety of outdoor activities perfectly suited to families. Many companies offer charters for freshwater or deep-sea fishing or diving, and others rent boats of nearly all types and sizes.

Celebrate the area's culture at the **Hispanic Heritage Festival** in mid-September at Freeport Municipal Park. Watch the parade, listen to mariachis, and enjoy folkloric dancers, cultural displays, food, and a carnival. Call (409) 548–3532.

If you can't beat 'em, celebrate 'em. That's the philosophy behind the **Great Texas Mosquito Festival** in Clute every July. The family event features arts-and-crafts and food booths, live entertainment, a carnival, fun runs, bike tours, kid contests, and a 25-foot mosquito (he's the bug wearing a cowboy hat and boots). Call (409) 265-8392 or (800) 371-2971.

SAN BERNARD NATIONAL WILDLIFE REFUGE (ages 4 and up)

On County Road 306, Freeport 77541, just southwest of Freeport (979–849–6062). Open during daylight hours.

The San Bernard National Wildlife Refuge is a 24,000-acre refuge between Cedar Lake Creek and the San Bernard River along the coast. You'll find more than 400 species of wildlife to watch, including at least 250 types of birds. Mammals include armadillos, bobcats, coyotes, raccoons, and river otters.

BRYAN BEACH STATE RECREATION AREA (ages 4 and up)

Off Farm Road 1495, Freeport 77541, 2 miles south of Freeport (800–792–1112; 512–389–8900 for camping reservations).

Your family can swim, fish, or camp at Bryan Beach State Recreation Area, 2 miles south of Freeport on Farm Road 1495, then 3 miles south on Gulf Beach.

QUINTANA BEACH COUNTY PARK (ages 4 and up)

Take Farm Road 1495 south from Route 288 in Freeport for 1.7 miles, then County Road 723 east 3 miles to the park (mailing address: 313 West Mulberry, Angleton 77515; 979–849–5711, ext. 1541 or 800–872–7578).

Even more outdoor fun is yours at Quintana Beach County Park. This park is located on a picturesque island with shaded pavilions, rest rooms, showers, a multilevel fishing pier, and a playground. Everything is connected by an elevated, wheelchair-accessible boardwalk. Historic Coveney House, in the park, has a museum and natural-history displays. There are also campsites and an RV park.

SEA CENTER TEXAS (ages 4 and up)

On Texas Highway 332 at Plantation Drive, Lake Jackson 77566 (979–292–0100; www.tpwd.state.tx.us/fish/hatch/seacentbr.htm). Open Tuesday through Friday 9:00 A.M. to 4:00 P.M., Saturday 10:00 A.M. to 5:00 P.M., Sunday 1:00 to 4:00 P.M. Hatchery tours are available by reservation. **Free**.

Sea Center Texas, an aquarium and educational center in Lake Jackson, showcases a 22,000-square-foot fish hatchery for redfish and speckled trout. "Touch tanks" are included specially for children, along with three aquariums that feature freshwater fish, bay fish, and Gulf fish in their natural habitats. The hatchery is surrounded by a five-acre wetland site with a nature walk for viewing birds and other wildlife.

BRAZORIA COUNTY HISTORICAL MUSEUM (ages 6 and up)
100 East Cedar Street, Angleton 77515 (979–849–5711). Open 8:00 A.M. to 5:00 P.M.

The first Anglo settlers in Texas started out here, and this museum, located in the renovated 1897 courthouse, has comprehensive exhibits on that period of history.

Texas Birds

The bird you're most likely to see while you're traveling Texas roads is the common turkey buzzard. These are the big black birds circling in the sky waiting for you to provide them with lunch. Along back roads, the buzzards become a nuisance as they will wait until the very last second while dining on roadkill before flying off as your vehicle approaches.

Bird-watching is good in Texas almost anywhere, anytime. No other state offers the variety of birds Texas does, with three-fourths of all known American birds represented—about 600 recorded species—many of them very rare like the Colima warblers and whooping cranes.

The state's resident population—varying from gulls to pelicans along the coast, roadrunners to eagles in the west, and flycatchers to woodpeckers in the east—is augmented by hosts of migratory birds in cooler months.

The **Great Texas Coastal Birding Trail** was completed in July 2000. It is a 700-mile marked trail from Port Arthur to Brownsville, including 300 public sites with maps and information on birds.

You can get a checklist of Texas birds, other birding information, and details on the Coastal Birding Trail at most state parks or from the Texas Parks and Wildlife Department, 4200 Smith School Road, Austin, TX 78744; (800) 792-1112.

BRAZORIA NATIONAL WILDLIFE REFUGE (ages 4 and up)

1212 North Velasco Street, Angleton 77515; take Route 332 south from Lake Jackson to Farm Road 523, go north on 523 about 5 miles to County Road 227 and east on 227 for 1.7 miles to the gate (979–849–6061).

Brazoria National Wildlife Refuge is another area full of wildlife waiting to be spotted. Brazoria is open to the public only on the first full weekend of each month or by special arrangement. Officials ask that before visiting the refuge you stop by the headquarters on Velasco Street in Angleton.

CENTER FOR THE ARTS AND SCIENCES (ages 4 and up)

400 College Drive, Clute 77531 (9-9–265–7661). Open Tuesday through Saturday 10:00 A.M. to 5:00 P.M., Sunday 2:00 to 5:00 P.M.

Kids will love the south's largest shell collection at the Center for the Arts and Sciences. But that's not all. The center has fascinating and fun natural-science displays, including dinosaur skeletons, planetarium shows, a nature trail, live theater productions (many specifically for children), and art exhibits and classes.

Where to Eat

Capt. Ken's Backyard. *629 Canal Street, Surfside Beach 77541 (979–233–6756).* Fresh seafood, steaks, Sunday brunch buffet. $$

Potato Patch. *1415 Highway 332 West, Clute 77531 (979–265–4285).* Everything fresh and homemade, including bakery items that are served hot every twenty minutes. $-$$

Smithhart's Downtown Grill. *104 That Way, Lake Jackson 77566 (979–297–0082).* Great Texas food. $-$$

Where to Stay

Best Western. *915 Highway 332, Lake Jackson 77566 (979–297–3031 or 800–722–5094).* Pool, **Free** continental breakfast. $$

Days Inn. *1809 North Velasco, Angleton 77515 (979–849–2173 or 800–325–2525).* Pool, spa, **Free** continental breakfast, and kids under sixteen stay **Free**. $$

La Quinta Inn. *1126 Highway 332 West at Lazy Lane, Clute 77531 (979–265–7461 or 800–531–5900).* Rooms are large and quiet, **Free** continental breakfast, children under eighteen stay **Free**. $$

Surfside Motel. *330 Coral Court, Surfside Beach 77541 (979–233–4585).* Kitchenettes, a couple steps from the beach. $$

Scenic Drive The 40-mile drive on Farm Road 3005 from Surfside Beach along barrier islands will certainly give you a close look at
the Gulf of Mexico. If you're traveling north, that's Christmas, West,
and Galveston Bays on your left, the surf of the Gulf on your right. For
most of the road, it's all sand dunes and seagulls. It's a peaceful, quiet,
sometimes almost secluded drive until you hit the four-lane on Galveston Island, then development picks up with beach homes, condomini-
ums, and, finally, large hotels.

You'll find several spots to access the beach along the road, including the totally undeveloped Christmas Bay State Park at the southern
end and Galveston Island State Park near the northern end.

For More Information

Palacios Chamber of Commerce.
312 Main Street, Palacios, TX 77465;
(361) 972–2615 or (800) 611–4567.

**Southern Brazoria County Visitors
Bureau.** *159 North Brazosport Boulevard,
Clute, TX 77531; (979) 265–2508 or
(800) WET–GULF.*

Houston

Houston is the fourth largest city in the United States, and you won't doubt it
for a minute when you drive its highways, a spaghetti-bowl mixture of over-
and-under passes where major thoroughfares like U.S. Highway 59 and I-10
and Loop 610 and I-45 converge and all the drivers seem to be in a hurry. Better know where you're headed beforehand. The city sprawls out from the Gulf
area nearly to the Piney Woods.

Houston, founded in 1836 by a couple of real estate developers of ques-
tionable ethics, was built up on the swampy banks of Buffalo Bayou and over
time has taken control of its own destiny in a big way by dredging up the
remarkable Houston Ship Channel to make the city one of the top ports in the
country. Then–Vice President Lyndon B. Johnson ensured that *Houston* would
be the first word spoken from the Moon when he wrangled for NASA's
manned spacecraft headquarters to be in the city (and NASA has returned the
favor by naming the Space Center after him). Oil and gas production made the
city boom, and its economy is still strongly based on these two Texas staples.

229

You'll find Houstonians almost universally pleasant and friendly and charged with a can-do spirit. Visitors will discover more than enough to fill their days with family amusement parks, first-rate museums, professional sports, top-notch performing arts, fun festivals, and lots of recreational possibilities.

Texas Trivia

Approximately 19.8 million people live in Texas, the second most of any state after California. Of those, 80 percent now live in urban areas. Texas now has twenty-one cities with more than 100,000 inhabitants. The top ten:

- Houston has 1,841,064 people.
- San Antonio has 1,123,626 people.
- Dallas has 1,085,614 people.
- Austin has 608,053 people.
- El Paso has 600,277 people.
- Fort Worth has 489,277 people.
- Arlington has 301,199 people.
- Corpus Christi has 276,712 people.
- Plano has 198,186 people.
- Garland has 193,475 people.

BRAZOS BEND STATE PARK (ages 4 and up)

On Farm Road 1462, Needville 77461, 25 miles south of Houston (979–553–3243; 512–389–8900 for camping reservations).

Brazos Bend State Park is 4,897 acres of Coastal Plain. This Brazos River bottomland has beautiful oaks draped in grapevines and Spanish moss, small lakes and a marsh, and abundant wildlife that includes migratory and shore birds and more than a few alligators. The park has campsites and screened shelters, picnic areas, a nature study and photography tower, fishing, 9 miles of hiking and bike trails, a gift shop and visitors center (open on weekends), and the **George Observatory.** The observatory features a 36-inch telescope that is open to public viewing on Saturday nights. For information on telescope viewing, call the **Houston Museum of Natural History** at (713) 639–4634.

STEPHEN F. AUSTIN STATE PARK (ages 4 and up)

Off I–10 at San Felipe, 25 miles west of Houston (mailing address: P.O. Box 125, San Felipe 77473; 979–885–3613; 512–389–8900 for camping reservations).

A portion of the park celebrates the history of Texas since the town of San Felipe was the center of American colonization in the Mexican state of Texas from 1824 to 1836. A number of old buildings are preserved here, along with historical exhibits. In the wooded, recreational portion of the park, your family can picnic, camp out, or enjoy themselves at the swimming pool or playground. Park facilities include some screened shelters with electricity.

ASTRODOME (ages 6 and up)

Loop 610 South at Kirby Lane, Houston 77098 (713–799–9544). Tours daily at 11:00 A.M., 1:00 P.M., and 3:00 P.M. unless a game or event is taking place inside; $4.00 adults, $3.00 children.

Houston's come a long way since it was just a riverboat landing on Buffalo Bayou in 1836. Today it's the fourth largest city in the United States, one of the largest ports in the country, the center of Texas's oil industry, and an important part of the American space program. Families will discover much to do here. For more than thirty years, Houston has been best known as home of the Astrodome, the world's first indoor sports stadium with the world's first artificial grass. Your family can tour behind the scenes and see a film on how the architectural wonder was built.

The Astrodome and adjacent AstroHall and AstroArena host several conventions and shows throughout the year, the best known being the annual boat and travel show in January and the **Houston Livestock Show and Rodeo** every February. The rodeo, one of the largest in the United States, features top competitors, with top music entertainers every night. While the cowboys and singers are going at it in the Astrodome, livestock competition is taking place in the adjacent buildings, where there are also art exhibits and sales booths. And the grounds are surrounded by a huge carnival. Call (713) 791-9000.

HOUSTON ASTROS BASEBALL (ages 4 and up)

501 Crawford Street, Houston 77002 (713–259–8000 for information, 713–627–8767 for tickets; www.astros.com). Tickets: $1.00 to $29.00.

The Astros moved into their new home, Enron Field, in 2000. The new downtown ballpark is more traditional looking than the Astrodome, their old home, and features real grass, a retractable roof,

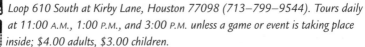

and a rushing locomotive that crosses the stands whenever the home team scores. Major-league baseball remains one of the last few bargains in professional sports, and this is especially true of the $1.00 seats the Astros continue to offer on game days only.

SIX FLAGS ASTROWORLD AND WATERWORLD (ages 4 and up)

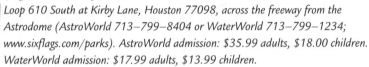

Loop 610 South at Kirby Lane, Houston 77098, across the freeway from the Astrodome (AstroWorld 713–799–8404 or WaterWorld 713–799–1234; www.sixflags.com/parks). AstroWorld admission: $35.99 adults, $18.00 children. WaterWorld admission: $17.99 adults, $13.99 children.

AstroWorld is one of the best amusement parks in the country, with more than one hundred shows, rides, and attractions. It also features the famous Texas Cyclone, one the best wooden roller coasters in the world, and several specialty steel coasters that go up, down, around, and backwards. For smaller kids, Bugs Bunny Land is filled with pint-size rides and activities. Adjacent WaterWorld is full of water slides, surf lagoons, swings, and a special water play area for children. Hours vary widely with seasons, so call for information.

HOUSTON ROCKETS BASKETBALL (ages 6 and up)

10 Greenway Plaza, Houston 77046 (713–627–DUNK; www.nba.com/rockets). Tickets: $25 to $105.

The Houston Rockets play basketball just up the road at the Compaq Center, off U.S. Highway 59. The Rockets, twice NBA champions, play from October to June. The Compaq Center—formerly called the Summit—is an intimate venue for roundball.

HOUSTON COMETS (ages 6 and up)

10 Greenway Plaza, Houston 77046 (713–627–WNBA; www.wnba.com/comets). Tickets: $8.00 to $140.00.

The Comets, in the new Women's National Basketball League, won the league's first four championships and are always contenders.

HOUSTON AEROS HOCKEY (ages 6 and up)

10 Greenway Plaza, Houston 77046 (713–974–7825; www.aeros.com). Tickets: $10.00 to $50.00.

Also quite popular locally, the Houston Aeros, a minor-league hockey team, play in the Compaq Center from October to April.

ADVENTURE BAY (ages 4 and up)

13602 Beechnut Drive, Houston 77083 (281–498–7946). Open Memorial Day through Labor Day, Monday through Thursday 10:00 A.M. to 6:00 P.M., Friday 10:00 A.M. to 7:00 P.M., Saturday and Sunday 11:00 A.M. to 7:00 P.M. Adults $17.99, children under 4 feet $13.99.

More family fun can be found at Adventure Bay. There are plenty of water slides and pools, a water coaster that blasts riders uphill, and the Pirates Cove children's area, with an interactive pirate ship.

CELEBRATION STATION (ages 4 and up)

I–45 at Rankin Road, Houston 77073 (281–872–7778) or U.S. Highway 59 at Hillcroft, Houston 77074 (713–981–7888). Open Sunday through Thursday 10:00 A.M. to 11:00 P.M., Friday and Saturday 10:00 A.M. to midnight. Admission varies with each ride or attraction, from $1.00 to $4.00. All-day passes to the Playland area are $16.99 for adults and $12.99 for children under 54 inches. Miniature golf is $4.99 per round.

Kids want more? Take them to one of the two Celebration Station locations, where they can play miniature golf, zip around on go-carts, try their skill at the batting cages, or play games in the video arcade.

FUNPLEX (ages 4 and up)

13700 Beechnut, Houston 77083 (281–530–7777). Open 11:00 A.M. to 10:00 P.M. daily. Cost is $3.75 to $6.25 for activities, and rides are $1.75 each.

FunPlex is an indoor family entertainment complex that features a roller rink, bowling, miniature golf, video arcades, three movie screens, and snack bars.

HOUSTON ARBORETUM AND NATURE CENTER (ages 4 and up)

4501 Woodway, Houston 77024 (713–681–8433). Trails open 8:30 A.M. to 6:00 P.M. daily. Visitors center open Monday through Saturday 9:00 A.M. to 5:30 P.M., Sunday 1:00 to 5:30 P.M. **Free**.

The Houston Arboretum is an environmental education center with classes and programs for children and adults and a preserve area for plants. Five miles of relaxing nature trails wind through 155 acres of woodlands, ponds, and prairie. Located near Memorial Park and the Galleria area.

CHILDREN'S MUSEUM OF HOUSTON (ages 4 and up)

1500 Binz Street (713–522–1138). Open Tuesday through Thursday and Saturday 9:00 A.M. to 5:00 P.M., Friday and Sunday noon to 5:00 P.M. Admission: $5.00.

The Children's Museum of Houston is a fun place, both to be in and to look at. The funky yellow, blue, and pink building, one of the five largest children's museums in the country, is in the heart of the city's museum district. Permanent and traveling exhibits focus on science and technology, environment and history, agriculture and archaeology, culture and art. Many of the displays are interactive and hands-on.

HOUSTON MUSEUM OF SCIENCE (ages 4 and up)

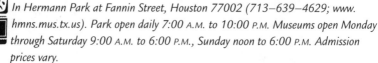

In Hermann Park at Fannin Street, Houston 77002 (713–639–4629; www. hmns.mus.tx.us). Park open daily 7:00 A.M. to 10:00 P.M. Museums open Monday through Saturday 9:00 A.M. to 6:00 P.M., Sunday noon to 6:00 P.M. Admission prices vary.

The Houston Museum of Natural Science, in Hermann Park at Fannin Street and Hermann Circle, is a first-rate collection of science museums tucked into a bucolic park setting in the middle of the city. Included are the following:

- The **Burke Baker Planetarium** is a sophisticated and entertaining place where your family can travel through a black hole or zip around constellations. On weekends, the planetarium shows rock-and-roll laser shows.

- A six-story glass house is home to the **Cockrell Butterfly Center** (713–639–4600), where more than 2,000 butterflies live in a tropical rain forest complete with a 40-foot waterfall.

- The **Cullen Gallery of Earth Science** displays a collection of more than 600 rare minerals and hundreds of gemstones.

- The **Hall of Health** features see-through mannequins and several hands-on exhibits.

- The **Wortham IMAX Theatre** shows exciting films projected onto a six-story-tall screen with incredible surrounding sound.

- A newer attraction at the Museum of Science is the **John P. McGovern Hall of the Americas,** a 12,000-square-foot series of galleries with exhibits designed to explain the ways humans inhabited the Western Hemisphere for thousands of years before Europeans dropped in. The hall has one of the best collections of pre-Columbian art and artifacts in the country. Many, such as the full-size Aztec gateway, are breathtaking. Call (713) 639–4629.

- Also in the park are the **Japanese Gardens,** a golf course, the **Houston Garden Center,** miniature golf and a regular golf course, a 4-mile hiking trail, paddleboats, a miniature train that runs around the park, and playground facilities.

HOUSTON ZOOLOGICAL GARDENS (ages 2 and up)

In Hermann Park, Houston 77002 (713–523–5888). Open daily 10:00 A.M. to 6:00 P.M. Adults $2.50, children 50 cents.

The Houston Zoo will thrill anyone in your family. Not a typical zoo, this one features a Tropical Bird House resembling an Asian jungle; where birds fly freely all around you; a hippo-dome; one of the best gorilla habitats in the United States; a large cat facility with rare white tigers; and an extensive collection of reptiles and vampire bats. The Wortham World of Primates is a 2.2-acre rain-forest habitat for the zoo's primates.

HOUSTON FIRE MUSEUM (ages 6 and up)

At Milam and McIlhenny Street, Houston 77002 (713–524–2526). Open Tuesday through Saturday 10:00 A.M. to 4:00 P.M. **Free**.

Your family can see the history of firefighting, from bucket brigades to horse-drawn pumpers to modern fire trucks, at the Houston Fire Museum, housed in a former fire station.

THE ORANGE SHOW (ages 4 and up)

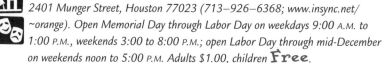

2401 Munger Street, Houston 77023 (713–926–6368; www.insync.net/ ~orange). Open Memorial Day through Labor Day on weekdays 9:00 A.M. to 1:00 P.M., weekends 3:00 to 8:00 P.M.; open Labor Day through mid-December on weekends noon to 5:00 P.M. Adults $1.00, children **Free**.

Any attempt to adequately describe the Orange Show would be impossible. The unique, Rube Goldberg–esque house and grounds were begun in the 1950s by owner Jeff McKissack, who had an obsession with everything orange—the fruit and the color. His stated goal was to encourage families to be healthier by drinking more juice and to be highly amused. Well, you'll definitely be amused here. This amazing place was opened to the public in 1979 and is now a park and performance center.

SPLASHTOWN (ages 6 and up)

21300 I–45, Spring 77373 (281–355–3300). Open April to October 10:00 A.M. to 8:00 P.M. Adults $20.99, children under 4 feet $14.99.

More water-based fun can be found at Splashtown, north of Houston in Spring. This is a large water park, one of the largest in Texas, with more than thirty-five different water slides and pools. It also has snack bars, picnic areas, and a bathhouse.

Texas Trivia The county with the largest population in Texas is Harris County (the Houston metropolitan area), with 3,087,153 people.

Where to Eat

Goode Company Barbecue. *5109 Kirby Drive, Houston 77098 (713–522–2530).* One of the best barbecue joints in Texas. Exceptional food, Texas-roadhouse atmosphere. Many unique items. $–$$

Shanghai Red's. *8501 Cypress, Houston 77012 (713–926–6666).* Seafood, steaks, and pasta are the highlights on the plate, but the huge ocean-going

ships turning in the Houston Ship Channel just outside are the big attraction. $$–$$$

Wunsche Bros. Cafe. *103 Midway Drive, Spring 77373 (281–350–1902).* Local favorite since 1949. Next door is **Old Town Spring,** a century-old railroad town that features a collection of more than 150 shops, boutiques, museums, and restaurants. $–$$

Where to Stay

La Quinta Inn–Astrodome. *Buffalo Speedway at Loop 610, Houston 77098 (800 NU–ROOMS).* Convenient location. Has eighteen other good hotels in town (call the same number). $$–$$$

Lexington Hotel Suites. *16410 I–45 North, Houston 77090 (281–821–1000*

or 800–53–SUITE). Full kitchens, pool, Free breakfast. $$–$$$

Shoney's Inn–Astrodome. *2364 South Loop West, Houston 77098 (713–799–2436 or 800–222–2222).* Within walking distance of AstroWorld, WaterWorld, and the Astrodome. $$–$$$

For More Information

Greater Houston Convention and Visitors Bureau. *801 Congress Avenue, Houston, TX 77002; (800) 365–7575 or*

(713) 227–3100. Visit the Web site at www.houston-guide.com.

Pasadena, Deer Park, and La Porte

Take Route 225 east from Houston.

The main highway from Houston through Pasadena, Deer Park, and La Porte isn't what most people would consider a scenic drive, but it is an interesting one. Route 225 cuts through the heart of the area's oil industry, the largest in the nation and the reason the Houston metropolitan region is as gigantic as it is. You'll see oil tanks and refineries of all sorts. It all takes on an eerie glow after sundown.

If you're in Pasadena in September, don't miss the **Pasadena Livestock Show and Rodeo.** It may not be as big as its cousin in Houston, but the cowboying is just as real, and you get a lot closer to all the competition at the Pasadena Fairgrounds (on Red Bluff Road at Fairmont) than in the Astrodome. Call (281) 487–0240.

DOW PARK AND BOTANICAL GARDENS (ages 4 and up)

P Street between Center and Luelle Streets, Deer Park 77536.

The forty-acre Dow Park and Botanical Gardens gives you a chance to cool off in a swimming pool or have a picnic, then stroll through a garden featuring more than 180 flower species, brick walkways, and wooden arches.

SAN JACINTO BATTLEGROUND STATE HISTORICAL PARK (ages 4 and up)

On Battleground Road, La Porte 77571 (281–479–2431). Park open daily 8:00 A.M. to 7:00 P.M., to 9:00 P.M. from March through October. Museum open daily 9:00 A.M. to 6:00 P.M. **Free**.

If your family cares anything at all about Texas history, don't miss San Jacinto Battleground. It was here on April 21, 1836, that Texas won its independence from Mexico. Historical markers provide details of the battle on the actual sites, while the museum, at the base of the monument, preserves hundreds of historical artifacts and documents. New to the museum is the Jesse H. Jones Theater for Texas Studies, where you can see the multi-image presentation *Texas Forever!! The Battle of San Jacinto.* You can also take an elevator ride to an observation room at the top of the monument for a breathtaking panorama of the area. To get to the park, take Route 225 east, then turn north on Battleground Road (Route 134). You can't miss the park: You'll see the San Jacinto Monument, towering higher than the Washington Monument, over the prairie. (By the way, although the correct Spanish pronunciation of this place is San Ha-ceen-to, Texans have always said it San Juh-cen-to.)

BATTLESHIP *TEXAS* (ages 6 and up)

At San Jacinto Battleground, La Porte 77571 (281–479–2431). Open daily 10:00 A.M. to 5:00 P.M., with specially guided tours on weekends. Adults $5.00, children 6 to 18, $3.00, children under 6 free.

The battleship *Texas* is the only surviving Navy warship that served in both world wars, and it was a pioneer in naval aviation. The ship has been moored at the San Jacinto Battleground since 1948 but only recently underwent significant restoration. You can now tour the dark-gray behemoth, seeing much of the ship and many excellent historical displays.

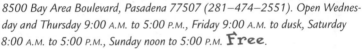

Texas Trivia The U.S.S. *Texas* had ten 14-inch deck guns that could fire a shell weighing as much as a compact car a distance of more than 12 miles.

ARMAND BAYOU NATURE CENTER (ages 4 and up)

8500 Bay Area Boulevard, Pasadena 77507 (281–474–2551). Open Wednesday and Thursday 9:00 A.M. to 5:00 P.M., Friday 9:00 A.M. to dusk, Saturday 8:00 A.M. to 5:00 P.M., Sunday noon to 5:00 P.M. free.

The Armand Bayou Nature Center is a rare place, a true wilderness in the middle of one of the largest urban areas in the United States. The 1,900-acre park showcases native plant and animal life in three different ecosystems that coexist within the park: hardwood forest, tallgrass prairie, and estuarine bayou.

The twisting arms of the bayou give your family the chance to get out in the middle of all the wildness in a canoe. Sightings of blue herons, ospreys, gars, and even alligators are common. Other attractions include the **Jimmy Martyn Farm** (a

Texas Trivia The state highway system has only one tunnel in the entire state—the 4,110-foot tunnel under the Houston Ship Channel that connects Baytown and LaPorte.

working century-old farm), hiking, picnic areas, and a visitors center with a number of nature exhibits. Located between Pasadena and Clear Lake City, **Windsurfing Sports,** 2300 NASA Road 1, conducts canoe trips up the bayou for $39.95 per person. Call (281) 291-9199.

Adjacent **Bay Area Park** is a favorite place for local families to get together. It has athletic fields, tennis courts, picnic areas with barbecue pits, and a nature walk. Open daylight hours. Call (281) 474-4891.

The Battle of San Jacinto

The Battle of San Jacinto It was all or nothing that April 26, 1836. Only a ragtag and undisciplined army of Texians, led by a cantankerous general called "Big Drunk" by the Native Americans, would face the man who called himself the "Napoleon of the West" and a regular army that would outnumber the insurrectionists two to one.

After suffering crushing blows delivered by the Mexicans at the Alamo and Goliad, Gen. Sam Houston took what was left of the army and ran. Many of his own men were on the verge of mutiny.

But Houston knew his small band of about 600 men was all that was left to preserve Texas independence, and he would wait to fight until he was certain of victory.

Gen. Antonio Lopez de Santa Anna's force of 1,300 camped on the banks of the San Jacinto River, leisurely awaiting reinforcements. Houston's force crossed Buffalo Bayou on rafts, and at 3:30 P.M. the Texians caught the Mexicans literally napping. The Mexicans were so surprised that many of their weapons were neatly stacked in front of their tents after the battle.

The Texas Army killed more than 600 and captured all the survivors, losing just nine men themselves. Now a captive, Santa Anna signed a treaty granting Texas its independence.

The battle lasted just eighteen minutes. Considering the amount of territory eventually decided by the victory—all of Texas and parts of New Mexico, Oklahoma, Kansas, Colorado, and Wyoming—it has been called by historians one of the most decisive battles ever fought.

For More Information

Pasadena Chamber of Commerce.
4334 Fairmont Parkway, Pasadena, TX 77504–3306; (281) 487–7871.

Clear Lake Area

Several cities all blend together in this area south of Houston, and you won't be able to tell whether you're in Clear Lake City, Webster, Nassau Bay, El Lago, League City, Clear Lake Shores, Taylor Lake Village, Seabrook, or Kemah if you miss one of the small street signs. The area is surrounded by bays and is full of good restaurants, nice shops and boutiques, and marinas galore. For information on marinas, boat rentals, and charters, call the Clear Lake NASA Area Visitors Bureau at (281) 488-7676.

SPACE CENTER HOUSTON (ages 4 and up)

1601 NASA Road One, Houston 77058 (281–244–2100 or 800–972–0369; www.spacecenter.org). Open Monday through Friday 10:00 A.M. to 5:00 P.M., weekends 10:00 A.M. to 7:00 P.M. Closed Christmas. Adults $11.95, children $8.50.

Space Center Houston is in Clear Lake City at the entrance to the **Johnson Space Center.** Your entire family will be fascinated by the exhibits and displays here, which track the past, present, and future of the U.S. manned-spacecraft program. Interactive exhibits, multimedia programs, shows, an IMAX film, and participation on several devices make space flight come alive. Visitors may also take tours of the **Manned Spacecraft Center** and visit **Rocket Park,** where some of the first rockets used in the space program are on display.

PUTT PUTT GOLF AND GAMES (ages 6 and up)

806 NASA Road One, Houston 77058, next to the Quality Inn (281–333–3200). Prices vary by activity.

Putt Putt Golf and Games offers your family miniature golf, bumper boats, go-carts, batting cages, and a game room.

Where to Eat

Frenchie's. *1041 NASA Road One, Houston 77058 (281–486–7144).* Where many astronauts and other Space Center folks like to eat Italian food. $-$$

Louie's on the Lake. *3813 NASA Road One, Seabrook 77586 (281–326–0551).*

The most famous seafood restaurant in all the state. The frog legs are legendary. $$-$$$

Outback Steakhouse. *481 West Bay Area Boulevard, Webster 77598 (281–338–6283).* Phenomenal steaks. $$

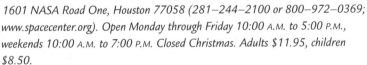

Texas Trivia The Great Storm of 1900 that struck Galveston on September 8 and 9 was the worst natural disaster in U.S. history, responsible for more than 6,000 deaths and hundreds of millions of dollars in damage. Once the second largest port in the nation and Texas's financial capital, Galveston would never completely recover from that hurricane.

Where to Stay

Holiday Inn–NASA. *1300 NASA Road One, Houston 77058 (281–333–2500 or 800–682–3193).* On the bay next to the Space Center, close to shopping and area parks. Has pool and exercise room, 𝓕𝐫𝐞𝐞 continental breakfast; children under nineteen stay 𝓕𝐫𝐞𝐞, children under twelve eat 𝓕𝐫𝐞𝐞. $$-$$$

Quality Inn–NASA. *904 NASA Road One, Houston 77058 (281–333–3737 or 800–221–2222).* Next to miniature golf; children under eighteen stay 𝓕𝐫𝐞𝐞. $$-$$$

For More Information

Clear Lake NASA Area Visitors Bureau. *1201 NASA Road One, Houston,* *TX 77058; (281) 488–7676 or (800) 844–LAKE.*

Galveston

Galveston's sand, surf, sunshine, and seafood are what draw visitors to the city. This island city has plenty of beaches, some public lands, some state park lands, some city parks, and some private parks. You'll find the beaches along Seawall Boulevard. Some are sandy and broad, others short and rocky. The most popular family-oriented beach is Stewart Beach, at Seawall Boulevard and Broadway on the north end of the island, which is alcohol-free. This area also has a water slide, a bathhouse, concession stands, go-carts, miniature golf, and bumper-boat rides.

On the first weekend in December the Strand area of Galveston turns into pre-Christmas Victorian England during **Dickens on the Strand.** Filled with shows, costumed characters, and hundreds of craft booths, it's a true step back in time. You'll find enough food booths that you'll gain weight just walking around smelling all the good stuff. Call (409) 765–7834.

 BAYOU WILDLIFE PARK (ages 4 and up)
5050 FM 517, Alvin 77511; on Farm Road 517 between Alvin and Dickinson, about midway between Houston and Galveston (281–337–6376). Open March through October 10:00 A.M. to 5:00 P.M., November through February 10:00 A.M. to 4:00 P.M. Adults $8.95, children $5.30.

Your kids can see and feed animals and birds from all over the world at Bayou Wildlife Park, which not only features exotic animals but has begun to collect endangered ones as well, like the very rare white rhinoceros, ring-tailed lemurs, Bactrian camel, addax, and scimitar-horned oryx. The animals roam free while you ride through the park on a tram with a guide. Frequent stops allow visitors to feed and pet some of the animals. At the **Children's Barnyard** kids can ride a horse and pet livestock. One bucket of animal food costs $2.00.

GALVESTON ISLAND STATE PARK (ages 4 and up)
At west end of Seawall Boulevard, Farm Road 3005, Galveston 77554 (409–737–1222; 512–389–8900 for camping reservations).

Galveston Island State Park is a 2,000-acre park of sandy beaches and Gulf breezes that spans the width of Galveston Island. Activities include swimming, fishing, picnicking, camping, beachcombing, birdwatching, and nature study along 4 miles of walking trails. Facilities include campsites, screened shelters, sixty sheltered picnic tables, a paved boat ramp, and an amphitheater where outdoor musicals are presented.

The **outdoor musicals** presented at the park's 1,700-seat outdoor theater are Broadway musicals that alternate nightly, except Sunday, at 8:00 P.M., June through August. Dinner is available from 5:30 to 7:30 P.M. Admission: $25 adults, $10 to $15 children. Call (409) 737-3440.

THE STRAND NATIONAL LANDMARK HISTORIC DISTRICT (ages 6 and up)
Along Strand Street, Galveston 77550 (409–763–4311 or 800–351–4237).

Once known as the "Wall Street of the Southwest" before the Great Storm of 1900 devastated most of Galveston, The Strand National Landmark Historic District is a portside area of Victorian buildings now filled with restaurants, shops, factory-outlet stores, jazz and reggae music clubs, art galleries, and more. Although lively anytime, the Strand puts on a great show twice a year, for Mardi Gras and for Christmas.

THE GREAT STORM (ages 6 and up)
Harborside Drive at Twenty-first Street, Galveston 77550 (409–763–8808). Open Sunday through Thursday 11:00 A.M. to 6:00 P.M., Friday and Saturday 11:00 A.M. to 8:00 P.M. Adults $3.50, children $2.50.

Feel the fury of the deadliest natural disaster in U.S. history at the **Pier 21 Theater** in a panoramic, multi-image documentary. Shows begin on the hour.

MARDI GRAS MUSEUM (ages 4 and up)

2311 Merchanic Street, Galveston 77550 (409–765–5930). Open Wednesday through Sunday 10:00 A.M. to 5:00 P.M. Adults $2.00, students $1.00.

Even if it's not Mardi Gras weekend, you can see some of the stunning floats and costumes at the Mardi Gras Museum. **Mardi Gras! Galveston** is too big for one parade, so there are about ten each year, along with masked balls, art exhibits, pageants, and costume contests. The festival, held throughout the town, runs for two weeks before each Fat Tuesday in February. The big parade and most of the festivities happen on the Saturday before Ash Wednesday. For information call (409) 765-7834.

COLONEL BUBBIE'S STRAND SURPLUS CENTER (ages 6 and up)

2202 Strand Boulevard (409–762–7397; www.colbubbie.com). Open Monday through Saturday 10:00 A.M. to 4:00 P.M. "usually," adds the colonel.

Most kids are bored with stores, but they won't be at Colonel Bubbie's. The good colonel's mazelike warehouse is literally jammed to the rafters with bona fide, genuine military surplus clothing and equipment from around the world. You've got to see this place, and smell the mothballs, to believe it.

TEXAS SEAPORT MUSEUM (ages 6 and up)

Located near the Strand Historic Area at Pier 21, Galveston 77550 (409–763–1877; www.pointecom.net/~tsm/). Open daily 10:00 A.M. to 5:00 P.M. Adults $6.00, students $4.00.

The Texas Seaport Museum is home to the *Elissa,* a three-masted sailing ship from the nineteenth century that serves as a symbol of Galveston and its port. The museum has a number of displays and a multiprojector slide show on what it's like to sail onboard the *Elissa.*

CENTER FOR TRANSPORTATION AND COMMERCE (ages 6 and up)

Twenty-fifth Street at Strand Boulevard, Galveston 77550 (409–765–5700). Open daily 10:00 A.M. to 5:00 P.M. except major holidays and Mardi Gras weekend. Adults $5.00, children $2.50.

Nostalgia and history run rampant at the Center for Transportation and Commerce. Known locally as the **Railroad Museum,** it showcases far more than railroads in its six multimedia theaters, which present a history of Galveston shipping, railroading, and commerce. A Santa Fe depot is restored to its 1932 pinnacle, full of life-size figures that speak to visitors. Sure to fascinate the kids are more than forty-six vintage railroad cars and steam engines on adjacent tracks.

OCEAN STAR OFFSHORE DRILLING RIG AND MUSEUM (ages 6 and up)

Harborside Drive at Twentieth Street on Pier 19, Galveston 77550 (409–766–7827). Open daily in the summer 10:00 A.M. to 5:00 P.M., in the winter until 4:00 P.M. Adults $5.00, students $4.00, children 6 and under Free.

The museum is located on an actual oil-drilling rig and showcases models, information, and interactive exhibits as well as a fifteen-minute orientation film. One of the city's newest attractions, it's one of the most impressive.

MOODY GARDENS (ages 2 and up)

One Hope Boulevard, Galveston 77554 (800–582–4673; www.moodygardens. com). Open Sunday through Thursday 10:00 A.M. to 6:00 P.M., Friday and Saturday 10:00 A.M. to 8:00 P.M. Admission varies per location, $7.50 to $11.00 for adults, $5.25 to $6.25 for children.

Your family can easily spend a day, even a few days, at the phenomenal Moody Gardens. You can't miss its central feature: a ten-story, 40,000-square-foot glass pyramid. The pyramid houses a tropical rain forest with waterfalls, cliffs, caverns, wetlands, and forests and is home to more than 2,000 species of exotic butterflies, birds, plants, fish, and bats. Other attractions include **Palm Beach,** a white sand beach and blue lagoon swim center for families; landscaped gardens and nature trails; and an **IMAX 3-D theater,** where fish seem to leap out of the six-story screen.

THE COLONEL (ages 4 and up)

One Hope Boulevard, Galveston 77554 (409–761–2618). Tours: $6.00 per person. Dinner/dance cruises: $27.50 adults, $15.00 children.

For a water-based tour of Galveston, step onto *The Colonel,* a triple-decked paddle-wheeler that takes one-hour sight-seeing cruises during the day and offers dinner and dancing cruises Friday and Saturday evenings. Departs from Moody Gardens.

TREASURE ISLE TOUR TRAIN (ages 4 and up)

2106 Seawall Boulevard, Galveston 77550 (409–765–9564). Tours: $5.50 adults, $3.00 children.

For a land-based tour of Galveston, step onto the Treasure Isle Tour Train, which tours new and historic sites on the island in about an hour and a half.

SEAWOLF PARK (ages 6 and up)

On Pelican Island, Galveston 77550; across the channel from the Port of Galveston (409–744–5738). Open daily dawn to dusk. Tours: $4.00 adults, $2.00 children.

Your kids can climb aboard an old World War II submarine or destroyer escort, a U.S. Navy jet, and other military vehicles at Seawolf Park. The park has a snack bar, picnic areas, and a playground. It also affords close looks at oceangoing cargo ships passing by. The fishing is good from the nearby pier. Take Fifty-first Street to the causeway.

Texas Trivia Karankawa Indians were the first inhabitants of Galveston. The earliest European settlement of the island was in 1817 by the pirate Jean Laffite; he called the place Campeachy. The U.S. Navy kicked him out in 1821.

Bolivar Peninsula

For less-crowded beaches, take the twenty-minute ferry ride from Galveston to the Bolivar Peninsula. These ferries are actually a part of the Texas highway system, so there's no charge. Follow Route 87 north to the dock. The same highway picks up on the other side at Port Bolivar. Kids will love the sand castle–building contests that are the star attraction of the **Texas Crab Festival,** every April in Crystal Beach. In addition, the festival has a crab cook-off, crab races, arts-and-crafts and food booths, a carnival, and a variety of beach games. Call (409) 684–5940 for more information on the area.

Where to Eat

Gaido's. *3800 Seawall Boulevard, Galveston 77550 (409–762–9625).* Locals believe Gaido's invented seafood, and it's the most popular place in the area. $$

Hill's Pier 19 Restaurant, Bar and Fish Market. *Twentieth Street and the Wharf, Galveston 77550 (409–763–7087).* A block from the Strand, overlooking the Galveston Ship Channel.

The adjacent fish market will custom cut and pack seafood for travel. Call the market at (409) 763-4618. $$–$$$

Mario's Italian and Seafood Restaurant. *628 Seawall Boulevard, Galveston 77550 (409–763–1693).* Gourmet pizza and pasta, seafood and chicken. $$–$$$

Where to Stay

Best Western Beachfront Inn. *5914 Seawall Boulevard, Galveston 77551 (409–740–1261 or 800–528–1234).* Walk across the street and jump in the Gulf. $$–$$$

Flagship Over the Water. *2501 Seawall Boulevard, Galveston 77550 (409–762–9000).* In the middle of everything, this hotel is built over the crashing surf into the Gulf. Unique. $$$

Victorian Condo Hotel. *6300 Seawall Boulevard, Galveston 77551 (409–740–3555 or 800–231–6363).* Convenient, quiet, and comfortable, with great views of the Gulf from private balconies. You'll also find a pool, barbecue area, playground, and tennis courts, kitchens, bunkbeds, and multibedroom suites. $$–$$$

For More Information

Galveston Convention and Visitors Bureau. *2106 Seawall Boulevard, Galveston, TX 77550; (888) GAL–ISLE or (409)* *763–4311, or the Strand Visitor Center at 2016 Strand; (409) 765–7834. Visit the Web site at www.galvestoncvb.com.*

Anahuac, Sabine Pass, and Port Arthur

ANAHUAC NATIONAL WILDLIFE REFUGE (ages 4 and up)
On Farm Road 1985, Anahuac 77514, south of Anahuac (409–267–3337).
Anahuac National Wildlife Refuge is one of the best places in the United States to see all nine species of rails and other marsh birds. Alligators are also common, and you also might see bobcats, river otters, muskrats, and nutria along the 12 miles of road through the refuge.

(The most common pronunciation is Anna-wack, but you'll hear old-timers say Anny-wack.)

MCFADDIN AND TEXAS POINT WILDLIFE REFUGES (ages 4 and up)

On Texas Highway 87, Sabine Pass 77655, between High Island and Sabine Pass (409–267–3337).

The McFaddin and Texas Point wildlife refuges are where thousands upon thousands of migratory geese and ducks use the marshlands. If you're hoping to see or photograph wildlife, you can certainly do it at one of these refuges. McFaddin also has one of the densest populations of alligators in Texas.

Sam Houston's Big Idea The idea for the Gulf Intracoastal Waterway was thought up by none other than Sam Houston in 1846, when he was serving in the U.S. Senate. Houston proposed construction of a navigable channel between the Sabine River and the Rio Grande to stimulate development of Texas's gulf coast. But grand ideas moved slowly in those days. Surveying didn't take place until 1873, ten years after Houston died. In 1913, the U.S. Army Corps of Engineers completed the first stretch, a 200-mile segment south from Galveston. The entire 426-mile length from Orange to Brownsville was finished in 1949.

SEA RIM STATE PARK (ages 4 and up)

Off Texas Highway 87, Sabine Pass 77655, 10 miles west of Sabine Pass (409–971–2559; 512–389–8900 for camping reservations).

Sea Rim State Park offers even more wildlife-viewing opportunities, in addition to beachcombing along the 5.2-mile shoreline. It also has a boardwalk and nature trail through the marshes, canoe trails, fishing, camping, and observation blinds in the 15,109-acre park. An altogether great place for a family to wander about in nature.

SABINE PASS BATTLEGROUND STATE HISTORIC PARK (ages 4 and up)

On Farm Road 3322, Sabine Pass 77655, off Route 87 (409–971–2559).

Union forces attempted to invade Texas at Sabine Pass in 1863 but were driven off by a much smaller force of Confederates. The site is now the Sabine Pass Battleground State Historic Park. Dominating the park is a large statue of Lieut. Dick Dowling, the Texan leader. The fifty-three-acre park also has a boat ramp, picnic facilities, a fish-cleaning shelter, and great views of ships on their way to and from Port Arthur and Beaumont.

MUSEUM OF THE GULF COAST (ages 6 and up)

At Procter Street and Beaumont Avenue, Port Arthur 77642 (409–982–7000). Open Monday through Saturday 9:00 A.M. to 5:00 P.M., Sunday 1:00 to 5:00 P.M. Adults $3.50, children 6 to 18 $1.50, children 5 and under, 50 cents.

The Museum of the Gulf Coast is filled with relics from this coastal area's past, surrounded by stunning murals. The musical-heritage room honors native daughter Janis Joplin, whose psychedelic-painted Porsche sits atop a spinning gold record, and other Port Arthur musical legends like J. P. "Big Bopper" Richardson, Richie Valens, and Tex Ritter. Interpretive displays include a number of children's interactive exhibits.

Texas Trivia The state stone is petrified palmwood.

For More Information

Port Arthur Convention and Visitors Bureau. *3401 Cultural Center Drive, Port Arthur, TX 77642; (800) 235–7822* or *(409) 963–1107. Visit the Web site at www.portarthurtexas.com/pavb.*

East Texas: The Piney Woods

It's a good thing the road signs for Texas's farm and ranch roads have a silhouette of the state on them, otherwise visitors to east Texas might not believe they're in the Lone Star State.

East Texas, often called the Piney Woods, is about as far from the stereotypical Texas landscape as you can get. When you see the red dirt and thick forests of tall pines, you might think you're in Georgia. When you visit the Alabama-Coushatta Indian Reservation, you might think you're in Oklahoma. When you see the multitude of large lakes and rivers, you might think you're in Minnesota. When you see thick moss hanging from trees around Caddo Lake or hear the Cajun lilt of people near Beaumont, you might think you're deep in Louisiana bayou country.

But it's all Texas, a region where timber and oil are king and queen. You won't find any metropolises here. What you will find are many small villages and cities filled with southern hospitality and a region where nature is a prized possession: More than 750,000 acres are set aside in four national forests and the **Big Thicket National Preserve.** If your family likes the outdoors, you're in for a real treat in east Texas.

Texas Trivia Trees cover approximately 13 percent of Texas's land area, or twenty-two million acres.

Orange

You'll find a lot of history in Orange, the first Texas city on I-10 from Louisiana. As one example of just how big Texas is, consider that if you started here and drove west along I-10, by the time you reached the western state line just past El Paso you'd have driven 880 miles.

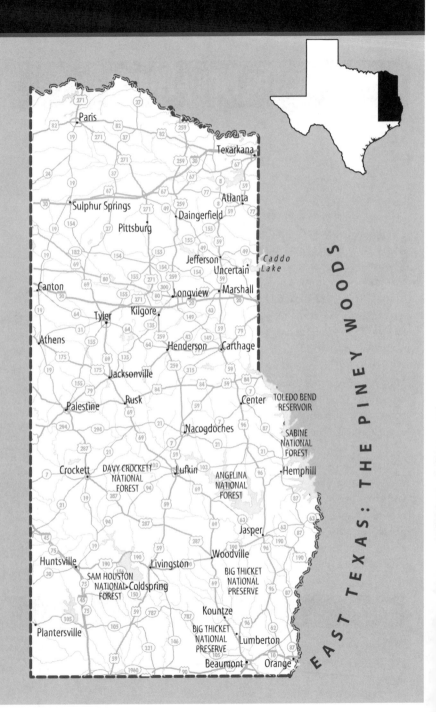

EAST TEXAS: THE PINEY WOODS

Allan's Top Annual Family Fun Events

- Dogwood Festival, Woodville, March (936–283–2632)
- Sam Houston Folk Festival, Huntsville, April (936–295–8113)
- Stagecoach Days, Marshall, May (903–935–7868)
- Tops in Texas Rodeo, Jacksonville, July (903–586–2217)
- Black-eyed Pea Jamboree, Athens, July (800–755–7878)
- Texas Renaissance Festival, Plantersville, October (800–458–3455)
- Southwest Canoe Rendezvous, Huntsville, October (936–295–8113)
- Fire Ant Festival, Marshall, October (903–935–7868)
- Texas Rose Festival, Tyler, October (903–597–3130)
- Wonderland of Lights Christmas Festival, Marshall, December (903–935–7868)

If your family likes Cajun food, don't miss the annual **International Gumbo Cook-Off** held the first weekend in May. Sample gumbo, enjoy the carnival rides, watch live entertainment, or wander around the arts-and-crafts booths. Call (409) 883-3536 or (800) 528-4906 for information, or visit the Web site at www.org-tx.com.

STARK MUSEUM OF ART (ages 6 and up)

700 West Green Street, Orange 77630 (409–883–6661). Open Tuesday through Friday 10:00 A.M. to 5:00 P.M., Sunday 1:00 to 5:00 P.M., closed major holidays. **Free**.

Some of the best western art in the country is in the collection at the Stark Museum. You'll find original Audubon bird sketches, sculpture by Remington and Russell, paintings by the Taos masters, Native American pottery and artifacts, and much more.

HERITAGE HOUSE MUSEUM (ages 6 and up)

905 West Division Street, Orange 77630 (409–886–5385). Open Tuesday through Friday 10:00 A.M. to 4:00 P.M., weekends by appointment. Adults $1.00, children 50 cents.

The Heritage House isn't some large mansion, as are many Registered Historic Landmarks. Instead, this simple home is a century-old middle-class house that features rotating exhibits of early Texas history and family life from a hundred years ago. The museum holds many historical and seasonal events throughout the year where you or the kids can take turns making crafts or participating in pioneer activities.

SUPER GATOR TOURS (ages 4 and up)

106 East Lutcher Stree, Orange 77632 (409–883–7725). Tours May through September 10:00 A.M. to 7:00 P.M., October to April 10:00 A.M. to 4:00 P.M. Adults $25.50, children $12.90.

I don't think anyone in your family will dislike touring the swamps in an airboat. Super Gator Tours will zip you through a true wilderness so you can see alligators, nutria, frogs, turtles, egrets, and a variety of visiting waterfowl.

CLAIBORNE WEST PARK (ages 4 and up)

On Cow Bayou, Orange 77630, west of Orange off I–10 (409–745–2255).

Get personal with nature at Claiborne West Park. This heavily wooded preserve has some of the best bird-watching around, along with nature and hiking trails, picnic areas, campsites, and a playground. You can fish for rainbow trout during the winter.

Beaumont

Beaumont is a city rich in Spanish and French tradition, a city where the Texas oil industry was born, and it's nestled close to both the Gulf of Mexico and the Big Thicket. You'll find a lot to do here, both in museums and outdoors.

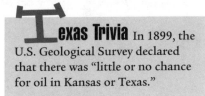

Texas Trivia In 1899, the U.S. Geological Survey declared that there was "little or no chance for oil in Kansas or Texas."

ART MUSEUM OF SOUTHEAST TEXAS (ages 6 and up)

500 Main Street, Beaumont 77701 (409–832–3432; www.amset.org). Open Monday through Saturday 9:00 A.M. to 5:00 P.M., Sunday noon to 5:00 P.M. Free.

The Art Museum of Southeast Texas has a permanent collection of art and hosts several traveling exhibits throughout the year.

JOHN JAY FRENCH TRADING POST (ages 6 and up)

2975 French Road, Beaumont 77706 (409–898–3267). Open Tuesday through Saturday 10:00 A.M. to 4:00 P.M., Sunday 1:00 to 4:00 P.M. Adults $2.00, children 50 cents.

The Trading Post is a collection of pioneer artifacts along with a blacksmith shop, tannery, corncrib, and smokehouse.

SPINDLETOP/GLADYS CITY BOOMTOWN (ages 6 and up)

On U.S. Highway 69 at University Drive, Beaumont 77705 (409–835–0823; www.spindletop.com). Open Tuesday through Sunday 1:00 to 5:00 P.M. Adults $2.50, children $1.25.

Your family can see where the oil business in Texas really got started at Spindletop. This wasn't the first well in the state, but the gusher Spindletop produced in 1901 made the industry a reality. You'll see the world's first boomtown re-created here, complete with wooden derricks.

TEXAS ENERGY MUSEUM (ages 6 and up)

600 Main Street, Beaumont 77701 (409–833–5100). Open Tuesday and Saturday 9:00 A.M. to 5:00 P.M., Sunday 1:00 to 5:00 P.M. Adults $2.00, children $1.00.

The Texas Energy Museum will show you just how the petroleum industry evolved, making Texas an oil giant. Displays include many hands-on and multimedia exhibits.

EDISON PLAZA MUSEUM (ages 6 and up)

350 Pine Street, Beaumont 77701 (409–839–3089). Open Monday through Friday 1:00 to 3:30 P.M. **Free**.

For the scientists in your family, visit the Edison Museum. This is the largest collection of Thomas A. Edison artifacts west of the Mississippi, including cylinder phonographs and a look at what some of his inventions have led to today and will lead to in the future.

FIRE MUSEUM OF TEXAS (ages 4 and up)

400 Walnut Street, Beaumont 77701 (409–880–3919). Open Monday through Friday 8:00 A.M. to 4:30 P.M. **Free**.

The Fire Museum displays antique bells, buckets, hoses and badges, photographs, and vintage fire trucks in a 1927 fire station.

BABE ZAHARIAS MUSEUM (ages 6 and up)

1750 I–10, Beaumont 77703, exit 854 (409–833–4622). Open daily 9:00 A.M. to 5:00 P.M., closed Christmas. **Free**.

Mildred "Babe" Didrickson Zaharias was the greatest American female athlete and the best athlete to come out of Texas. She could do it all: win Olympic medals, play championship basketball, and play championship golf. The Babe Zaharias Museum honors this pioneer with many of her trophies and personal memorabilia.

JULIE ROGERS THEATRE (ages 8 and up)

765 Pearl Street, Beaumont 77701 (409–880–3749 or 800–392–4401). Prices vary with the event.

Beaumont may be a small city, but it is justly proud of its performing-arts organizations. The Julie Rogers Theatre, across from the Civic Center, is home to the Beaumont opera, symphony, and ballet.

CLIFTON STEAMBOAT MUSEUM (ages 6 and up)

7777 Fannett Road, Beaumont 77701 (409–842–3162). Open Tuesday through Saturday 9:30 A.M. to 5:15 P.M., Sunday 1:00 to 5:00 P.M. Adults $5.00, children $4.00.

The museum honors military and civilian heroes from the Battle of San Jacinto to the Persian Gulf War, along with steamboats.

Where to Eat

Carlito's. *890 Amarillo Street, Beaumont 77701 (409–839–8011).* Extremely popular for steaks and Mexican food such as shrimp enchiladas. $$

Don's. *2290 I–10 South Beaumont 77707 (409–842–0686).* Texans know Don's is the place for great, authentic seafood and steaks done up with a flavorful Cajun twist, heavy on the crawfish. $$

Willy Ray's Bar-B-Q and Grill. *145 I–10 North, Beaumont 77702 (409–832–7770).* Not your typical barbecue joint, this one features great pork loin, pepper turkey and key lime cheesecake. $-$$

Where to Stay

Best Western. *1610 I–10 South, Beaumont 77703 (409–842–0037).* Pool, **Free** continental breakfast. $$

La Quinta. *2201 I–10 North, Beaumont 77707 (409–838–9991).* Pool, **Free** continental breakfast. $$

For More Information

Beaumont Convention and Visitors Bureau. *801 Main Street, P.O. Box 3827, Beaumont, TX 77704; (800) 392–4401 or* *(409) 880–3749. Visit the Web site at www.beaumontcvb.com.*

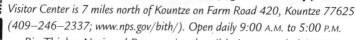

Kountze and Lumberton

BIG THICKET NATIONAL PRESERVE (ages 4 and up)

Visitor Center is 7 miles north of Kountze on Farm Road 420, Kountze 77625 (409–246–2337; www.nps.gov/bith/). Open daily 9:00 A.M. to 5:00 P.M.

Big Thicket National Preserve is a bewildering, wooded 96,000 acres where eight ecosystems converge to make up what biologists call the "biological crossroads of North America," with thousands of animal and plant life forms. The Big Thicket was designated a Man and the Biosphere Reserve by the United Nations in 1981, giving you an idea of just how unique this place is. The park features nine hiking trails ranging from .75 mile to 18 miles. You can also enjoy canoeing, swimming, and fishing. Guided hikes, children's programs, lectures, and boat tours are **Free**, but reservations are required.

Timber Ridge Tours will customize a boating, hiking, or camping trip into the Big Thicket just for your family. The company specializes in canoe trips on Village Creek. Call (409) 246-3107.

VILLAGE CREEK STATE PARK (ages 4 and up)

10 miles north of Beaumont on Highway 96 (Alma Drive), Lumberton 77711(409–755–7322; 512–389–8900 for camping reservations).

Village Creek is a very popular flat-water stream among Texas canoeists. The 63-mile-long creek flows through the heart of the Big Thicket to the Neches River. You'll find a wildness here that is difficult to match. The woods are very thick, dotted with baygalls (a kind of miniature swamp) and larger cypress and tupelo swamps. Wildlife like deer, raccoons, armadillos, alligators, rabbits, and possums are common. Birds are plentiful, too. Facilities include tent campsites, a canoe launch ramp, picnic areas, a playground, and plenty of hiking trails.

For More Information

Hardin County Tourist Bureau. *210 West Main Street, P.O. Box 1859, Kountze, TX 77625; (800) 835–0343 or (409) 246–3413.*

Lumberton Chamber of Commerce. *140 South Main Street, P.O. Box 8574, Lumberton, TX 77657; (409) 755–0554.*

Plantersville and Huntsville

If you're lucky enough to be in Huntsville during mid-April, don't miss the **Sam Houston Folk Festival,** a rousing family event that features costumed characters, demonstrations of pioneer skills and crafts, an arts-and-crafts fair, and entertainment. For information call (409) 295-8113, or visit the Web site www.chamber.huntsville.tx.us/visitor.html.

TEXAS RENAISSANCE FESTIVAL (ages 4 and up)

On Farm Road 1774, Plantersville 77363, 6 miles south of Plantersville (800–458–3435; www.texrenfest.com). Adults $19.95, children $8.95.

On seven weekends in October and November, 237 wooded acres of the Piney Woods are transformed into something out of the Middle Ages. The Renaissance Festival is a wonderful family event, full of parading entertainers, jousting, dancing, entertainment stages, plenty of food booths, and an arts-and-crafts fair.

SAM HOUSTON MEMORIAL MUSEUM AND PARK (ages 6 and up)

1836 Sam Houston Avenue, Huntsville 77320 (936–294–1832; www.shsu. edu/~smm_www). Open Tuesday through Sunday 9:00 A.M. to 4:30 P.M. **Free.**

Huntsville is one of the state's oldest cities, home to the biggest Texas hero of them all, Sam Houston. After Houston won independence for Texas and served as president of the republic and governor of the state, he settled here. You can visit his home at the Sam Houston Memorial Museum and Park, near Sam Houston State University. It's also hard to miss that huge statue of Houston, a good place for photos. The statue is the tallest in the world to depict an American hero.

TEXAS PRISON MUSEUM (ages 6 and up)

1113 Twelfth Street, Huntsville 77340 (936–295–2155). Open Tuesday through Friday noon to 5:00 P.M., Saturday 9:00 A.M. to 5:00 P.M., Sunday noon to 5:00 P.M. Adults $2.00, children $1.00.

Huntsville is also home to the state's most famous prison. It's here where most of the hard cases go, and its dirty red walls are terrifying. The Texas Prison Museum displays many artifacts pertaining to outlaws and historic methods of punishment. The shop features crafts made by prisoners with a lot of time on their hands.

Texas Trivia Sam Houston may have had the most unusual career of any politician. As a Tennessee resident, he was elected to the U.S. Congress and served as that state's governor. After moving to Texas, he was elected president of the republic, then to the U.S. Senate, then as governor of his adopted state.

SAMUEL WALKER HOUSTON CULTURAL CENTER (ages 6 and up)

341 Old Madisonville Road, Huntsville 77320 (936–295–2119). Donations requested.

The Samuel Walker Houston Cultural Center honors a prominent black educator and son of Joshua Houston, a former slave of Sam Houston's. The center depicts life for blacks in the city after the Civil War. Next door is a children's playground.

HUNTSVILLE STATE PARK (ages 4 and up)

Exit 109 off I–45, 6 miles south of Huntsville (mailing address: P.O. Box 508, Huntsville 77342; 936–295–5644; 512–389–8900 for camping reservations).

Huntsville State Park is a beautiful area in the midst of loblolly and shortleaf pines with a lake right in the middle of it all. The park has 11 miles of hiking and biking trails where wildlife and birds can easily be seen. Facilities include campsites, screened shelters, picnic areas, and an amphitheater where rangers give nature talks. You might even see an alligator around the lake. Even if you don't, make sure to get a picture of the DO NOT FEED OR HARASS ALLIGATORS sign.

The park's Lake Raven is the site of the **Southwest Canoe Rendezvous,** held in early October. This is an event where anyone in your family, regardless of skill level or age, can try out canoes and kayaks, learning from experts. Call (936) 295-8113.

Scenic Drive Several roads through the forest provide you with great woodland beauty. Drive along Farm Road 1374 and Farm Road 1375 and you'll see a Texas you may not have known existed, one of the prettiest drives in the state. The route goes through the heart of Huntsville State Park and Sam Houston National Forest, with so much cooling shade in the summer that you might not want to leave.

The pines are abundant, but they're interspersed with willow and oak, elm, black gum and green ash, some dogwood, maple, and sassafras. This thick forest is also thick with wildlife, so drive carefully so the kids can get a glimpse of the white-tailed deer, raccoons, possums, and armadillos that seem to always be alongside the roads.

SAM HOUSTON NATIONAL FOREST (ages 4 and up)
Between Huntsville and Livingston (936–344–6205).

Sam Houston National Forest has a number of hiking and mountain-biking trails and recreation areas. It's an exceptionally beautiful area of Texas, seldom visited except by locals and others in the know.

The **Lone Star Hiking Trail** is one way to get the family out enjoying nature without crowds or traffic. This is actually several trails that wind for a total of 140 miles through Sam Houston National Forest. You can do short stretches or overnight hikes. Either way, you'll be deep in the Piney Woods, listening to hawks and woodpeckers, feeling cool breezes, and smelling the pungent odor of pine.

For general information on all four of the national forests in east Texas, call the U.S. Forest Service office in Lufkin at (409) 639–8501.

Where to Eat

Catfish Place. *3400 Texas Highway 19, Huntsville 77320 (936–295–8685).* The best place to taste this Piney Woods staple. $–$$

Chili's. *1406 I–45, Huntsville 77320 (936–295–3018).* This Texas chain serves up scrumptious food with a Southwestern flavor. Special kids' meals. $$

Where to Stay

La Quinta. *1407 I–45 North, Huntsville 77320 (936–295–6454).* Pool, **Free** continental breakfast. $$

Sam Houston Inn. *3296 I–45 South, Huntsville 77320 (936–295–9151).* Pool, **Free** continental breakfast. $$

Crockett

DAVY CROCKETT NATIONAL FOREST (ages 4 and up)

Between Crockett and Groveton on U.S. Highway 287 (mailing address: P.O. Box 130, Apple Springs 75926; 936–831–2246, 936–544–2046, or 936–639–8501).

Davy Crockett National Forest is the largest of Texas's four national forests, its primary boundary formed by the scenic Neches River. The forest has only a few developed areas but many backpacking trails and primitive campsites. Canoeists in the family will like the **Big Slough Canoe Trail.**

For More Information

Walker County Chamber of Commerce. *Look for the giant statue of Sam Houston at exit 109 from I–45, P.O. Box 538, Huntsville, TX 77342; (800) 289–0389 or (4936) 295–8114. Visit the Web site at www. chamber.huntsville. tx.us/visitor.html.*

Texas Trivia Huntsville is the seat of Walker County, originally named for U.S. Treasury Secretary Robert J. Walker, an early Texas patriot. But the state legislature withdrew the honor in 1863 because Walker was a Union sympathizer. Then the legislature renamed the county for Samuel H. Walker, an early Texas Ranger, scout, and codeveloper of the Walker Colt revolving pistol.

Palestine

This Palestine is pronounced "Pal-es-teen" by natives.

So many dogwoods bloom in this part of Texas that Palestine celebrates with a three-weekend event in late March through early April. The **Texas Dogwood Trails** includes parades, an arts-and-crafts fair, tours of historic homes, domino tournaments, model-train shows, and hikes and drives through the heart of dogwood country. Call (903) 729-7275 or (903) 723-3014. Visit the Web site www.palestine-online.org.

ENGELING WILDLIFE REFUGE (ages 4 and up)

20 miles northwest of Palestine on U.S. Highway 287, Palestine 75801 (903–928–2251).

Engeling Wildlife Refuge has more than 10,000 heavily wooded acres that are home to several species of birds and many deer, fox, rabbits, squirrels, and wolves.

MUSEUM FOR EAST TEXAS CULTURE (ages 6 and up)

400 Micheaux Street, Palestine 75801 (903–723–1914; www.palestine-online.org/tourism/tourism.html). Open Monday through Saturday 10:00 A.M. to 5:00 P.M., Sunday 1:00 to 4:00 P.M. Adults $1.00, children 50 cents.

The Museum for East Texas Culture is a regional museum housed in a circa 1915 high school. Featured are displays on the railroads, local architecture, schools, and pioneers, as well as traveling exhibits.

DAVEY DOGWOOD PARK (ages 4 and up)

On North Link Street, Palestine 75801, just north of town (903–729–6066).

Near the Museum for East Texas Culture is Davey Dogwood Park, a 200-acre natural area with 5 miles of scenic roads and hiking trails through a forest of dogwood and other trees. There are several picnic areas.

FAIRFIELD LAKE STATE PARK (ages 4 and up)

On Park Road 64, Fairfield 75840, south of U.S. Highway 287, about 20 miles west of Palestine or off Farm Road 2570 east of Palestine (903–389–4514; 512–389–8900 for camping reservations).

Get the family wet at Fairfield Lake State Park. You'll find rolling hills of hardwood forest surrounding the lake. Facilities include boat ramps, campsites, picnic areas, a

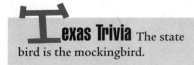
Texas Trivia The state bird is the mockingbird.

sandy swimming area, and 6 miles of hiking trails. You can see beaver here and, in the winter, bald eagles.

For More Information

Palestine Chamber of Commerce. *502 North Queens Street, Palestine, TX* *75801; (903) 729–6066. Visit the Web site at www.palestine-online.org.*

Rusk

About 30 miles east of Palestine on U.S. Highway 84.

 TEXAS STATE RAILROAD (ages 4 and up)
Depots in Rusk/Palestine units of the state park, Rusk 75785 (903–683–2561 or 800–442–8951). Round-trip fares are $15.00 adults, $9.00 children; one-way fares are $10.00 adults, $6.00 children.

The state's most unusual state park is the Texas State Railroad. This century-old steam train runs for a 50-mile round-trip through scenic forests and pastures and across the Neches River between Rusk and Palestine, over twenty-four bridges. The depots at each end of the trip re-create early twentieth-century stations, and the Rusk depot has a theater that shows a film detailing the railroad's history. This rail line was begun in 1896 using convict labor, and prisoners renovated it when it became a state park in 1972. Engines date from 1901 to 1927.

 RUSK/PALESTINE STATE PARK (ages 4 and up)
 On U.S. Highway 84, Rusk 75785, 3 miles west of Rusk and 4 miles east of Palestine (903–683–5126; 512–389–8900 for camping reservations).

Adjacent to the depots, you'll discover Rusk/Palestine State Park, which has playgrounds and picnic areas. The Rusk unit also offers overnight camping, fishing, and hiking. The Palestine unit is a day-use facility with excellent hiking.

 JIM HOGG HISTORICAL PARK (ages 4 and up)
Fire Tower Road off Highway 84, Quitman 75783, 2 miles northeast of Rusk (903–683–4850).

It seems Rusk is full of state parks. This park is named after James Hogg, the state's first native-born governor. There's a scale replica of Hogg's birthplace here, as well as the family cemetery, picnic areas, nature trails, and a children's playground.

 MISSION TEJAS STATE PARK (ages 4 and up)
 Off Highway 69 on Texas Highway 21, Grapeland 75844, about 20 miles south-west of Rusk (903–687–2394; 512–389–8900 for camping reservations).

Mission Tejas was one of the first Spanish settlements in the area. Historic structures here will transport your family to days of rustic tranquillity. The Civilian Conservation Corps built one log building to commemorate that early mission. The other log building is the Rice family home, which was moved here and restored. Facilities include camping, hiking, and picnicking, with fishing in a pond near the picnic area.

CADDOAN MOUNDS STATE PARK (ages 4 and up)

On Texas Highway 21, Alto 75925, about 20 miles southwest of Rusk (409–858–3218).

Caddoan Mounds is a fascinating place, encompassing a Native American village site and the earthen burial grounds of Caddo Indians. The park has two temple mounds in addition to the burial mounds. The park is currently day-use only, and picnicking and camping are not allowed.

Where to Eat

Golden Corral. *2036 Crockett Road, Palestine 75801(903–729–8841).* Order from the varied menu or graze to your stomach's content at the many food, bakery, potato, and dessert bars. Food is fresh, good, plentiful. Lunches are a special bargain. $-$$

Where to Stay

Bailey Bunkhouse. *Off Texas Highway 155, Palestine 75801, 8 miles north of Palestine (903–549–2028).* Spacious log cabin has two bedrooms downstairs and extra beds upstairs, with kitchen. Rustic location offers excellent fishing on the grounds. $$

Parker House Bed and Breakfast. *304 North Maple Street, Trinity75862 (409–594–3260 or 800–593–2373).*

Centrally located, allowing your family to travel all over on day trips and return to a comfortable, gracious home in the evening. The B&B is a restored home more than a hundred years old, furnished with antiques. There's even an antique crib for infants. You're served a full country or Mexican-style breakfast with the cost of the room. Horseback riding, river tours, waterskiing, and wilderness hiking available. $$

For More Information

Rusk Chamber of Commerce. *415 North Main Street, P.O. Box 67, Rusk, TX 75785; (800) 933–2381 or (903) 683–4242.*

Jacksonville, Athens, and Canton

Rodeo is always family fun, and the **Tops in Texas Rodeo** in Jacksonville will provide you with some of the best in mid-July. Even though the city is small, the rodeo attracts top Professional Rodeo Cowboy Association riders. The event also boasts a parade, an arts-and-crafts festival, and special children's activities. For information call (903) 586-2217.

The city of Athens has its own festival about a week after the Jacksonville rodeo: the **Black-eyed Pea Jamboree.** People compete for cash prizes for cooking black-eyed peas, eating black-eyed peas, shelling black-eyed peas—well, you get the idea. There's also a carnival, a parade, and the usual arts-and-crafts and food booths. Call (800) 755-7878 or (903) 675-5181.

 ### LAKE PALESTINE (ages 4 and up)
13 miles northwest of Jacksonville on U.S. Highway 175, Jacksonville 75766 (903–729–6066).

Go from the woods to the water at Lake Palestine. Here are boating, fishing, hunting, picnicking, skiing, and swimming on a 22,500-acre lake well stocked with fish.

 ### LAKE JACKSONVILLE (ages 4 and up)
Off U.S. Highway 69, Jacksonville 75766, 4 miles south of Jacksonville (903–586–4160).

Water-ski, fish, have a picnic, camp out, swim, or just relax on the shore of the this 1,320-acre lake, which is also rated as one of the best bass lakes in all of Texas.

 ### FIRST MONDAY TRADE DAYS (ages 6 and up)
Off U.S. Highway 64, Canton 75103, near the courthouse (903–567–6556; www.cantontx.com).

Your family has probably never seen anything like First Monday Trade Days in Canton, with parking at the Route 19 intersection. Like many small towns in Texas, Canton holds a monthly market day where vendors sell everything from antiques to art, crafts to junk. But Canton's is by far the largest in the country: More than 5,000 dealers gather on a hundred acres to sell their wares the first weekend and Monday of every month. And they've been doing it since 1850. There's something for everyone here. The grounds are full of food and drink booths, and ATM machines, to keep you going.

PURTIS CREEK STATE PARK (ages 4 and up)

On Farm Road 316, Eustace 75124, about 15 miles southwest of Canton (903–425–2332; 512–389–8900 for camping reservations).

When the family's shopped out, head to Purtis Creek State Park to relax. Good fishing and shady campsites and picnic areas are the attraction here. Facilities include boat ramps, fishing piers and cleaning stations, a playground, and a trout pond.

Texas Trivia Next time your family has a round of hamburgers, thank the town of Athens. More specifically, Fletcher Davis, who, in the 1880s, served up a ground meat patty topped with mustard, onion, and pickles between two slices of bread at Stirman's Drug Store. It was a local favorite for lunch, and in 1904 Davis introduced the hamburger to the world at his booth at the St. Louis World's Fair.

For More Information

Athens Chamber of Commerce. *1206 South Palestine Street, Athens, TX 75751; (903) 675–5181.*

Canton Chamber of Commerce. *315 First Monday Lane, Canton, TX 75103; (903) 567–2991. Visit the Web site at www.cantontx.com.*

Jacksonville Chamber of Commerce. *526 East Commerce Street, Jacksonville, TX 75766; (800) 376–2217 or (903) 586–2217.*

Tyler

MUNICIPAL ROSE GARDEN AND ROSE CENTER (ages 4 and up)

420 South Rose Parkway, Tyler 75701 (903–531–1212). Garden open daily 6:00 A.M. to 10:00 P.M.; visitors center open daily 9:00 A.M. to 5:00 P.M.; museum open Tuesday through Saturday 9:30 A.M. to 4:00 P.M., Sunday 1:00 to 4:00 P.M. **Free**.

Tyler is famous throughout Texas for its roses. One-fifth of all commercial rose bushes in the United States come from this area. The **Texas Rose Festival** in October celebrates the flower with a parade and show.

All you can imagine about roses is at the Municipal Rose Garden and Rose Center. The garden has 38,000 rose bushes of 500 varieties. The museum features educational exhibits about the rose-growing industry.

BROOKSHIRE'S WORLD OF WILDLIFE MUSEUM AND COUNTRY STORE (ages 6 and up)

1600 Loop 323, Tyler 75701 at Old Jacksonville Highway (903–534–2169). Open Tuesday through Friday 9:00 A.M. to noon and 1:00 to 4:00 P.M., Saturday 10:00 A.M. to 4:00 P.M. **Free**.

The museum preserves 250 specimens of animals, reptiles, and fish from Africa and North America while the store depicts what grocery stores were like in the 1920s, including a 1926 delivery truck and antique fire truck.

TYLER MUSEUM OF ART (ages 6 and up)

1300 South Mahon Street, Tyler 75701 (903–595–1001). Open Tuesday through Saturday 10:00 A.M. to 5:00 P.M., Sunday 1:00 to 5:00 P.M.; closed July 1 through August 15. **Free**.

The Tyler Museum, near Tyler Junior College, is always changing its exhibits, focusing on a special artist or collection, so you'll never see the same thing twice.

CALDWELL ZOO (ages 2 and up)

2203 Martin Luther King Boulevard, Tyler 75702 (903–593–0121). Open October through March daily 9:30 A.M. to 4:30 P.M., April through September until 6:00 P.M. **Free**.

The Caldwell Zoo started as a backyard menagerie, but it's now a thirty-five-acre zoo with elephant and giraffe houses, a monkey island, birds, bears, and alligators. That the zoo was designed especially for children is evident in the milk-cow exhibit.

TYLER STATE PARK (ages 4 and up)

On Farm Road 14, Tyler 75706 10 miles north of Tyler (903–587–5338; 512–389–8900 for camping reservations).

Like other east Texas towns, Tyler has its own family outdoor getaway, Tyler State Park, where you'll find a spring-fed lake surrounded by a pine and hardwood forest. You can camp, fish, have a picnic, swim, watch wildlife, or wander along the 2.5 miles of hiking trails and the self-guided nature trail.

Where to Eat

Black-Eyed Pea. *322 Loop 323 (903–581–0242).* Down-home cooking. $$

Golden Corral. *420 Loop 323 (903–534–0281).* Steaks plus all-you-can-eat bountiful buffet. $–$$

Luby's Cafeteria. *1815 Roseland Boulevard (903–597–2901).* Luby's is legendary in Texas. $–$$

Where to Stay

Best Western. *Loop 323 at U.S. Highway 69 (903–595–2681).* Pool, Free breakfast. $$

La Quinta. *1601 Loop 323 (903–561–2223).* Pool, Free breakfast. $$

For More Information

Tyler Convention and Visitors Bureau. *407 North Broadway Street, Tyler, TX 75702; (800) 235–5712 or* *(903) 592–1661. Visit the Web site at www.tylertexas.com/cvb.*

Allan's Top
Family Fun Ideas

1. Alabama-Coushatta Indian Reservation, Woodville
2. Super Gator Tours, Orange
3. Caddo Lake canoeing, Uncertain
4. Big Thicket tours, Beaumont
5. Texas State Railroad, Rusk
6. Hiking the Lone Star Trail, Huntsville
7. Depot Museum and Children's Discovery Center, Henderson
8. Babe Zaharias Museum, Beaumont
9. *Graceful Ghost* boat tour, Uncertain
10. Discovery Place, Texarkana

Pittsburg and Daingerfield

North of Tyler on Texas Highway 11.

Getting to these small cities, you'll discover you are surrounded by a heavily timbered area that's a center for farming, poultry, and livestock. You'll also find berry farms almost everywhere, and several offer pick-your-own deals in season. Pittsburg is also one of the largest peach-producing areas in Texas.

*S*cenic Drive One of the more unusual drives in Texas is the route between Daingerfield State Park and Caddo Lake, mainly because it doesn't look like what most people figure Texas should look like. Along the way you'll see thick forests, trees turning colors in the fall, scenic lakes and bayous, and, finally, the mysterious looking Caddo Lake, with its thick cypress-crowded waters.

Take Park Road 17 out of Daingerfield State Park to Texas Highway 49, head east to Farm Road 250, and drive south. Continue south, then east on Farm Road 729 and east on Farm Road 134 out of Jefferson to Uncertain and Caddo Lake, with its moss-draped cypress and numerous side sloughs.

NORTHEAST TEXAS RURAL HERITAGE CENTER AND MUSEUM (ages 6 and up)

At the train depot on Marshall Street, Pittsburg 75686 (903–856–0463). Open Thursday through Saturday 11:00 A.M. to 5:00 P.M. Adults $3.00, children $2.00.

Housed in the old Cotton Belt Railroad Depot, the museum's exhibits include historical artifacts from the time of the town's founding in 1854 along with antique farm equipment and other memorabilia.

LAKE BOB SANDLIN STATE PARK (ages 4 and up)

On Texas Highway 21, Pittsburg 75686, about 12 miles north of Pittsburg (903–572–5531; 512–389–8900 for camping reservations).

Are you outdoored out yet? Don't be, because you're in the middle of the best outdoor recreation in the state. Another place where you can find camping, fishing, picnicking, and swimming is Lake Bob Sandlin State Park. The park features many campsites, screened shelters, a fishing pier and cleaning station, and 3.5 miles of hiking trails.

DAINGERFIELD STATE PARK (ages 4 and up)

Off U.S. Highway 259 on Texas Highway 11, Daingerfield 75638; 10 miles east of Daingerfield (903–645–2921; 512–389–8900 for camping or cabin reservations).

Families will find an abundance of sights and activities in the park's 550 pine-covered acres, and a spring-fed lake offers excellent fishing and swimming. Hiking trails provide 2.5 miles of wildlife-watching opportunities. Springtime brings blossoming flowers throughout the park. Facilities include campsites, cabins with kitchenettes, picnic areas, and a playground.

Sulphur Springs and Paris

SOUTHWEST DAIRY MUSEUM (ages 4 and up)

1210 Houston Street, Sulphur Springs 75482 (903–439–6455). Open Monday through Saturday 9:00 A.M. to 4:00 P.M. 𝐅𝐫𝐞𝐞.

Sulphur Springs is the largest dairy-producing area in Texas, and your family can get a fascinating look into the industry at the Southwest Dairy Museum. Find out how milk gets from cow to your refrigerator and how it was done a century ago, and help yourself to ice cream at the old-fashioned soda fountain. The museum has several interactive exhibits for children.

MUSIC BOX GALLERY (ages 4 and up)

201 North Davis Street, Sulphur Springs 75482 (903–885–4926). Open Monday through Wednesday and Friday 9:00 A.M. to 6:00 P.M., Thursday noon to 8:00 P.M., Saturday 9:00 A.M. to noon. 𝐅𝐫𝐞𝐞.

More things to fascinate your family can be found at the city library, where you'll find the largest collection of music boxes in the world on the first floor houses in the Music Box Gallery.

HOPKINS COUNTY MUSEUM AND HERITAGE PARK (ages 6 and up)

416 North Jackson Street, Sulphur Springs 75482 (903–885–2387). Open Tuesday through Sunday 1:00 to 4:00 P.M. Adults $2.00, children $1.00.

Over at the Hopkins County Museum and Heritage Park, you'll find many restored homes and shops from the nineteenth century which were relocated to this eleven-acre site. The museum has displays of area pioneer artifacts.

GREAT PARIS TRAIN RIDE (ages 4 and up)
1651 Clarksville Street, Paris (903–784–2503 or 800–727–4789). Train leaves at 10:00 A.M. on the second Saturday of each month April through October and returns at 5:00 P.M. Fare is $15.

The Great Paris Train Ride is a nice way for the family to spend the day. It takes you on a seven-hour round-trip from the depot in Paris to Hugo, Oklahoma, aboard a period locomotive.

 MINIATURE GOLF (ages 4 and up)
Paris is almost a miniature-golf heaven. You've got your choice of three courses here:

- **Chisum Golf,** 3701 Lamar Avenue, Paris 75462, (903) 785–2145
- **Culbertson Golf,** 1520 Neathery Street, Paris 75460, (903) 784–8088
- **The Gopher Hole,** 2810 Loop 286 North, Paris 75460, (903) 784–0752

Texarkana and Atlanta

Texarkana is one of those few cities in the United States that are split between two states. The name comes from three states, however: TEXas, ARKansas, and LouisiANA. The Louisiana state line is south of the city. For an amusing picture of the kids, head to **Photographers Island,** in front of the Federal Building at 100 North State Line Avenue. Half the building is in Texas, half in Arkansas, and so as not to play favorites, its address is Texarkana, USA 75501. The island in front of the building shows the state line.

 CRYSTAL SPRINGS BEACH (ages 4 and up)
 On U.S. Highway 67, Texaskana 75501, 18 miles west of Texarkana (903–798–3000). Open 10:00 A.M. to 7:00 P.M. weekends in May, daily Memorial Day through Labor Day.

Family park surrounding a twelve-acre lake. Features include water slides and paddle boats, video arcade and picnic areas.

 TEXARKANA HISTORICAL MUSEUM (ages 6 and up)
219 State Line Avenue, Texarkana 75501 (903–793–4831). Open Tuesday through Saturday 10:00 A.M. to 4:00 P.M. Adults $2.00, children $1.00.

The Texarkana Historical Museum has a little something for all tastes. Featured are not only the history of the area, from Caddo Indians to the railroad, but memorabilia honoring native son Scott Joplin, the father of ragtime music.

ACE OF CLUBS HOUSE (ages 6 and up)

420 Pine Street, Texarkana 75501 (903–793–7108). Open Tuesday through Saturday 10:00 A.M. to 4:00 P.M. Adults $5.00, students $3.50.

The unusual Ace of Clubs House was built in 1885 with winnings from a poker game. The Victorian house has a central octagonal stairhall with three octagonal wings and one rectangular wing, giving it the distinctive shape of an ace of clubs. Each room represents a specific period in the history of the house, providing insight into the families that lived here.

DISCOVERY PLACE (ages 4 and up)

215 Pine Street, Texarkana 75501 (903–793–4831). Open Tuesday through Saturday 10:00 A.M. to 4:00 P.M. Admission: $4.00.

The kids can amuse themselves and learn something at the same time at Discovery Place, featuring hands-on science and history exhibits, lab demonstrations, and audiovisual presentations and lectures.

ATLANTA STATE PARK (ages 4 and up)

South of Texarkana on Park Road 42 via Highway 59 and Farm Roads 96 and 1154, 14 miles northwest of Atlanta (mailing address: Route 1, Box 116, Atlanta 75551, 903–796–6476; 512–389–8900 for camping reservations).

Atlanta State Park is nestled in the pine forests bordering Lake Wright Patman. Activities on the lake include boating, fishing, skiing, and swimming, and the park has a number of hike and bike trails where you can see abundant wildlife. Facilities include campsites, picnic areas, and a playground with basketball and volleyball courts.

Where to Eat

Bob's Smokehouse. *2504 Richmond Road, Texarkana 75503 (903–832–3036).* Lucious hickory smoked barbecue. $$

Old Tyme Burger Shoppe. *1205 Arkansas Boulevard, Texarkana 71854 (870–772–5775).* The best burger in town. $

Ole Feed House. *2701 Arkansas Boulevard, Texarkana 71854 (870–773–0595).* Down-home country cooking with seafood, gumbo, chicken and dumplings. Special kids prices. $–$$

Where to Stay

Best Western Northgate. *400 West Fifty-third Street, Texarkana 75503 (903–793–6565).* Pool, children's pool, and playground. $$

La Quinta. *5201 North State Line Avenue, Texarkana 75503 (903–794–*

1900). Pool, **Free** continental breakfast. $$

Motel 6. *I–30 at Summerhill, Texarkana 75501(903–793–1413).* Pool, kids under eighteen stay **Free**. $$

For More Information

Texarkana Chamber of Commerce. *819 State Line Avenue, Texarkana, TX 75501; (903) 798–3000 or (903)*

792–7191. Visit the Web site at www.texarkana.org/visitor.html.

Jefferson

They call Jefferson "the Belle of the Bayous," and you might think you're in Louisiana or Mississippi here rather than in Texas. The town was once a bustling metropolis, one of the gateways to Texas in the nineteenth century, when it shipped plenty of timber and cotton on passing steamboats. Visit the Web site at www.jeffersontexas.org.

JEFFERSON HISTORICAL SOCIETY AND MUSEUM (ages 6 and up)

223 West Austin Street, Jefferson 75657 (903–665–2775). Open daily 9:30 A.M. to 5:00 P.M. Adults $3.00, children 50 cents.

Your family will discover a lot about east Texas at the Jefferson Museum. The museum is housed in a restored 1888 Federal building where exhibits fill three floors and the basement. Among the interesting displays are Civil War artifacts; family and household items; Native American artifacts; early tools, weapons, and furniture; an art gallery; and a special collection of children's toys and clothing on the third floor.

JEFFERSON AND CYPRESS BAYOU RAILROAD STEAM TRAIN (ages 4 and up)

Depot on East Austin Street, Jefferson 75657 (903–665–8400). Adults $7.89, children $4.89. Schedules vary with seasons.

To reinforce all that history, take a trip on the Jefferson and Cypress Bayou Railroad Steam Train. The steam locomotive pulls the train beside Big Cypress River and by many historic sites.

JEFFERSON GENERAL STORE (ages 6 and up)

113 East Austin Street, Jefferson 75657 (903–665–2222).

While you're in downtown, don't miss the Jefferson General Store. It has not only an old-fashioned soda fountain, but an authentic atmosphere complete with a nickel jukebox, a nickel cup of coffee, and games of checkers. You can even buy an old jukebox or soda machine, if you'd like one.

JEFFERSON RIVERBOAT TOURS (ages 4 and up)

1001 Bayou Street, Jefferson 75657 (903–665–2222). Tours are every two hours daily, 10:00 A.M. to 4:00 P.M. Adults $6.50, children $4.00.

For a close-up look at Big Cypress bayou, once a major steamboat route that connected Texas to New Orleans, take a ride on the Jefferson Riverboat. The guided tour provides information on the area's history, nature, and wildlife.

For More Information

For dining and lodging suggestions, see the listings for nearby Caddo Lake.

Marion County Chamber of Commerce. *119 West Lafayette Street, Jefferson, TX 75657; (888) GO–RELAX or (903) 665–2672. Visit the Web site at www.jeffersontexas.org.*

Uncertain

Isn't Uncertain a great name for a town? It developed because boat captains had a difficult time landing their steamships here. A bit of trivia: Lady Bird Johnson was born in the neighboring town of Karnack.

Whatever you do, don't miss a chance to take the family out on **Caddo Lake,** the most beautiful lake in Texas and one of the few natural lakes in the state. Caddo Lake crosses into Louisiana, but the whole lake feels as if it belongs there, with its moss-laden cypress trees, maze of bayous and sloughs, and swamplands. A canoe trip through the early morning mist is an unforgettable, almost mystical, experience. For canoe or pontoon boat rentals, call (903) 679–3743. For guided canoe tours call (903) 665–2911.

GRACEFUL GHOST (ages 4 and up)

Taylor Island on Bois d'Arc Lane, Uncertain 75661 (903–789–3978 or 888–325–5459). Departs 5:00 and 7:00 P.M. Friday; 1:00, 3:00, 5:00, and 7:00 P.M. Saturday; 3:00 and 5:00 P.M. Sunday. Adults $15, children $12. Trips may also be scheduled during the week and are one-third off regular fares.

Your family is certain to enjoy a tour of Caddo Lake on the *Graceful Ghost*, a genuine paddlewheel steamboat. By steamboat or by canoe are really the only ways to enjoy this lake that seems lost in the mists of time.

The Texas Badlands

You'll find Caddo Lake so quiet and peaceful today that often the loudest sound you'll hear will be the plop of a jumping fish or squawk of a swamp bird. But once this place was full of outlaws, pirates, thieves, and ne'er-do-wells of all sorts.

Seems like after the Louisiana Purchase in 1803, Caddo Lake was the central area of a disputed portion of the purchase. The United States and Spain both claimed it and finally agreed to let it remain neutral territory until the matter was formally decided, barring any immigration by either side. But immigrants came anyway, usually of the nefarious sort. When a man went bad in the United States, he was said to have "gone to Texas," and this area was where he usually came first. The swampy Caddo Lake territory became known as the Texas Badlands, and it had so many outlaws living in it that a common form of greeting was, "What was your name before you came to Texas?"

After Texas won its independence, Caddo Lake remained in dispute, this time by the people living there, who divided into two groups: Regulators and Moderators, who had their own civil war in the early 1840s. Sam Houston finally ended the war with a personal appearance in the area, but many families continued feuding for several decades.

Civilization came to the lake then, with steamboats plying the maze-like bayous and sloughs of the 30,000-acre lake that straddles the Texas and Louisiana border.

CADDO LAKE STATE PARK (ages 4 and up)

Off Farm Road 2198 on Park Road 2, Karnack 75661, 3 miles from Uncertain (903–679–3351; 512–389–8900 for camping reservations).

Caddo Lake State Park was built by the Civilian Conservation Corps in the 1930s, and the period architecture all around only adds to the mystery of the lake itself. The park has campsites, screened shelters, fully furnished cabins, picnic areas, nature and hiking trails, and facilities for boating, fishing, or swimming in the lake.

Where to Eat

Bayou Landing. *300 Cypress Drive, Uncertain 75661 (903–789–3394).* Steaks and seafood. $$

Lamache's Pasta Depot. *126 West Austin Street, Jefferson 75657 (903–665–6177).* Real Italian comfort food; children's menu. $$

Sleepy Hollow. *On U.S. Highway 59, Jefferson 85657, about 8 miles north of Jefferson (903–665–1148).* Steak and that east Texas staple, catfish. $$

Where to Stay

Hotel Jefferson. *124 West Austin Street, Jefferson 75657(903–665–2631).* One of the most historic inns in Texas. A cotton warehouse from 1861 to 1900, when it was converted to a hotel. Rooms are furnished with century-old antiques. $$

Maison Bayou Bed and Breakfast. *300 Bayou Street, Jefferson 75657 (903–665–7600).* Relax at this plantation with waterfront cabins, bunkhouses, unusual railcar and steamboat rooms, hiking and biking trails, and fishing. $$$

The Texas Experience. *On Blackjack Road, Jefferson 75657, off U.S. Highway 59, 6 miles from Jefferson (903–938–8019).* Camp outside with cowboys or stay in a cabin; trail rides, hayrides, chuckwagon cooking around a campfire on Las Brisas Ranch. $$$

For More Information

Marion County Chamber of Commerce. *119 West Lafayette Street, Jefferson, TX 75657; (888) GO–RELAX or (903) 665–2672. Visit the Web site at www.jeffersontexas.org.*

Marshall and Longview

Celebrate Marshall's history with the Miss Loose Caboose contest, Cow Patty Bingo, parades, arts-and-crafts and food booths, and historical reenactments at **Stagecoach Days** in mid-May. This is one of east Texas's most popular festivals. Call (903) 935-7868.

In mid-October, don't miss the tongue-in-cheek **Fire Ant Festival.** Gather the most ants in the Fire Ant Roundup or try your hand at the Rubber Chicken Chunking Contest. Arts-and-crafts and food booths, entertainment, and children's games mean lots of fun. Call (903) 935-7868.

Then, all through December, Marshall really lights up to celebrate the holidays. The **Wonderland of Lights Christmas Festival** is famous throughout the state, even prompting other communities to try to imitate it. In addition to lights everywhere, entertainment is featured Tuesday and Thursday through Saturday. Call (903) 935-7868.

The Capital of Missouri Used to Be in Texas

Marshall served as the capital of Missouri during the Civil War. Missouri governor Claibourne Jackson, fearing a Union invasion, moved his staff to Marshall in 1861 and conducted affairs of state there. He was followed by large numbers of Southern sympathizers after several battles were fought in Missouri. When Jackson died in 1862, Lt. Gov. Thomas Reynolds took office and continued running Missouri from Marshall until Lee surrendered in 1864.

Today, a historical marker commemorates the Missouri capital at South Bolivar and Crockett Streets.

MARSHALL POTTERY AND MUSEUM (ages 6 and up)
4901 Elysian Fields Road, Marwshall 75672 (903–938–9201; www. marshallpottery.com). Open Monday through Saturday 9:00 A.M. to 8:00 P.M., Sunday 10:00 A.M. to 6:00 P.M. **Free** *factory tours.*

Marshall is home to the largest manufacturer of red clay pots in America. Marshall Pottery is more than a hundred years old now, still making pots and selling them in addition to glassware, china, collectibles, pillows, gourmet foods, housewares, books, gadgets, candles, wrought iron, baskets, and more at the giant shop.

MARTIN CREEK LAKE STATE PARK (ages 4 and up)

On County Road 2183, Tatum 75691, off Texas Highway 43 about 20 miles south of Marshall (903–836–4336; 512–389–8900 for camping reservations).

Caddo, Choctaw, Cherokee, and Kickapoo Indians dominated this area until the 1850s, and from the lake's fishing pier visitors can still see Trammel's Trace, a Native American trail that became a major immigration route for Anglo settlers traveling from Arkansas into Texas. Facilities include campsites, screened shelters, picnic sites, hiking and mountain-bike trails, boat ramps, and a lighted fishing pier. You can take a guided tour of the lake or rent a boat from the store. Kids will enjoy the "perch-jerk" contest on Labor Day Saturday. Worship services are held in the park every Sunday morning from Memorial Day to Labor Day.

GREGG COUNTY HISTORICAL MUSEUM (ages 6 and up)

214 North Fredonia Street, Longview 75601 (903–753–5840). Open Tuesday through Saturday 10:00 A.M. to 4:00 P.M. Adults $2.00, children $1.00.

If your family would like to know what life was like in the 1800s, the Gregg County Museum is a good place to find out. The museum re-creates business offices, a dental office, a school, and several homes, along with offering hands-on activities for the kids.

Where to Eat

Aunt Bea's Home Cookin'. *2804 Judson, Longview 75605(903–663–3999).* Good family-style food. $$

Bear Creek Smokehouse. *On Texas Highway 154, Marshal 75672, 9 miles northwest of Marshall (800–950–BEAR).* Irresistible smoked meats of all sorts. $$

Golden Corral. *440 West Loop 281, Longview 75605 (903–757–8779).* Steaks or a bountiful, all-you-can-eat buffet can't be beat. $–$$

Where to Stay

Best Western. *I–20 at U.S. Highway 59, Marshall 75672 (903–935–1941).* Pool, **Free** continental breakfast. $$

Days Inn. *3103 Estes Parkway, Longview 75602 (903–758–1113).* Pool, **Free** McDonald's breakfast, and children under eighteen stay **Free**. $$

Econo Lodge. *3103 Estes Parkway, Longview 75602 (903–753–4884).* Pool, kitchenettes, **Free** McDonald's breakfast, and children under eighteen stay **Free**. $$

For More Information

Longview Convention and Visitors Bureau. *401 North Center Street, Long-view, TX 75606; (903) 753–3281. Visit the Web site at www.easttexas.com/ longview.*

Marshall Chamber of Commerce. *213 West Austin Street, Marshall, TX 75670; (903) 935–7868. Visit the Web site at www.etnet.net/marshall.*

Kilgore

In early April Kilgore is ablaze with red, white, and pink azaleas, so don't miss the annual **Azalea Trail,** featuring some of the area's most beautiful homes and gardens. For information call (903) 984–5022.

RANGERETTE SHOWCASE (ages 6 and up)

Broadway at Ross, Kilgore 75662 (903–983–8265; www.kilgore.cc.tx.us/ attr/ranshow/ranshow.html). Open Tuesday through Friday 10:00 A.M. to noon and 1:00 to 4:30 P.M., weekends 2:00 to 5:00 P.M. **Free**.

Kilgore is famous in Texas as home of the Kilgore College Ran-gerettes. You've probably seen a photo of them: cowgirls in white hats cocked to one side of their heads, high-stepping like the Rockettes at Radio City Music Hall. The Rangerette Showcase, on the college cam-pus, displays the group's history in film, photos, scrapbooks, and other displays.

Lost Pirate Treasure Most tales of Texas treasure are myths, but one is very real. In 1816, pirate Jean Laffite took $2 million worth of silver bars from a Spanish ship in Matagorda Bay. He sent the treasure north in a wagon train, hoping to reach St. Louis, but Mexican troops overtook the wagons at Hendricks Lake, near Longview. In an attempt to save the silver, the wagon master drove the six wagons into the water, where they sank.

The silver was never found again. However, three bars were hauled up by fishermen in 1928. Portions of the wagons were discovered in 1959 and 1975, but the silver had apparently settled into the muck. Laf-fite's loot is still down there, tempting treasure hunters to this day.

EAST TEXAS OIL MUSEUM (ages 6 and up)
U.S. Highway 259, Kilgore 75662, at Ross (903–983–8295). Open Tuesday through Saturday 9:00 A.M. to 4:00 P.M., Sunday 2:00 to 5:00 P.M. Adults $4.00, children $2.00.

Your family can see more conventional history at the East Texas Oil Museum, also on the Kilgore College campus. The museum re-creates an entire boomtown from the 1930s, accompanied by dioramas, artifacts, and films. Don't miss the simulated elevator ride to oil formations 3,800 feet underground.

For More Information

Kilgore Chamber of Commerce. *813 North Kilgore Street, P.O. Box 1582, Kilgore, TX 75663–1582; (903) 984–5022.*

Visit the Web site at www.ci.kilgore.tx.us/home.

Henderson and Carthage

Families will enjoy the **Potlatch** festival in Carthage every October. It celebrates the area's heritage with Native American dances, an arts-and-crafts fair, hands-on art exhibits, fun runs, and even an old-time dunking booth. Call (903) 693–6634.

   DEPOT MUSEUM AND CHILDREN'S DISCOVERY CENTER (ages 4 and up)
514 North High Street, Henderson 75652 (903–657–4303). Open Monday through Friday 9:00 A.M. to 5:00 P.M., Saturday 9:00 A.M. to 1:00 P.M. Adults $2.00, children $1.00.

Hundreds of hands-on and interactive science and history exhibits will keep the kids busy at the Depot Museum and Children's Discovery Center. Housed in a 1901 Missouri-Pacific Railroad depot, the museum also has a restored caboose, a log cabin, and the fanciest outhouse anyone in your family has ever seen, including great-grandma.

 TEX RITTER MUSEUM/JIM REEVES MEMORIAL (ages 6 and up)
300 West Panola Street, Carthage 75633 (903–693–8578 or 903–693–6634; www.panola.cc.tx.us/Carthage-PanolaCounty/ritter.htm). Free.

Cowboy singer and actor Tex Ritter (father of actor John Ritter) and country singing legend Jim Reeves were both born in Panola County. Ritter is honored in the museum in a restored bank building in downtown Carthage. Reeves has a memorial statue 3 miles east of downtown on U.S. Highway 79.

LAKE MURVAUL (ages 4 and up)
On Farm Road 1970, Carthage 75633, 12 miles southwest of Carthage (903–693–6634).

Lake Murvaul offers boating, camping, picnicking, swimming, and waterskiing. The panorama is a wonder: a pristine blue lake meeting deep blue skies surrounded by the Piney Woods. It's easy to relax here.

For More Information

Panola County Chamber of Commerce. *300 West Panola Street, Carthage, TX 75633; (903) 693–6634.*

Rusk County Chamber of Commerce. *201 North Main Street, Henderson, TX 75652; (903) 657–5528. Visit the Web site atwww.hendersontx.com.*

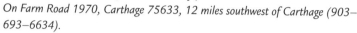

Center and Hemphill

Center, on U.S. Highway 96, is another area known for its timber mills and poultry. Hemphill, at the junction of U.S. Highways 259 and 79, is a commercial lumber center and a gateway to the Toledo Bend Reservoir.

SHELBY COUNTY MUSEUM (ages 6 and up)
Thomas at Pecan Street, Center 75935 (936–598–3613). Open Monday through Friday 1:00 to 4:00 P.M. **Free**.

Shelby County is one of the original counties in the Republic of Texas, so its history goes back a long way, and it's all preserved here, from bearskins to bottles, spinning wheels to warbonnets. The museum is housed in a 1905 historic home.

Texas Trivia The largest reservoir in the state is Toledo Bend Reservoir, with 185,000 surface acres.

TRAIL BETWEEN THE LAKES (ages 4 and up)
201 South Palm Street, Hemphill 75948 (936–787–3870).

If your family enjoys hiking, take them to Trail Between the Lakes, a 28-mile hiking trail that winds through the Sabine National Forest. It extends from the Lakeview Recreation Area on Toledo Bend Reservoir to Route 96 near the Sam Rayburn Reservoir. The scenery is gorgeous, and many sections are near streams frequented by wildlife. Bicycles and horses are not allowed on the trail. For more information, check the district ranger's office on Palm Street in Hemphill.

TOLEDO BEND RESERVOIR (ages 4 and up)
Between Jasper and Center off Texas Highway 87, Center 75935 (936–565–2273).

Toledo Bend Reservoir is a paradise for fisherfolk and families who want to have fun or relax on a big lake. The reservoir impounds the Sabine River and stretches into Louisiana. It's the largest man-made body of water in the United States, covering about 185,000 acres. With 1,200 miles of shoreline, you can do just about anything here: boating, camping, fishing, hiking, hunting, picnicking, and swimming. Public and private facilities cover the shores.

Nacogdoches

Nacogdoches (pronounced Nack-ah-doe-chis) is the oldest town in Texas and was occupied for centuries before Europeans ever settled it. French explorer La Salle passed through in 1687, followed by Spanish missionaries in the early 1700s, and the settlement became a city in 1779. The state's first newspaper was published here, the first oil well pumped here, and Sam Houston, Jim Bowie, and Davy Crockett all slept here. The city is also home to Stephen F. Austin University.

Texas Trivia The first oil well in the state known around the world for its petroleum reserves and refining was drilled in 1866 near Nacogdoches, with production beginning in 1889.

STONE FORT MUSEUM (ages 6 and up)
Griffith at Clark Street, Nacogdoches 75961 (409–468–2408). Open Tuesday through Saturday 9:00 A.M. to 5:00 P.M., Sunday 1:00 to 5:00 P.M. **Free**.

The Old Stone Fort on the SFA campus is where Texas's first two newspapers were set in type. The museum also has many artifacts from a nearby archaeological excavation and other exhibits on pioneer life in the area.

MILLARD'S CROSSING (ages 6 and up)

6020 North Street, Nacogdoches 75961 (936–564–6631). Open Monday through Saturday 9:00 A.M. to 4:00 P.M., Sunday 1:00 to 4:00 P.M. Adults $4.00, children $2.00.

Millard's Crossing is a collection of nineteenth-century homes, including a Methodist chapel and parsonage. Interiors are furnished with antiques and pioneer artifacts.

For More Information

Nacogdoches Convention and Visitors Bureau. *513 North Street, P.O. Box 631918, Nacogdoches, TX 75963; (888)* *564–7351 or (936) 564–7351. Visit the Web site at www.visit.nacogdoches.org.*

Lufkin

At the intersection of U.S. Highways 59 and 69.

Lufkin is the heart of the Piney Woods, surrounded by tall timber and between two national forests and the huge Lake Sam Rayburn.

MUSEUM OF EAST TEXAS (ages 6 and up)

503 North Second Street, Lufkin 75901 (936–639–4434). Open Tuesday through Friday 10:00 A.M. to 5:00 P.M., weekends 1:00 to 5:00 P.M. **Free**.

Discover east Texas history at the Museum of East Texas, housed in a 1905 church. In addition to many exhibits on area pioneers, the museum has an extensive collection of works by east Texas artists.

TEXAS FORESTRY MUSEUM (ages 6 and up)

1905 Atkinson Drive, Lufkin 75902 (936–632–TREE). Open Monday through Saturday 10:00 A.M. to 5:00 P.M., Sunday 1:00 to 5:00 P.M. **Free**.

If you're in Lufkin, you already know you're in the midst of one of the most heavily wooded areas in the country, certainly the most in Texas. The family can learn all about timber in the Piney Woods at the Forestry Museum. You'll find exhibits of machinery and tools, an antique logging train, lumber oxcarts, a fire lookout tower, and displays on area plant life, wildlife and the lumberjacks who work the timber.

ELLEN TROUT ZOO (ages 2 and up)

Loop 287 North at Martin Luther King Drive, Lufkin 75904 (936–633–0399). Open daily 9:00 A.M. to 5:00 P.M. September through March, to 6:00 P.M. otherwise. Adults $2.00, children $1.00.

The Ellen Trout Zoo began with a hippopotamus donated as a gag gift and has now grown to include hundreds of animals from around the world, like ruffed lemurs, Siberian tigers, clouded leopards, bald eagles, Hawaiian geese, Siamese crocodiles, and Jamaican boas.

Texas Forests

Yes, Texas has forests—lots of them. More than twenty-three million acres are woodlands in the state, and much of it is open for recreation in the form of park lands, preserves, or wilderness areas.

Also, four national forests covering 635,000 acres offer abundant opportunities for outdoor family recreation, whether for day use or over several days. Each forest has its own lakes, streams, and hiking trails.

- Angelina National Forest—Home to Boulton Lake, Boykin Springs, Caney Creek, Harvey Creek, Sandy Creek, Lake Sam Rayburn, and the Sawmill Hiking Trail
- Davy Crockett National Forest—Home to Ratcliff Lake, Big Slough, Alabama Creek, and the 4C Hiking Trail
- Sabine National Forest—Home to Red Hills Lake, Toledo Bend Reservoir, and the Trail Between the Lakes
- Sam Houston National Forest—Home to Double Lake, Kelly Pond, Lake Stubblefield, Lake Conroe, and the Lone Star Hiking Trail

For information on the national forests in Texas, contact the Forest Supervisor, Homer Garrison Federal Building, 701 North First Street, Lufkin, TX 75901; (936) 639-8501.

ANGELINA NATIONAL FOREST (ages 4 and up)

On U.S. Highway 69, Lufkin 75901, 14 miles southeast of Lufkin (936–639–8620 or 409–639–8501).

Angelina National Forest surrounds Sam Rayburn Reservoir, creating 560 miles of shoreline and offering great places for families to camp, picnic, swim, fish, water-ski, or just relax. Because of the lake, there are a number of developed sites in the forest.

Texas Trivia Angelina County is the only Texas county named for a woman. She was a Hasinaii Indian raised at Mission Tejas in the late seventeenth century. She was named "little angel" (*Angelina* in Spanish) by the mission priests. She was later an interpreter for explorers in the area.

For More Information

Angelina County Chamber of Commerce. *1615 South Chestnut Street, Lufkin, TX 75904; (800) 409–5659 or* *(936) 634–6644. Visit the Web site at www.chamber.angelina.tx.us.*

Livingston and Coldspring

LAKE LIVINGSTON (ages 4 and up)
Between Livingston and Huntsville on U.S. Highway 190, Livingston 77351 (936–327–4929 or 800–766–LAKE; www.lakelivingston.com).

Lake Livingston is a mecca for outdoor recreation in the area, drawing families from as far away as Houston. Reaching it is easy from either I-45 or Highway 59, or Highway 190, which connects the two. You can play on the 93,000 acres of lake or relax along the 450 miles of wooded shoreline, which has many public and private recreational facilities.

LAKE LIVINGSTON STATE PARK (ages 4 and up)
On Farm Road 3126, Livingston 77351, 7 miles southwest of Livingston via Farm Road 1988 (936–365–2201; 512–389–8900 for camping reservations).

Lake Livingston State Park has a fishing pier, fish cleaning stations, boat ramps, campsites, screened shelters, picnic areas, and about 4 miles of hike and bike trails through the pine and oak forests surrounding the lake. You can get bait, groceries, and gas at the park store.

DOUBLE LAKE (ages 4 and up)
On Texas Highway 150, Coldspring 77331, 4 miles south of Coldspring (409–653–2795).

For families with small children, Double Lake can't be beat. This is a relatively small area in Sam Houston National Forest that has campsites, picnic areas, a beach house, canoe and paddleboat rentals, a boat ramp, a quiet hiking trail that loops around the lake, and a 5-mile trail that leads to the **Big Creek Scenic Area** with access to the **Lone Star Hiking Trail.**

For More Information

Livingston Chamber of Commerce. *505 North Drew Street, Livingston, TX* *77351; (936) 327–4929. Visit the Web site at www.lakelivingston.com.*

Woodville

Woodville is a quiet little city tucked away in a beautiful forest of pines and dogwoods. The city celebrates its natural heritage with the annual **Dogwood Festival,** which covers several weekends in late March through early June. Each weekend features different activities, like an antique car show, fun run, arts-and-crafts fair, parade, historical play, rodeo and trail ride, Western dance, quilt show, and bluegrass music. This is a rousing, old-time celebration. For information call (409) 283-2632.

Texas Trivia The largest lake completely in the state is Lake Sam Rayburn, with 114,500 surface acres. Other principal lakes are Amistad, Falcon, Livingston, Texoma, and the Highland Lakes of the Hill Country.

HERITAGE VILLAGE MUSEUM (ages 6 and up)
On U.S. Highway 190, Woodville 75979, 1 mile west of Woodville (409–283–2272). Open daily 9:00 A.M. to 5:00 P.M. except Christmas and New Year's. Adults $4.00, children $2.00.

This is a collection of pioneer buildings and artifacts depicting life in the 1800s, including a giant clock, a blacksmith shop, churches, physician's and apothecary shops, a schoolhouse, a railroad depot, and much more. A gift shop, picnic areas, and a restaurant await upon your exit.

In May the Heritage Village hosts **Ghosts of Texas Past,** an evening of storytellers presenting legends and folktales of early east Texas that's sure to delight children and fascinate adults. Call the village for dates.

ALABAMA-COUSHATTA INDIAN RESERVATION (ages 4 and up)
On U.S. Highway 190, Livingston 77351, midway between Livingston and Woodville (936–563–4391 or 800–444–3507). Open Monday through Saturday

9:00 A.M. to 6:00 P.M., Sunday 12:30 to 6:00 P.M. in summer; open Friday and Saturday 10:00 A.M. to 5:00 P.M., Sunday 12:30 to 5:00 P.M. in spring and fall; closed December through February. Each event is $3.00 per person.

The Alabama-Coushatta Indian Reservation is one of the oldest reserves in the nation, established by Sam Houston in the 1850s. The tribes offer swamp-buggy or train tours through the Big Thicket, tours of the reservation, colorful dances every day, and a nice gift shop and restaurant. The gift shop features the lovely, delicate baskets made here. Prices in the restaurant are low and the food is quite good, making it the perfect place for lunch in the area. There are also camping, picnic, and swimming areas. Don't miss the annual powwow if you're around the first weekend in June.

For More Information

For dining and lodging suggestions, see the listings for Jasper.

Tyler County Chamber of Commerce. *201 North Magnolia Street, Woodville, TX 75979; (409) 283–2632.*

Jasper

At the junction of U.S. Highways 190 and 96.

Jasper lies just south of both Angelina National Forest and Sabine National Forest. The city is in the middle of one of the most heavily forested areas of Texas; about 85 percent of the surrounded land grows pines and hardwoods.

ANGELINA NATIONAL FOREST (ages 4 and up)

On Texas Highway 63, Jasper 75951, 13 miles northwest of Jasper (409–384–5716).

Jasper is on the southern end of Lake Sam Rayburn, which is famous in Texas for its great fishing, thanks to the lake's many coves. In addition to fishing, you'll find prime swimming and waterskiing. The shores are covered in dogwood and pine, magnolia and azalea. The lake lies within Angelina National Forest.

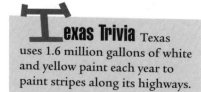

Texas Trivia Texas uses 1.6 million gallons of white and yellow paint each year to paint stripes along its highways.

MARTIN DIES JR. STATE PARK (ages 4 and up)

On U.S. Highway 190, Jasper 75951, 12 miles west of Jasper (409–384–5231; 512–389–8900 for camping reservations).

More lake recreation can be found at Martin Dies Jr. State Park. The park has numerous creeks and the 15,000-acre B. A. Steinhagen Reservoir. The area is filled with beautiful trees like cypress, willow, beech, and magnolia. Facilities include boat ramps, campsites, canoe rentals, hiking trails through the bottomland forest, and screened shelters. Bald eagles winter here.

Where to Eat

Casa Olé. *2120 North Wheeler, Jasper 75951 (409–383–8800).* Claimed to be the best Mexican food in all of the Piney Woods. $–$$

Inn of the Twelve Clans. *On the Alabama-Coushatta Indian Reservation, Livingston 77351 (936–563–4391).* Some of the best food around; try the fry bread. $–$$

Pickett House. *In Heritage Village, Woodville 75979 (409–283–3371).* Housed in an old one-room schoolhouse, this restaurant is extremely popular thanks to all-you-can-eat staples like chicken-fried steaks, chicken and dumplings, and its "mess of greens." $$

Where to Stay

Best Western Inn. *205 West Gibson Street, Jasper 75951 (409–384–7767).* Pool and spa, **Free** breakfasts, special parking accommodations if you happen to be towing a boat or trailer. You can even check out late on Sunday. $$

Woodville Inn. *201 North Magnolia Street, Woodville 75979 (409–283–3741).* Pool; surrounded by beautiful dogwood trees in spring. $$

For More Information

Jasper Chamber of Commerce. *246 East Milam, Jasper, TX 75951–4136; (409) 384–2762. Visit the Web site at www.jaspercoc.org.*

Index

N

O